Scarecrow Film Score Guides
Series Editor: Kate Daubney

1. *Gabriel Yared's* The English Patient: *A Film Score Guide*, by Heather Laing. 2004.
2. *Danny Elfman's* Batman: *A Film Score Guide*, by Janet K. Halfyard. 2004.
3. *Ennio Morricone's* The Good, the Bad and the Ugly: *A Film Score Guide*, by Charles Leinberger. 2004.
4. *Louis and Bebe Barron's* Forbidden Planet: *A Film Score Guide*, by James Wierzbicki. 2005.
5. *Bernard Herrmann's* The Ghost and Mrs. Muir: *A Film Score Guide*, by David Cooper. 2005.
6. *Erich Wolfgang Korngold's* The Adventures of Robin Hood: *A Film Score Guide*, by Ben Winters. 2007.
7. *Mychael Danna's* The Ice Storm: *A Film Score Guide*, by Miguel Mera. 2007.

Mychael Danna's
The Ice Storm

A Film Score Guide

Miguel Mera

Scarecrow Film Score Guides, No. 7

The Scarecrow Press, Inc.
Lanham, Maryland • Toronto • Plymouth, UK
2007

SCARECROW PRESS, INC.

Published in the United States of America
by Scarecrow Press, Inc.
A wholly owned subsidary of
The Rowman & Littlefield Publishing Group, Inc.
4501 Forbes Boulevard, Suite 200, Lanham, Maryland 20706
www.scarecrowpress.com

Estover Road
Plymouth PL6 7PY
United Kingdom

British Library Cataloguing in Publication Information Available

Library of Congress Cataloging-in-Publication Data

Mera, Miguel.
  Mychael Danna's The ice storm : a film score guide. / Miguel Mera.
    p. cm. — (Scarecrow film score guides ; no. 7)
  Includes bibliographical references and index.
  ISBN-13: 978-0-8108-5941-8 (pbk. : alk. paper)
  ISBN-10: 0-8108-5941-6 (pbk. : alk. paper)
  1. Danna, Mychael. Ice storm. I. Title. II. Title: Ice storm.

ML410.D167M47 2007
781.5'42—dc22
                                        2007007339

∞™ The paper used in this publication meets the minimum requirements of
American National Standard for Information Sciences—Permanence of
Paper for Printed Library Materials, ANSI/NISO Z39.48-1992.
Manufactured in the United States of America.

To Claire.

Mychael Danna. Courtesy of Mychael Danna.

Mychael Danna and editor Pia Di Ciaula. Sketched by director Gillies
MacKinnon during the recording sessions for *Regeneration* (1997).
Courtesy of Gillies MacKinnon.

Contents

Figures

Tables

Editor's Foreword

The Scarecrow series of Film Score Guides is dedicated to drawing together the variety of analytical practices and ideological approaches in film musicology for the purpose of studying individual scores. Much value has been drawn from case studies of film scoring practice in other film music texts, but these guides offer a substantial, wide-ranging, and comprehensive study of a single score. Subjects are chosen for the series on the basis that they have become and are widely recognized as a benchmark for the way in which film music is composed and experienced, or because they represent a significant stage in the compositional development of an individual film composer. A guide explores the context of a score's composition through its place in the career of the composer and its relationship to the techniques of the composer. The context of the score in narrative and production terms is also considered, and readings of the film as a whole are discussed in order to situate in their filmic context the musical analyses which conclude the guide. Furthermore, although these guides focus on the score as written text, bringing forward often previously unknown details about the process of composition as they are manifested in the manuscript, analysis also includes exploration of the music as an aural text, for this is the first and, for most audiences, the only way in which they will experience the music of the film.

As the series has become established, two issues have begun to surface through the scholarship of the guides which challenge some of the previously well-established tenets of film musicology. One of these is the notion of singular authorship by the composer, in parallel with filmic models of the *auteur*. The guides are titled in a format which implies that a score belongs to a composer in some way—Mychael Danna's *The Ice Storm*—and it is a format which was established to foreground the essential interpretative function a composer has in writing the music for a film. Giving the composer possession of the film in this way highlights the very particular nature of their relationship with the film in its pre- and post-scored states, and the way that relationship is handed on to the audience of the film. But the nature of film music composition is and always has been collaborative to some degree, and the guides have explored the different manifestations of this collaboration, from Erich Korngold's team of orchestrators, through Steve Bartek's processing of Danny Elfman's manuscripts, to Mychael Danna's incorporation of improvised Native American flute performances into his score. What emerges in this volume is just how extensive this notion of collaboration can be and, as with Ben Winters's volume on Korngold's score for *The Adventures of Robin Hood* (1938), Miguel Mera's analysis of Danna's compositional processes forces us to interrogate our comfortable assumptions.

The second issue which emerges in particular from this volume is an equally well-established conceit established by some of the earliest composers, that music is naturally and principally in the service of the film. This conceit is in most cases, however, a mask for an additional assumption that composers must be permitted to preserve their hallmark sound in the score. Again, this series seems almost to accept that hallmark as a prerequisite for scholarship, legitimizing the search for the composer's voice within their response to a film. But as Miguel Mera shows, Mychael Danna's approach to film music is rather different in that it is the same processes which are consistently identifiable in Danna's music, not Danna himself. In searching only for the right sounds for the film, in matching music to the underlying concept of the film—its structure, its mood, its emotional message—anything is possible. There are no prerequisites of structure, tone or instrumentation, leaving Danna freer than composers who must live up to their own reputation.

The Ice Storm is an unusual and significant film which challenges the audience to engage with it, just as the score leaves us unexpected room to experience that engagement. Whatever the reader's level of musical knowledge or understanding, this volume provides an insightful, challenging, and important guide to the part the score plays in shaping both the film and its audience.

Dr. Kate Daubney
Series Editor

Acknowledgments

I am indebted to numerous people and organizations that have assisted in the preparation of this book. First and foremost thanks must go to Mychael Danna, who has been more generous than I could possibly have imagined. He provided me with scores, notes, and computer files, in fact, with every piece of source material relating to *The Ice Storm* in his possession. His honesty and willingness to engage with my questions helped me understand his compositional processes from the inside. Any inaccuracies or errors exist only because of my own weaknesses of interpretation and not because of a lack of information.

The Royal College of Music awarded me a period of study leave to commence the project. My line manager, David Burnand, gave me his full support and also read early drafts of the first two chapters.

In a field where source materials are often scarce and can hardly ever be located in libraries or established archives, I am grateful to individuals who have helped me secure unique primary sources. Jeremy Bell at Wilfrid Laurier University provided me with a recorded interview of Mychael Danna and Atom Egoyan. Mark Hasan provided me with a transcript and video of an interview with Danna at the Toronto Film Festival, as well as access to some early Danna works. Paul Tonks provided me with further interview materials, and Pam Price at Gordon Price Music Ltd. helped me locate rare published scores.

I have been fortunate to interview a number of people who were involved with *The Ice Storm* and/or who have worked with Mychael Danna. These include: Walter Buczynski, Jeff Danna, Nicholas Dodd, Mark Duggan, Atom Egoyan, John Greyson, Jamie Hopkings, Jeanne Lamon, Andrew Lockington, Mira Nair, John Potter, James Schamus, Alex Steyermark, Philip Stockton, and Tim Squyres. Their insights are much appreciated.

Securing copyright clearances and licenses for this book was, at times, extremely complicated and included numerous unproductive searches and circular journeys. I am deeply indebted to the people who assisted me, often beyond the call of duty; they include: Anikah McLaren and Daniele Bernfeld at Focus Features; Payal Sethi at Mirabai Films; Marcy Gerstein at Ego Film Arts; Robin Cass at Triptych Media; Ted Spellman, Veronica Lemcoff, and Andy Bandit at Fox Searchlight; Anne-Sophie Chollot and Benedicte Viallet at Studio Canal Image; Adeela Sharif and Isabelle Lhérondel at Icon Entertainment; Louis Meisel at the Louis K. Meisel Gallery; Karen Kadlecsik at the Marlborough Gallery; Aimee Gessner at BMW Group; Nick Hern at Nick Hern Books; Julie McDowell and Jennifer Chartier at the Hal Leonard Corporation; Diane Hayes and Betul Al-Bassam at Fairwood Music; Burt Harris and Jane Sibbery at Sheeba; Ann Dawson and Steven Joyce at Boosey and Hawkes; Gabrielle Fastman at Cherry Lane Music; and The Tragically Hip.

In particular, I would like to thank Kate Daubney. I could not have asked for a more helpful and generous editor. She persuaded me to embark on the project and was thoroughly supportive throughout. She read numerous drafts, provided insightful comments, and offered encouragement, even when I missed deadline after deadline. Without her persistence and enthusiasm this book would not have been conceived or completed.

My wonderful wife, Claire, read the entire draft text and, as ever, provided detailed and perceptive comments as well as much needed emotional support.

Introduction

The Ice Storm (1997) is a film that could be described as something of a buried treasure. Despite widespread critical acclaim for the delicately crafted, exquisitely acted study of suburban morality in 1970s America, the cinematic release of the film was limited and consequently it performed poorly at the box office. The film made relatively little impact on the American society that it so incisively explores. Outside the United States the film was well received: Sigourney Weaver won a BAFTA for her acting performance and writer/producer James Schamus won Best Screenplay at the Cannes Film Festival, but in general *The Ice Storm* has been undervalued. One can only wonder whether, with greater initial exposure, it might have reached a wider audience and achieved greater industry approval. The aim of this book, then, is to provide a map with which this treasure can be unearthed. Recognizing *The Ice Storm* as a film of striking significance is a process that already has considerable momentum as new audiences come to the work through television broadcasts, DVD sales, and increased interest in the director, Ang Lee, as his career continues its meteoric rise.

However, this is also a book about film music and specifically about the composer Mychael Danna, who in *The Ice Storm* created arguably one of the most distinctive scores of the 1990s. Danna counts, by almost any measurement, as an unconventional film composer. His scoring aesthetic constantly aims to challenge perceptions of the form and function of film music and he is known for borrowing musical ideas from other cultures and incorporating them into his own musical language, as well as for insightful scoring of dramatic subtext. His approach leads to an idiosyncratic, subtle, and eclectic musical voice. However, it is not an egotistical notion of nonconformity which drives Danna, but rather a sense of frustration with many of the traditional, structural, and representative aspects of film scoring practice that he believes an increasingly cine-literate audience no longer requires.

There is relatively little extant writing on the composer and, consequently, the biographical information contained in chapter 1 explores the context and experiences from which Danna's approach emerged. Given that filmmaking is a collaborative process, there is also a focus on the pivotal people and moments that have shaped Danna's compositional career. Chapter 2 draws from a range of examples and illustrates some of the techniques and stylistic features central to Danna's music. It also highlights the ways in which Danna explores the compositional freedom provided by the postmodern condition. In combination, these two chapters demonstrate the remarkable breadth of Danna's compositional language and how musical resources are tailored to the specific needs of a given project.

The film itself is the subject of chapter 3. In preparation for the analysis of the music used in *The Ice Storm* presented in chapter 5, the central narrative, structural, and aesthetic themes are explored. This reading shows how aspects such as visual style and production context impact on the ultimate design of the soundtrack.

Chapter 4 provides a detailed evaluation of the evolution of the score from initial sketches through to the completed product. Unprecedented access to the composer's MIDI sequencer files reveals radical changes in concept, style, and instrumentation as the score developed over a four-month period. Understanding this journey provides a valuable insight into the form and function of the music, and also demonstrates how the politics of filmmaking interacts with creativity. The numerous layers of creative collaboration employed in the making of the film challenge the notion of the composer as *auteur* and provide a useful link between intention and interpretation.

Chapter 5 considers the aural features of the completed soundtrack: the sound design, the use of preexistent pop songs, a song that was specifically arranged for the film by David Bowie, and Danna's score. In particular, this analysis will demonstrate how restraint is the principal device employed by the filmmakers in generating a powerful emotional arc.

There are a number of score examples used throughout this book. They serve to illustrate aspects of compositional technique, structural design, or the development of materials, but are by no means designed to replace the experience of watching and listening to the films themselves. *The Ice Storm*, in particular, both merits and reaps the rewards of repeated viewing.

Chapter 1

Mychael Danna's Musical Background

Having an idea of where you stand in the whole history of making music, that is really important to me. That's a sense that I carry into the work that I do as well. I try to be very aware of music from different places and from different times. I feel perfectly able and like I have the right to use those in my music-making and draw from them at any point.[1]

Mychael Danna was born into a music-loving family in Winnipeg, Canada, on September 20th 1958. When he was only three weeks old the family moved southeast to the city of Burlington which banks onto the north shore of Lake Ontario. Mychael's father, Frank Danna, was a chartered accountant and also a keen amateur operatic tenor. He had seriously considered becoming professional, but had decided that the life of a freelance musician was too "unpredictable for a family man."[2] Mychael's mother, Edith (née) Broadhurst, played the piano and sang in local choirs. Danna's formative years were surrounded by performances of opera, operetta, musicals, and choral concerts. The excitement of the musician's lifestyle—garnered through the various family concert trips, and the behind-the-scenes events—had a profound effect on Danna. Furthermore, the fact that Mychael's parents could make music together instilled musical performance as a central family activity. Like many musical children Danna was drafted into the local church choir, but despite parental influence he never had any inclination to be a singer himself.

The family also owned a large collection of recordings in which the young Danna immersed himself, though he did not always share his parents' tastes in music. Even at a young age he had defined individual musical preferences, including an intense dislike of the extensive household collection of jazz 78s from the 1930s. Danna recalls that the jazz music he heard as a child never "took root" and did not touch him emotionally, a prejudice that he still holds to this day.[3] However, what did move him was music of the Baroque era, specifically George Frideric Handel: "I remember very clearly, I just loved Handel. I remember thinking from a very early age 'that is what I would love to do, write music like that guy.'"[4] This passion for Baroque music was fuelled by the fact that Frank Danna frequently sang the tenor solos in Handel's *Messiah*. The young Danna also listened obsessively to the "overblown but still somehow appropriate"[5] recording of Handel's *Water Music* and *Music for the Royal Fireworks* conducted by Leopold Stokowski (1959), as well as Herbert von Karajan's recordings of the complete Beethoven Symphonies with the Berlin Philharmonic (1961–62).[6]

At eight years of age Danna began piano lessons, but was disappointed that they did not "have anything to do with writing music."[7] When he confronted his teacher, James Gunton, about this issue, Danna recalls that "it seemed to be a lot more important to put the dime on the back of my hand and play a scale without it falling off."[8] Despite the obvious pains in the pursuit of technical proficiency, Danna held a deep affection for his teacher who excited him with his great enthusiasm and who "would tell me all kinds of stories about composers."[9] As Danna grew into his teens his pianistic skills developed such that he began to entertain notions of a career as a performer. His playing had introduced him to a wide range of musical styles and historical periods and, coupled with continued detailed listening, he had gained enough confidence to begin writing his first short piano pieces. He had also broadened his musical horizons beyond classical music and planned to join a band as the keyboard player.

Just days before his sixteenth birthday in 1974, a single event impelled Danna to pursue composition more vigorously. It was during his after-school cleaning job in a local church that Danna fell—hand first—through a window, tearing nine tendons, an artery, and two nerves. The accident put an end to any serious notions of a performance career. The decreased functionality of the left hand must have been devastating to the sixteen-year-old, however, Danna's desire to continue making music was manifested in more focused compositional activity and increased production of solo piano pieces. Danna's growing proficiency is acknowledged by the fact that some of the pieces he wrote between the ages of sixteen and nineteen were published in the grade six, seven, and eight examination books of the Royal Conservatory of Toronto. These pieces allowed Danna the opportunity to explore techniques for the formation of coherent musical structures, the organic development of musical materials, and for sensitivity and clarity of notation. The works provide a useful picture of Danna's evolving technique. Compositions such as *Pietà* (dedicated to James Gunton), *Shadows*, and *Fantasy* demonstrate imagination, rhythmic energy, and idiomatic instrumental writing.[10] Despite the fact that he had not received any formal compositional training, Danna was already establishing himself as a promising composer. Yet, at this stage, he had no desire to become a film composer. Danna recalls enjoying the music to the film *Ben Hur* (1959) which he saw as a teenager and "seemed to have a harmonic language that [he] had not heard before."[11] However, in general, Danna had very little interest in films and most film music made little impression on him.

Synthesizers and Studies

Even though Danna's pianistic skills were now somewhat limited, he had not abandoned the idea of playing in a rock band and "luckily, synthesizers in those days were monophonic. The left hand really only had to twiddle knobs, so [he] ended up doing that for a while, playing in bands, being a synth guy."[12] Danna played keyboards, Mellotron,[13] and synthesizers with a group called the Oh No's, who subscribed to the non-conformist "prog-rock" movement of the mid-1970s with music that was "really pretentious: no song less than seven minutes long, no less than forty-seven themes, and lyrics in Italian; hilarious now."[14] The band provided him with an outlet for performance that had been restricted by his accident, but also increased his familiarity with the inner workings of synthesizers, which would become fundamental to his future compositional career.

Indeed, Danna had begun to share his ideas about the creative uses of music technology with a like-minded eleventh grade chemistry student and fellow band member, Tim Clément. At this time, synthesizers were difficult to set up, use, and maintain, and generating sounds required nothing short of obsession. Danna and Clément were excited by the possibilities that the technology provided and, alongside the Oh No's, they experimented and created multi-layered soundworlds through "rhythmless jamming, guitar, synths, and tape, and getting more involved in what later became known as ambient music."[15]

In 1977 at the age of nineteen, Danna wanted to consolidate what he had learned through his years of exposure to music, technology, performance, and self-directed learning, and went to McMaster University in Hamilton to read music. However, this educational experience was short-lived. The singer in the Oh No's started writing very different material and the band made a sudden shift from progressive rock to the opposite end of the musical spectrum, which was new wave, early electro-pop. They became relatively successful, and Danna suspended his studies after only one year, in order to go on tour and perform "short, snappy, catchy little pop songs."[16] Danna and Clément continued to share ideas and work together enthusiastically on pieces purely for their own private enjoyment, because they had a "complete lack of faith that anyone else would want to hear what [they] were doing."[17] The Oh No's eventually disbanded, but Danna and Clément's musical collaboration flourished.

The birth of MIDI (Musical Instrument Digital Interface) in 1983 was one of the most significant developments in the history of music technology. Various manufacturers from around the world cooperated to create a standard digital language that allowed electronic musical instruments and related devices to communicate with one another: computers and electronic musical instruments could be connected and synchronized, it became possible to change voices and modify control parameters (such as pitch bend or velocity) on several instruments at once, and so on. MIDI democratized and revolutionized electronic music production, and Danna and Clément seized the newfound opportunities that it provided. Between 1982 and 1984 they worked on an album entitled *A Gradual Awakening*, a "haunting collection of tone poems which celebrate Canadian nature," and immediately followed this with *Summerland* (1985).[18] The music is relaxing, atmospheric, and tonally centered with slowly shifting and evolving textures. It is in the tradition of ambient music as pioneered and defined by artists such as Brian Eno and Harold Budd. Eno explains that ambient music was designed to be environmental, but without the negative connotations or derivative nature of muzak: "Whereas the extant canned music companies proceed from the basis of regularizing environments by blanketing their acoustic and atmospheric idiosyncrasies, ambient music is intended to enhance these."[19] However, unlike Eno whose work was based on tape loops of synthesized sounds, Danna and Clément featured environmental sounds as part of their compositional material and process. For example, *Summerland* fuses synthesizers, guitars, Appalachian harp, recorders, and flutes with the sound of rushing water, insects, church bells, and the cries of timber wolves. What Danna contributed compositionally, Clément balanced with detailed manipulation of natural soundscape recordings, creating a strong collaborative partnership. Clément explains that the incorporation of natural sounds adds "more color to the internal sensations we're trying to convey. This is typical of our work together—as opposed to exotic inspiration, it's all been pretty much Canadian with us."[20] For Danna and Clément, ambient music was inspired by, and was representative of, Canada's space and natural environment.

While Danna was enjoying his work with Clément, he also craved a new direction. An encounter with Tim Clark, the composer in residence at the McLaughlin Planetarium in Toronto, provided a new focus. Danna thought that writing music for planetarium productions would be an excellent way to make a living, but he was sure "government bureaucracy" would require any candidate for the job to have a composition degree.[21] Consequently, Danna returned to his studies, this time at the University of Toronto, with the hope that on completion he might be able to apply for the planetarium post. He also believed that he had a variety of musical talents and experiences that needed to be united into a coherent structure in order to allow further musical progress.

Danna had mixed feelings about his second university experience, finding his course fascinating and pointless in equal measure. There were certain areas of the curriculum that he found more useful than others. He reveled in the increased knowledge brought about by the study of music history, in particular cherishing the early music courses, and he also became intensely interested in ethnomusicology. Music of other cultures had always caught his ear, but it was at university that he first began to study the aesthetic conceptions and construction of a variety of world musics. Danna immersed himself in the music of other cultures through extensive listening, concert attendance, and record collection, as well as practical experimentation, including learning to play the *bîn*.[22] In addition, Danna was living in Toronto at a time when it was exploding as a multicultural city. Over and above the long history of ethnic diversity, extending back to Confederation, the Canadian Government created proactive immigration policies. Oriental Exclusion Acts were removed from the statute books in 1949, which meant that many religious and racial barriers to immigration were removed.[23] Consequently, Indian, African, and Asian migrants increased steadily throughout the 1960s and diversified the largely West-European ethnic melting pot.

The mixture of influences on Danna during his university years meant that he came away "loving early music, ethnic music, and minimalism."[24] At this time, in the early-to-mid 1980s, the North American minimalist movement had gathered considerable momentum.[25] Significantly, many of the minimalist composers had sought inspiration from and had studied the music of non-Western cultures, writing music that emphasized rhythm, timbre, and repetition. This approach appealed to Danna, although he did not write music in this style at that time. Despite the fact that his course encouraged the study of world music, Danna did not feel able to draw on these resources as tools for composition. Indeed, one of the most frustrating aspects of his degree was the perceived stylistic prescription of the composition tutors. Danna felt that the kind of music that was fashionable in academic circles was "certainly not anything I was interested in."[26] Yet, like many composition students of this era, he concluded that there was no choice but to write in a modernist style and that minimalism was strictly forbidden; whenever he did try and write in a minimalist style "it was not accepted."[27]

> It depended on who your professor was—I had several, I went through a few of them. . . . out of survival, you had to figure out what it was that they wanted you to do and then do that.[28]

Danna clearly excelled at this game of compositional appeasement, winning the Glenn Gould Composition Award in 1985. The cash prize was awarded annually to a student in any year of the composition program who had demonstrated excellence in both academic and music studies. Although Danna did not fully appreciate it at the time, he later acknowledged one tutor who had made a particular impression on him, the Polish-Canadian composer Walter Buczynski who had studied with Milhaud and Boulanger, and was also an acclaimed pianist. Buczynski recalls that Danna was "an older student (about twenty-four or twenty-five)" in a class of five composers who were otherwise aged nineteen or twenty. Buczynski believed that Danna's "background in classical music was weak," and that he "was not that advanced compared to the other classmates."[29] Nonetheless, Danna worked hard at his composition exercises and Buczynski "encouraged him and felt very sympathetic to his cause," and was impressed by his "desire to learn and curiosity about how to make things work."[30] Buczynski's compositional sensitivities were also less modernist than many of his colleagues. However, it was not Buczynski's own compositional technique or style that was inspirational, but his method of critique.

> He was very disciplined about every note. Every note had to have a justification, a reason, and you had to really think before you wrote. You had to be able to explain what it was you were doing, you could not just write notes on a page. You had to have a skeleton of structure and philosophy underneath what you were doing.[31]

This conceptual detail—the insistence on purposeful economy of musical material and structural coherence—are compositional features that have remained with Danna and which he continues to bring to his film work. Indeed, Danna acknowledges the importance of Buczynski on his daily compositional processes: "I still can hear the words of one of my professors in my ears while I'm writing. Just having your music criticized every week and torn apart, it is very useful and basically in film that is what your whole life will be."[32] Equally deferential, Buczynski believes that Danna has "*that* thing for film music, invention, and not the crass and the ordinary. I have great respect for the distance he has taken."[33]

As an antidote to the stylistic limitations that he felt were imposed on him, Danna also sought ways to express different compositional ideas by writing music for the University Graduate Studies Theatre Department and the Hart House Theatre. Danna composed and arranged music, and selected preexistent recordings for a variety of different productions including plays by Joe Orton and new student works. These projects allowed him to use "traditional" melody and harmony and to explore ways of using ethnic instruments and music technology in dramatic contexts. Aside from the freedom to experiment, Danna also cites pragmatic reasons for working on theatre productions at this time. As an undergraduate approaching the end of his course he was fuelled by the knowledge that there were only "a handful of ways for a composer of non-lyric driven music to make a living."[34] Even at this stage, film music did not seem to be a plausible option, as Danna "hated the romantic, bombastic sound that kept living on in film scores," which was reason enough for him to temporarily reject it.[35] Although it did not pay well, theatre scoring seemed to provide Danna with a great deal of compositional freedom and enjoyment. Significantly, the experience of shaping a score for a play or experimental theatre piece provided him with valuable insights into narrative structure, emotional shading, timing, and short-form musical development, as well as collaboration and communication skills. Danna believes that his experience of writing for theatre was "probably the most important thing [he] got out of university,"[36] not least because of a number of contacts that would later prove significant to the development of his career as a film composer. Indeed, it was through theatre contacts that Danna met one of his most significant future collaborators, Atom Egoyan.

Towards Film

Extraordinarily, Atom Egoyan had been an International Relations student at the University of Toronto at the same time as Danna. Egoyan had also written and directed a number of plays for the theatre department and was very interested in music, being a proficient classical guitarist. Given these factors, it seems remarkable that the two men knew of each other only in passing and had not met or worked together. Egoyan had also made a number of short films such as *Howard in Particular* (1979), *Peepshow* (1981), and *Open House* (1982), and one feature film, *Next of Kin* (1984). These films demonstrated a variety of developing techniques including visual styles drawn from experimental film traditions and fascination with detailed, textural scripts and non-linear narratives that had already established Egoyan as a distinctive filmmaker of great promise.

The two men were introduced in the fall of 1986 just as Egoyan was about to make his second feature film, *Family Viewing* (1987). A mutual friend from the university theatre department gave the director a tape of Danna's music and Egoyan "felt a great affinity with it, particularly some of the work he was doing with instruments from other places."[37] Egoyan was also acutely aware that the emotions of the characters in his films were often restrained and reserved. He thought it would be interesting to "create a dynamic where the music was indicating something that the images were not immediately relating back; that would create an alchemy that I could use in the dramatic structure of my storytelling."[38] Danna recalls meeting Egoyan at his office and discussing ideas through an exploration of each other's record/cassette collections. Like Danna, Egoyan was fascinated by early music and had an impressive record collection including Renaissance music by Dufay performed by the Early Music Consort and the recorder player David Munrow. Egoyan observes that his enjoyment of early music is based upon "the lack of self, the notion of the identity of a composer not really existing before the Baroque," coupled with "a plaintive quality."[39] This detailed appreciation, understanding, and personal response to early music clearly endeared Egoyan to Danna and gave both men a shared focus for discussion. Egoyan recalls listening to one particular troubadour-style composition that

> had a very intoxicating rhythm and there was something mesmeric about the piece, and Mychael responded to that and he played me back some music that he was excited by at that time, and we just connected. I think that is basically what it comes down to.[40]

Having discovered that Egoyan was born in Cairo, Danna played some of his favorite Egyptian music to ignite further discussions. The fact that Egoyan also disliked the melodramatic nature of the traditional Hollywood score allowed for further empathy between the two men. This first encounter already highlights a pattern of creative iteration that is fundamental to Danna and Egoyan's collaborative process.

Sharing music, musical enthusiasms, and the joy of new discoveries is a central feature of their scoring process. In addition, the fact that Egoyan is musically literate allows this process to be more evenly balanced than in many composer/director partnerships. Through his collaboration with Egoyan, Danna was beginning to see a means of working in films; however, according to Danna both men were extremely naïve about filmmaking at this stage: "[We] started out together knowing absolutely nothing. . . . He came up through theatre and I had never watched films."[41] This supposed naïveté allowed both men to be free from political and economic pressures of filmmaking practice. They searched for solutions to problems as they perceived them, not as an industry had taught them to perceive them. Consequently, the score for *Family Viewing* is a continuation of Danna's compositional interests and explorations, combining electronica, African percussion, Indonesian drums, strings, and woodwinds. Danna notes that he had "no idea that you weren't supposed to put that kind of material in films—I didn't know any better."[42] Had it not been for Egoyan's encouragement and his particular approach to filmmaking, Danna may not have pursued film composition as a career. Egoyan is effectively responsible for Danna's entry into film music.

One of Danna's initial reasons for returning to his studies at the University of Toronto had been to apply for the post of composer in residence at the McLaughlin Planetarium, which was part of the Royal Ontario Museum. The residency became available in September 1987, just as *Family Viewing* was being screened at film festivals, and Danna was offered the job. Given his background in ambient electronic music, this is not as unusual a career move as it may first appear. Indeed, it was an obvious way for a composer favoring electronic resources to make a living. Danna explains what was involved:

> The planetarium would put educational star shows together, and they would have an audio soundtrack with narration and some suitably 'spacey' electronica. So, my job was primarily a technician but also composing the background music. It was all electronic and it was a lot of fun.[43]

The star shows required him to respond to a script, mold music around dialogue, and react to moving images, albeit of planetary orbits. Furthermore, the audience would sit in a darkened room watching a combination of moving images, sound design, and music, much like cinema. The music that Danna wrote for these productions survives on two recordings, *Planets, Stars and Galaxies* and *Mars: The Journey Begins.*[44] It is clear that by this stage he had become an extremely sophisticated user of analog synthesizers, sequencers, and samplers, and was very comfortable with the techniques of additive and subtractive synthesis, signal and dynamic processing. The result is an elaborately constructed soundworld with rich, varying textures alternating with rhythmically propulsive percussive sections.

Family Viewing was critically successful, winning the Locarno International Critics Prize and the Best Canadian Feature at the Toronto International Film Festival, as well as being nominated for eight Genie Awards including Best Motion Picture, Best Achievement in Direction, and Best Music Score. The film also acquired considerable notoriety when Wim Wenders declined the jury prize at the Montreal Film Festival for his own film *Wings of Desire* (1987) and instead offered it to Egoyan. With increasing confidence that their approach was artistically profitable, Danna and Egoyan continued their working relationship with films such as *Speaking Parts* (1989), *The Adjuster* (1991), the television film *Gross Misconduct* (1993), and the extremely influential *Exotica* (1994).

Exotic Ice: Developing Career

The stylistic fusion of Middle Eastern and Indian music that Danna created for *Exotica*, which is discussed further in chapter 2, had captured the attention of a number of directors including Mira Nair, who was working on her latest film, *Kama Sutra: A Tale of Love* (1996). Nair had been given the *Exotica* soundtrack CD as a birthday present and thought it was "markedly original and haunting, but in the madness of shooting [had] put it aside."[45]

> Then Mychael wrote to me in New York and in his letter he referred to Guru Dutt, who is one of my all-time favorite directors, and *Umrao Jaan*. This was very contemporary and knowledgeable stuff that he was writing about. I was amazed that a Canadian would have his finger on the pulse of these two specific references that I happened to be thinking about constantly.[46]

Danna met Nair in New York and was shown a rough cut of *Kama Sutra*. He intended to travel to India to record musicians, as he had done with *Exotica*, but because the production team wanted to be very "involved in the music and hear what was going on at every step," musicians were flown into recording studios in New York.[47] Each theme in the film was created from a different improvised *raga*,[48] and shaped to specific scenes under Danna's direction. The materials could then be edited and a full score shaped around these elements. A wide range of performers covering all of the instrumental families of Indian music were used. These included non-membranous percussion (*ghan*), membranous percussion (*avanaddh*), blown wind (*sushir*), plucked strings (*tat*), and bowed strings (*vitat*). The ensemble was predominantly North Indian in its construction featuring instruments such as the *sitar, surbahar, shehnai, bansuri, sarangi, tanpura*, and a wide range of membranous percussion including *tabla, pakhawaj*, and *dholak*, as well as vocals provided by Shubha Mudgal. However, instruments traditionally associated with South Indian music were also used, such as the *ghatam*, violin, and *kanjira*. The cultural melange was further compounded by the addition of bass guitar, mandolin, flutes, and synthesized elements creating a contemporary Indian sound.[49]

Given that the bulk of the initial material appears not to have been physically 'created' by Danna, his approach challenges notions of authorship and expectations of compositional practice. Critics of this method argue that improvisation and composition are distinct procedures, but Bruno Nettl contests this notion, suggesting that improvisation and composition are "opposite aspects of the same process."[50] For musicians who work within an oral rather than a notated tradition, materials are almost always generated through improvisation. Danna's approach therefore was dictated by the performers, but his role in shaping performances and structuring musical resources should not be underestimated simply because it does not conform to traditional notions of how composers instigate and project their ideas. Danna's skill at drawing useful materials from performers is manifested in a great deal of his work and is central to his compositional approach.

While working with Mira Nair in one of the editing rooms at the Brill Building in Manhattan, which had long been the heart of New York's music scene, Danna's next project suddenly surfaced.[51] Work on *Kama Sutra* was close to completion when music supervisor, Alex Steyermark, introduced himself. In American production, music supervisors are responsible for all film music activities and personnel, including working closely with the director to select songs and instrumental music for the film soundtrack, recommending and auditioning composers and recording artists, and the preparation of film music budgets. According to Danna, Steyermark had been working in the next room and was curious about the music he had heard "through the wall."[52] However, Steyermark recalls a more resolute decision about which composer to hire: "We were all familiar with and big admirers of Atom Egoyan, and *Exotica* had come out right before; to us that was a really ground-breaking score. As a result we wanted to try and work with Mychael."[53] Danna was eventually invited to score the film on which Steyermark was working, Ang Lee's *The Ice Storm* (1997).

The importance Steyermark ascribed to the film *Exotica* suggests that world music was the focal point for *The Ice Storm* score from the very outset. However, although *The Ice Storm* eventually featured gamelan ensemble and Native American flute, this was not where the soundworld originated. Initially, the 1970s suburban Connecticut setting was represented, somewhat literally, through an analog synthesizer score. The music underwent a series of striking transformations which will be examined in chapter 4.

Danna found the collaborative working process on *The Ice Storm* brutal in its rigorous attention to detail and, as he had not worked with Lee before, it took quite some time to get inside the mind of the director. Danna explains that Lee is very subtle and a "man of very few expressive moments. . . . There's a lot going on in his mind, but he doesn't necessarily communicate in a way that is really obvious."[54] *The Ice Storm* remains one of the most challenging projects on which the composer has worked, and Lee's perfectionist attitude appears to have stretched Danna compositionally.

> He is very driven to make sure that everything under his control is the best. He is difficult to work for in that way, and you do have to keep going back and trying again. You throw things out that you feel you would keep for other people. But I am always really happy with the things I write for him, so it is worth it.[55]

Furthermore, the project was demanding because the film edit was constantly revised and restructured: "Ang was really wrestling with the film, trying to come to some kind of a structure that he felt comfortable with."[56] While this process required numerous score revisions, it also led to an extremely detailed and intimate understanding of every single moment in the film and a thoroughly unified soundtrack. Vera John-Steiner observes that: "An individual learns, creates, and achieves mastery in and through his or her relationships with other individuals."[57] It is significant that through his work with Ang Lee, Danna defined further concepts for the precise control of emotion through film scoring, the use of restraint, and for the articulation of subtext as a compositional device. As such, *The Ice Storm* was an artistic milestone for Danna and marked a compositional coming-of-age.

After the Storm

The year 1997 continued to be productive with Danna scoring both Gillies MacKinnon's *Regeneration* and Atom Egoyan's *The Sweet Hereafter*. It was as if *The Ice Storm* had marked the end of Danna's apprenticeship and his newfound self-assurance was manifested in intriguing, carefully conceived and constructed scores, each with their own unique soundworld. *Regeneration* consisted of a hollow score for string-based ensemble with violin and boy soprano soloist, and *The Sweet Hereafter* successfully combined a variety of Medieval instruments and Persian *ney* flute.[58] The distinctiveness and maturity of the scoring of these three films had not gone unnoticed, and Danna was beginning to gain greater industry recognition for his work and approach. In particular, widespread critical acclaim for *The Sweet Hereafter*, which received an Academy Award nomination and won the jury prize at the Cannes Film festival, helped Danna's next career move. Danna had made enough of an impact to be offered his first Hollywood feature film, *8MM* (1998) directed by Joel Schumacher and produced by Columbia Pictures. Danna observes that: "Schumacher is well-known for finding people in the independent world and bringing them into the big-budget world."[59] However, the approach to *8MM* was no different to any other project: "I see the film and I meet with the director and start trying to get inside what the film is about on a fundamental level, what its essence is, without having any preconceptions."[60] In the case of this contemporary film noir, dealing with private investigator Nick Welles's increasingly out-of-control descent into the seedy world of snuff movies, Danna attempted to find an appropriate musical soundworld that could elucidate the film's main themes and ideas. Supported by Schumacher's initial direction to "be bold, go crazy,"[61] Danna opted for the percussive drive of traditional Moroccan music that uses the "constant speeding of rhythms, which seem to spin almost like a whirlpool, and draw you in."[62] The score was equally seductive and dangerous, and the conceptual framework allowed Danna to "play with places that we think we know."[63] Unexpected sounds color narrative locations that seem familiar on the surface, yet which hide dark secrets. Danna spent weeks on the outskirts of Marrakech working individually with nine different provincial Moroccan vocal and instrumental groups, as well as some Algerian Tetuan flute performers. All of the music was recorded with a portable DAT machine and a simple two microphone set-up in a hotel conference room. Danna reacted and responded to the music that was played to him and shaped it through discussion and improvisation with the musicians themselves. The recordings could later be manipulated in Danna's studio in Toronto and electronic elements added. The resulting cocktail was then used as a backdrop for the orchestra, which was recorded in New York.

By the late nineties and early noughties, Danna seemed to have achieved an enviable career balance. He continued to work with his longtime collaborator Egoyan on films such as *Felicia's Journey* (1999), further developed his collaborative relationships with Ang Lee in *Ride With the Devil* (1999) and *Chosen* (2001), and Mira Nair on *Monsoon Wedding* (2001), but he was also involved in a number of mid-to-low budget Hollywood projects such James Mangold's *Girl, Interrupted* (1999).

With Ang Lee's film *The Hulk* (2003), Danna's transition from arthouse to mainstream cinema seemed complete. Not only was it a big-budget Hollywood feature, but also intended as Universal Pictures' summer blockbuster. The marketing strategies of the High Concept movie were, therefore, embedded in the film's creation. High Concept is a style of filmmaking based on the simplification of narrative and character which can be easily pitched and easily understood, frequently favors lavish visual effects and/or big-name stars, and aims to reach a large youth audience.[64] The financial risks inherent in such blockbuster movies are greatly reduced, as Tino Balio explains, by a variety of interrelated factors: they constitute media events, lend themselves to promotional tie-ins, create profit in ancillary divisions such as games and video, are easy to distribute, and stand to make profits in foreign markets.[65] The computer game and film of *The Hulk* were released simultaneously, and a DVD of the 1970s television series was re-released just prior to the film's première. A range of toys including the obligatory action figure and electronic hulk hands were created. More than three-hundred licensees worldwide produced *Hulk* related products designed to build brand recognition and profit from the release of the film. Despite the avowed intent of the High Concept movie to be ground-breaking, critical detractors stress the extent to which they "rely on replication and combination of previously successful narratives."[66] Hence, *The Hulk* built on the format and style of a variety of films inspired by comic superheroes and monster characters such as *Godzilla* (1998), *X-Men* (2000), and *Spiderman* (2002). Furthermore as Justin Wyatt argues, high concept movies do not require the viewer to engage in the responsibility of reading the film's narrative, but rather "the viewer becomes sewn into the 'surface' of the film, contemplating the style of the narrative and the production. The excess created through such channels as the production design, stars, music, and promotional apparatus enhances this appreciation of the film's surface qualities."[67] These complicated social and political factors do not favor a composer like Mychael Danna who, as has been seen, frequently employs oblique compositional strategies that incorporate ethnic instruments, as well as the scoring of subtext. The huge financial outlays involved and the centrality of the summer season to the major studios' economic success tend to demand conventional and familiar, if visually and aurally striking, narratives and production processes. When mainstream concerns are at stake, mainstream scoring is expected and stylistic assimilation is key. It is hardly surprising, therefore, that Danna's approach to *The Hulk* did not meet with the approval of the studio and he was fired days before the intended recording sessions. Danna explains: "Ang and I were mostly done with a pretty cool score with a lot of ethnic touches, including, with perhaps some poor political timing, Arabic singing. The studio was not thrilled when they heard it."[68] The poor political timing is a reference to the fact that, just prior to the release of the film, American troops were engaged in the second Gulf War against Iraq. In the previous year Taliban and Al Qaeda targets in Afghanistan had been bombed in response to the terrorist attacks on America on September 11th 2001. The notion of a powerful green monster—a threat to civilized society—being represented through the use of Arabic-influenced music at this time was simply too delicate an issue. Any inherent self-reflective irony would have been unwelcome by the politically correct studio. As Richard Maltby observes, even though globalization and convergence have resulted in an American film industry that is no longer exclusively owned by Americans, the cinematic product has "if anything, become more exclusively American in perspective."[69] What room, then, is there for a composer such as Danna within the mainstream system?

Following the disappointment of *The Hulk*, Danna has continued to work on a number of fascinating and varied projects. Among many others, these include: *Shattered Glass* (Ray, 2003), *Vanity Fair* (Nair, 2004), *Being Julia* (Szabó, 2004), *Capote* (Miller, 2005), *Water* (Mehta, 2005) *Where the Truth Lies* (Egoyan, 2005), *Little Miss Sunshine* (Dayton and Faris, 2006), *The Nativity Story* (Hardwicke, 2006), and *Tideland* (Gilliam, 2005), which he composed with his brother Jeff.[70] Whatever the political factors that continue to affect cinema production and whatever boundaries exist, either perceived or real, between mainstream Hollywood, independent, low budget, and art film, Mychael Danna will continue to pursue projects where "the music has something important to say."[71]

Chapter 2

Danna's Film Scoring Language

Well, if you're living in a building and you're looking out of it, you don't necessarily know what it looks like. You can start putting it together, maybe, by what other people's reactions are. I don't know if there is [a Mychael Danna sound] or not. I'm told there is. I hear a lot of the same descriptive words over and over again from people.[1]

Identifying the stylistic traits of individual composers has become a mainstay of musicological analysis and composition teaching, yet Danna's understandable difficulty in classifying the precise nature of his own musical sound highlights a number of challenging questions that are central to contemporary film scoring practice. Given the wide variety of genres and differing approaches to filmmaking, it is axiomatic that compositional versatility and stylistic eclecticism are vital tools for composers who work with more than one director or in more than one type of production system. Defining a film composer's musical language, then, can be complicated because a number of factors are involved in the selection of an appropriate soundworld for a given film: genre, narrative structure, visual style, the relationships between the score and other aural elements, and interactions with the production team. This is not unique to Danna, but is particularly acute in his case because he has an extremely broad musical palette and range of compositional techniques at his disposal. Danna's musical reach extends from Medieval-influenced music to twenty-first-century dance styles. He is equally comfortable working with an orchestra as he is with a sequencer, with improvisation as with precisely conceived and prepared structures, and with all of the methodologies that those processes require. Furthermore, Danna's knowledge extends beyond a series of Western idioms and draws on a vast array of world music cultures. This expertise allows him to select appropriate musical materials for differing film projects and to respond flexibly to a wide range of narrative and emotional situations. Attempting tidy definitions of Danna's compositional style, therefore, is comparable to explaining what a chameleon looks like. In either case, the background or context is a fundamental articulator of appearance. This is not to say that Danna, or indeed any other film composer, is suffering from an identity crisis, but rather that stylistic variety has become as much a defining feature of contemporary composition as the previous rigorous adherence to one individual style. It is a position that is clearly postmodern.

Jonathan Kramer puts forward the idea (following Jean-François Lyotard and Umberto Eco) that musical postmodernism is not so much a historical period or surface style as an attitude.[2] It is this attitude that is clearly reflected in Danna's work. Danna's music does not accept boundaries between sounds and techniques of the past and present, or between music of different traditions and cultures; it challenges the barriers between "high" and "low" art and between elitist and populist values; it considers technology as central to its production and character, not just as a means of transmission; and, importantly for this study, his music presents multiple meanings and trusts the perceiver(s) in the construction of meaning.

A closer understanding of Danna's musical language can only be achieved through an awareness of the particular contexts in which he works and the thinking behind certain stylistic choices, as well as by examining recurrent aural features and scoring choices. Within this context, the notion of the composer's "voice," an essential facet of traditional musicology, seems less relevant than how a film composer responds to given situations. The way Danna uses sound says a great deal about what he believes his role as a film composer should be; he truly puts music at the service of the film, without prejudice or precedent. Danna is not a composer who writes music for films but a filmmaker who specializes in music, a genuine collaborator. This chapter will, therefore, explore the extraordinarily diverse musical territories that he has covered, starting with a discussion of the importance of contextual and subtextual frameworks, the means by which Danna finds pathways into the center of a film. This will be followed by a focus on Danna's recurrent approaches such as the use of music from "other" cultures, referentialism, and the influence of both early music and popular music. Many of the examples discussed here post-date *The Ice Storm*, partly because that film acted as a springboard for Danna's fully developed methodology, but also because Danna's technique is not in evolution in the same way that one might find in composers who are more concerned with constructing their own musical identity rather than a musical identity for the given film. This chapter will prepare for the case study analysis of *The Ice Storm* by providing an investigation of Danna's musical-narrative language and the contexts in which it is framed.

Concept and Subtext

Virtually any Danna scoring process is dominated by an initial period of conceptualization; "the first step is not to do anything. You have to think."[3] By arriving at an intimate understanding of the film's aims, themes, subtle allusions, and structural connections the purpose, style, and form of the music can be discovered. This process of conceptualization can, on occasion, last considerably longer than the physical act of composition itself. For example, on *Felicia's Journey* (Egoyan, 1999) it took Danna three months to discover the conceptual framework, but only two weeks to write the actual score. The period of conceptualization is not, of course, a passive process; it involves experimentation, acceptance and rejection of ideas, and attempts to find conduits into a film that allow music the opportunity to make dramatically intelligent and emotionally perceptive comments. Inevitably, this approach leads to the scoring of subtext rather than surface narrative, as there seems to be little point in "repeating what the drama is already saying on the screen."[4] The aim is to avoid patronizing what Danna believes to be a highly cine-literate audience, allowing them the freedom to engage in a personal way with the content of the film. It is a mode of scoring that intends to evoke rather than to represent and creates what Walter Murch describes as a "perceptual vacuum into which the mind of the audience must inevitably rush."[5] Of course, some films do not allow this process to take place as they convey only limited layers of meaning. While Danna enjoys watching those types of film, he finds them less challenging and interesting to work on. Locating methods that create what I shall call "layers of signification," therefore, lies at the heart of Danna's scoring technique. Due to the fact that Danna struggled with the creation of the score for *Felicia's Journey*, it provides a useful example of how the discovery of an appropriate conceptual framework leads to music that creates layers of signification, rather than opting for more easily encountered solutions.

Based on William Trevor's novel of the same name, *Felicia's Journey* is a subtle take on the serial killer movie. A seventeen-year-old Irish Catholic girl, Felicia, arrives in an industrial English town looking for Johnny, her former lover and father of her unborn child. Refusing to accept rumors that he has joined the British Army, she longs for a reunion with him and dreams of an idealistic future family life.

Felicia's own family cannot cope; her father rejects her when he discovers she is pregnant, branding her a whore; her mother is dead; and her great grandmother is too ill to notice what goes on around her. While searching for Johnny Felicia meets Hilditch, a meticulous catering manager, who takes on the mantle of father figure and offers to help her. However, Hilditch's ultimate motive is far from charitable. He eventually persuades and pays for Felicia to have an abortion. The film's most disturbing discovery is that Hilditch wishes to murder Felicia, like numerous vulnerable girls before her, but he cannot bring himself to kill the unborn fetus. Once that obstacle has been removed he can once again set about his task. Hilditch is also obsessed with his own dead mother, the presenter of a 1950s cookery program, which he watches every night on videotape. He prepares the extravagant meals according to her instruction then dines with her ghostly image. What connects Hilditch and Felicia is the fact that they are both searching for a utopian past that never existed in reality.

Egoyan's initial ideas for music in the film consisted of ballroom orchestra music by bandleaders such as Victor Sylvester and singers like Helen Shapiro and Alma Cogan. This music was intended to be reflective of the world in which Hilditch was raised as a child. The director eventually decided to use, as source music, a number of songs by the little-known, androgynously voiced singer Malcolm Vaughan, who had a handful of hits in the mid-1950s. Danna found himself compositionally blocked because he was not close to the reference material that Egoyan brought to him; he was struggling to understand what the function of the score should be within the film. The first breakthrough came by fully appreciating the meaning and importance of the diegetic songs to Hilditch. What Danna initially may have perceived as an indictment of Hilditch's bad taste, was in fact the key to his character. Hilditch needs the syrupy 1950s source music in order to conjure his utopian world, and does not perceive it as kitsch because "he thinks of that music as very comforting, very suave, and gentle, just like he sees himself. He's built this kind of cocoon, this velvety covering around his inner real character, which we discover by the end of the film."[6] In order to represent this saccharine sheen, a Mantovani-esque piece of orchestral library music entitled Cascade Waltz, composed by Ray Davies, is used during the film's opening titles (Figure 2.1).[7] The music with an abundance of major-seventh harmonies, sumptuous melody, and heavy use of reverberation is hypertonal, explicit in its sweetened and gushing overenthusiasm.

Figure 2.1: *Felicia's Journey*. Cascade Waltz.
© 1991, Cavendish Music Co. Ltd.
Reproduced by permission of Boosey and Hawkes Music Publishers Ltd.

Danna's focus on compositional subtlety and his dislike of declamatory scoring means that he has always found it difficult to compose music of excess. Hence rather than attempting to pastiche Mantovaniesque music without sincerity, Danna's solution was to treat the existing library music track as raw material for manipulation using a variety of audio processing techniques throughout the film. Consequently, the music is frequently reversed, time stretched or compressed, pitch shifted, filtered, and distorted. In a scene that crosscuts between both the adult and child Hilditch stealing money, Danna takes one of the central production characteristics of Mantovani's music, the heavy use of reverberation, to an uncomfortable extreme such that the sweet music becomes an indistinct wash and its tonal center is disrupted. Danna further adds atmospheric, distorted electronica that help scrub away Hilditch's ingratiating gloss, as he becomes more devious in his attempts to control Felicia.[8]

At the same time, Danna had begun to compose music that related to the character Felicia. Felicia's musical material needed to be a locus from which the eponymous journey could develop both spiritually and geographically. One scene where Felicia speaks in Gaelic with her bed-ridden great grandmother seemed to provide the spark for the idea of using a female Irish vocalist. Egoyan observes that "the use of the language was important," particularly in creating a generational link between Felicia, her dead mother, and her great grandmother.[9] The use of the ancient Gaelic folk tune *"Coinleach Ghlas an Fhomhair"* ("The Green Autumn Stubble"), underscored with an undulating electronic wash, helps to connect the three women. Furthermore, the text of the folksong resonates with Felicia's narrative development. In particular, the last two lines—"Alas that we're not married/Or on board ship sailing away"—provide a direct reflection of her actions and her journey across the English Channel to find Johnny.[10] The ethereal reverberation effects added to the singer's voice are notable because they are designed to enhance the inherited cultural memory implicit in the scoring concept.

The representative nature of the voice provides a fascinating example of what Michel Chion describes as the *acousmêtre*.[11] Developing Schaeffer's concept about a sound that is heard without its source being seen, Chion explains:

> When the acousmatic presence is a voice, and especially when this voice has not yet been visualized—that is, when we cannot yet connect it to a face—we get a special being, a kind of talking and acting shadow to which we attach the name *acousmêtre*.[12]

The disembodied singing voice in *Felicia's Journey* is never specifically connected to anyone's face, although it could be linked to Felicia's great grandmother through association of the Gaelic language; a disembodied voice with a disembodied language. The voice could also represent Felicia's mother speaking from beyond the grave.[13] Egoyan explains that use of the voice was symbolic and speaks to Felicia like a spirit "singing to her and lulling her."[14] Whoever the voice represents, or even if it is perceived as a double *acousmêtre*, it lacks one of the four powers that Chion identifies as central facets of the acousmatic voice: panopticism, ubiquity, omniscience, and omnipotence.[15] The disembodied Gaelic voice has the ability to see Felicia and appear to her at any time and it calls to her whenever she needs comfort and support; it knows all because it reappears during her abortion, or when she is wandering around an industrial estate in Birmingham looking for her ex-lover who has abandoned her. What the voice cannot be is omnipotent. It can lull, comfort, encourage, or support, but it does not seem to have the power to forewarn, to change events or alter Felicia's fate. Interestingly, the *acousmêtre* in this case is never de-acousmatized, that is, its source is not revealed. It remains nondiegetic as if emanating from Felicia's own memory; it is the voice of her past, a link to her home and family. I do not wish to suggest that these issues were consciously discussed by Danna and Egoyan, but the conceptual depth inherent in their instinctual decision allows for many layers of subconscious meaning to be created.

The two types of music already described were working well, but lacked the ability to present the very darkest side of Hilditch's character. This was partly because the saturated string music, even when digitally treated and manipulated, still presented the world from Hilditch's point of view. Another musical strand was required which could present the truth about the serial killer. Egoyan observes that in the meeting of the two musical worlds "a sense of rupture" was required.[16] This concept seems to have grown out of the inclusion of an extract from the 1953 film version of *Salome* (Dieterle), used in a scene when Hilditch watches television in hospital. Egoyan had directed Richard Strauss's opera *Salome* with the Canadian Opera Company during the 1996–97 season and he thought that the inclusion of a scene from the opulent 1950s film could provide some useful references. He also tried to temp the film with some of the music from Strauss's opera, which failed to create the appropriate sense of rupture. However, this approach did propel Danna's thought processes in a different direction. If we consider Strauss's music as the supreme example of fin-de-siècle chromatic Romanticism, then it stretches tonal language to such an extreme that the music can move freely in any harmonic direction at any time. It is this idea that appealed to Danna and he extended it to its full conclusion by writing music that had no recourse to key whatsoever; serial music.[17] Ironically, the music that he had been forced to compose as a student and hated became a highly appropriate and central articulator of the instability central to the representation of Hilditch.

Danna's tone row first appears on the solo cello as Felicia wanders ineffectually around Birmingham looking for a lawnmower factory (Figure 2.2). This links her destiny to Hilditch from the very opening of the film.

Figure 2.2: Tone Row
from the Motion Picture *Felicia's Journey.*
Music by Mychael Danna.
Copyright © 1999 Music Icon Publishing Inc. (BMI)
Worldwide Rights for Music Icon Publishing Inc. Administered by Cherry River Music Co.
International Copyright Secured. All Rights Reserved.

The octave displacement at the very beginning of Danna's row is a fascinating conceptual decision that has a number of implications. First, it demonstrates a sense of playfulness with the rules of serial technique; there are thirteen notes in Danna's initial statement of the row. More importantly, however, transpositions, retrogrades, and inversions of the row begin or end with an octave that will help the listener to locate phrases. Furthermore, the tritone between the first and second pitches of the row (D and G♯) is invariant when subjected to inversion. This means that any retrograde of the row ends with a tritone and every transposition or inversion begins with one. The effect is to demarcate the start and end points of phrases, which contradicts the fundamental aim of serial technique: the emancipation of dissonance and the equality of all pitches. Danna's tone row contains a clear home pitch whose function is analogous to a capital letter or period in a sentence (Figure 2.3).

	I^0	I^6	I^{10}	I^9	I^3	I^7	I^2	I^5	I^4	I^{11}	I^2	I^8	
P^0	D	G♯	C	B	F	A	E	G	F♯	C♯	D♯	A♯	R^0
P^6	G♯	D	F♯	F	B	D♯	A♯	C♯	C	G	A	E	R^6
P^2	E	A♯	D	C♯	G	B	F♯	A	G♯	D♯	F	C	R^2
P^3	F	B	D♯	D	G♯	C	G	A♯	A	E	F♯	C♯	R^3
P^9	B	F	A	G♯	D	F♯	C♯	E	D♯	A♯	C	G	R^9
P^5	G	C♯	F	E	A♯	D	A	C	B	F♯	G♯	D♯	R^5
P^{10}	C	F♯	A♯	A	D♯	G	D	F	E	B	C♯	G♯	R^{10}
P^7	A	D♯	G	F♯	C	E	B	D	C♯	G♯	A♯	F	R^7
P^8	A♯	E	G♯	G	C♯	F	C	D♯	D	A	B	F♯	R^8
P^1	D♯	A	C♯	C	F♯	A♯	F	G♯	G	D	E	B	R^1
P^{11}	C♯	G	B	A♯	E	G♯	D♯	F♯	F	C	D	A	R^{11}
P^4	F♯	C	E	D♯	A	C♯	G♯	B	A♯	F	G	D	R^4
	RI^0	RI^{10}	RI^9	RI^3	RI^7	RI^2	RI^5	RI^4	RI^{11}	RI^1	RI^8	RI^9	

Figure 2.3: *Felicia's Journey*. Tone Row Matrix.

The importance of the pitch D to Danna's musical design is foregrounded in one of the film's climactic moments. Hilditch has just prepared a cup of cocoa laced with sleeping tablets for Felicia, which he carries up the stairs ready to give to her as a nightcap.[18] We know that he plans to kill her when the drugs have taken effect (Figure 2.4). The viola and cello play a pedal D in octaves while violin 2 has the row in retrograde (R^0), the piccolo likewise plays a pattern derived from the last five notes of R^0, the oboe has the row in inversion (I^0), and the tone row proper is played by the clarinet. The fact that these rows appear in a prime form is because of their direct association with the pitch D. In addition, the sequence also has a great deal of tritone movement between D and G♯, which further demarcates the prime pitch of the row. The climactic *fortissimo* woodwind chord coincides with the moment when Hilditch steps unnervingly out of the diegesis and stares directly at the camera and at us the audience; a horrific moment of realization. The score in this section is punctuated by a hideously distorted version of the saccharine library music creating a truly ugly and chaotic soundworld.

Figure 2.4: Hilditch Climbs the Stair
from the Motion Picture *Felicia's Journey.*
Music by Mychael Danna.
Copyright © 1999 Music Icon Publishing Inc. (BMI).
Worldwide Rights for Music Icon Publishing Inc. Administered by Cherry
River Music Co.
International Copyright Secured. All Rights Reserved.

Why would Danna create a row that has clear tonal implications when one of the aims of the score is to create a dissonant frenzy? The reason becomes apparent towards the end of the film when Hilditch realizes the monster that he has become and decides to free Felicia. The abundance of rising minor/major thirds and perfect fifths in the row now become articulators of harmonic direction. The row is used in its prime form but its latent tonality is revealed by the accompaniment.

The shroud is removed at the moment of Hilditch's self-revelation. It is a musical device that allows redemption to rise out of the chaos (Figure 2.5).

Figure 2.5: Redemption Theme
from the Motion Picture *Felicia's Journey*.
Music by Mychael Danna.
Copyright © 1999 Music Icon Publishing Inc. (BMI).
Worldwide Rights for Music Icon Publishing Inc. Administered by Cherry River Music Co.
International Copyright Secured. All Rights Reserved.

Ethnicity

One of the most recognizable features of a Danna score is the use of instruments and music from other cultures. These influences appear regardless of whether a film has a Western or non-Western context, but always with rigorous justification. The importance of conceptual frameworks to Danna's method is what marks him apart from many film composers who use ethnic music. There is nothing perfunctory about Danna's approach; when world music is used it always forms the nucleus of his score, rather than starting with an orchestra and affixing token world instruments afterwards. This depth arises from a complete immersion in the music and traditions of other civilizations. As Andrew Lockington explains, Danna is an "anthropologist when it comes to the culture he is drawing from. He really needs to understand that culture, in more ways than just the music."[19]

It is surely no coincidence that Danna's long-term collaborators Atom Egoyan, Mira Nair, and Ang Lee are all directors associated with diaspora (Armenia, India, and Taiwan, respectively). Each director also has a different relationship to the representation of otherness. Egoyan's films, for example, deal directly with characters that come from "different worlds or carry the baggage from different worlds and are carrying spirits which are very often not present in real time."[20] Nair's early films such as *Mississippi Masala* (1991) also deal with the notion of cultural identity in diaspora, but her work with Danna has been more about the reclamation and representation of Indian culture, even in films that lack obvious Indian cultural references such as *Vanity Fair* (2004).[21] Indeed, Nair could not have imagined working with a non-Indian composer on *Kama Sutra* (1996) or *Monsoon Wedding* (2001), but explains that Danna's depth of understanding is such that he "only looks Canadian, but is actually Indian."[22] Lee's work with Danna (*The Ice Storm*; *Ride With the Devil*, 1999; *Chosen*, 2001) examines American culture and history with the cool objectivity of an outsider's perspective. Lee presents a consistent "pattern of people who are on the outside,"[23] a position with which he clearly has some empathy: "I'm a sort of foreigner everywhere. It's hard to find a real identity."[24] In all of these cases it is easy to understand the appeal of Danna's chosen compositional approach. The potential for musical representation of otherness, dislocation, exoticism, and identity as well as geographical location is a powerful dramatic and narrative tool.

In some cases it is simply the sound quality of a particular type of ensemble, musical style, or instrument that draws Danna to it. If the particular timbre of a melody played on *duduk* is a more powerful articulator of a dramatic idea than the same melody played on a flute, Danna sees no reason not to use it. The difficulty in "resisting the tendency to read domination and subsumption into any and all musical appropriation" sometimes challenges the Western audience to view the use of ethnic instruments without further cultural meaning.[25] In *Family Viewing*, for example, a mixed African and Indonesian percussion ensemble is used to create frenzied driving movement. This music accompanies, or rather dominates, a scene where the father, Stan, frenetically searches the empty north wing of a hotel for his mother-in-law, whom he believes has been hidden there by his son, Van. The propulsive brutality of the music is out of proportion with the scene's physical action, but it creates a powerful sense of the aggression central to the film's overarching design as an "oedipal conflict played out in a technological arena."[26] The cultural mélange of the varied ensemble has no direct referential meaning, except that its sound quality helps to create the necessary sense of dramatic delirium; musical otherness as plain aesthetic difference.

In *Exotica*, however, the mixing of musical styles and cultures has a clear conceptual purpose. The film deals with the intertwined lives of characters that work at or frequent a Toronto lap-dancing club. The first line of the film's dialogue: "You have to ask yourself, what brought the person to this point?" is the question that the film addresses consistently as the various characters act out their obsessions and fantasies. The club Exotica is where the characters seek to exotify their own experience and "sedate themselves or lose themselves in another place."[27] Danna's aim, therefore, was to create "somewhere that should only exist in an imaginary world."[28] For that reason, the score fuses Middle Eastern and Indian instruments with contemporary pop techniques to create "a dreamlike amalgamation of styles."[29] The literal crossing of musical boundaries complements the characters' move into an enticing, unusual, and unreal world.

The opening title music, for example, already defines the disturbing and peculiar cultural mix (Figure 2.6). The main theme is first heard on a *shehnai*; a type of North Indian oboe. However, the lascivious melody is based around the Arabic mode *nagrīz* on F♯ (F♯–G♯–A–B♯–C♯–D♯–E). The piano accompaniment's drone-like assertion of the F♯ starting pitch (*mabdā*) is unsettled by Danna's recurrent and idiomatic focus on the fourth degree of the mode, B♯. It is music that to a Western listener sounds uncomfortably displaced and unresolved. This is arguably because the melodic line can also be heard as a Western C♯ melodic minor scale. If the B♯ is heard as a leading note, then its recurrent usage emphasizes an unfulfilled desire to resolve onto C♯. In effect, the music plays out a battle between F♯ and C♯ as the home pitch of the piece; the *shehnai*'s B♯ and the piano drone F♯ pull the score in different directions. It is Danna's understanding of both Middle Eastern and Western musical cultures that allows him to create this effect. He respects the original use and function of the mode, but also understands *how* the film's predominantly Western audience will hear it. Of course, the aim is not to use the mode authentically, but to be deferential to the culture from which the musical idea is borrowed:

"If you're going to stretch the boundaries or bend the rules, you should know that you are doing that. As opposed to doing it by accident."[30]

Figure 2.6: *Exotica*. Opening Titles (transcribed).
© 1997, reproduced by permission of Mychael Danna and Ego Film Arts.

The use of ethnic music and musicians can raise questions about exploitation of other cultures. What happens to an original cultural product when it is appropriated and used within a different context? Who profits from this kind of cultural assimilation? Such debates have long raged in ethnomusicology and cultural studies, with many scholars drawing on Edward Said's seminal work *Orientalism* as a means of constructing arguments about postcolonialism and racial condescension.[31] A whole school of thought, consequently, argues that hybridity and cultural imperialism are inextricably linked, that discourses on world music both ideological and economic are "inseparable from discourses on indigineity and domination."[32] For example, John Hutnyk's charge against the appropriation of exotic music deftly encapsulates the field.

> The preparation of content for the liberal multiculturalism of the cultural smorgasbord implicates both well meaning Third Worldists and livelihood seeking Third Worlders. Good intentions caught within a sometimes quite restricted and apolitical horizon transmute into an advertising programme for international capital hegemony.[33]

The problem with this type of interpretation is that it implies that anybody ("well meaning" or "livelihood seeking") who draws on ethnic influences is somehow an agent of cultural domination. The love of the "other" is understood only as "part and parcel of the evil dynamic of capitalist exploitation."[34] This seems to me a rather reductivist critique that paints every creative musician with the same sweatshop-exploitation brush regardless of content or context. There would be no option but to judge all hybrid works as at the mercy of the global condition and, consequently, as artistically bankrupt. Studies of local practice, conversely, tend to highlight the fact that musical styles constantly develop, and have constantly developed through a process of borrowing and syncretism; that hybridity is a feature of all music. The notion of traditional music as a pure, immutable form is unfounded, because, as Simon Frith explains, "tradition is always a matter of invention and reinvention."[35]

The opening title sequence of *Monsoon Wedding* highlights this very evolution by using a reinvented Indian musical form. In Hindu marriage ceremonies the *Baraat*, or groom's wedding procession, accompanies his official arrival at the *milni* (meeting point) where he is received by the bride's family. The jubilant procession is led by family and friends and a loud, rowdy brass band. *Baraat* bands were formerly comprised of indigenous Indian instruments, but during the British colonial rule widespread adoption of Western military brass by Indian musicians became commonplace.[36] As the popularity of Indian film song grew from the 1930s onwards, so the *Baraat* band repertoire evolved from light "classical" *raga*-based music, to raucous arrangements of Hindi film songs which held significant referential meanings. For example, the song "*Aaj Mere Yaar Ki Shaadi Hai*" ("Today Is My Best Friend's Wedding"), which was first used in the film *Aadmi Sadak Ka* (1977), is considered an indispensable part of the modern Hindu wedding ceremony.[37] While such appropriation inevitably changes the repertoire, it also alters the nature and meaning of the mediated music. The development of the *Baraat* band could be viewed as the result of contamination by British colonialist rulers, but its quintessentially Indian embrace also announces triumph over oppression, or simply ownership of the musical materials in question. Previously mediated music is altered socially and economically by musicians to suit a new function.[38]

For the vivid graphics of *Monsoon Wedding*'s opening titles, then, Danna takes the film's main theme and composes a *Baraat*-style piece for clarinet, two trumpets, two trombones, tuba, and mixed percussion (including a prominent part for snare drum). The decision to create this energetic street sound was influenced by Mira Nair's desire to construct an "Indian version of Nino Rota, to tell the audience that they are in for a really good time."[39]

Figure 2.7: *Monsoon Wedding. Baraat*, Thematic Material (a).
© 2001, reproduced by permission of Mychael Danna and Mirabai Films.

Figure 2.8: *Monsoon Wedding. Baraat*, Thematic Material (b).
© 2001, reproduced by permission of Mychael Danna and Mirabai Films.

Figures 2.7 and 2.8 show the basic thematic material from which Danna's *Baraat* is constructed. The music consists of recurrent bass lines and melodic patterns, around which the performers were encouraged to improvise. The vibrancy of the music, therefore, comes from the sense of playfulness and buoyant freedom in the performance. The musicians take Danna's simple material and cast themselves in the role of street band by employing over-the-top *glissandi*, rhythmic discontinuities, and individual flights of fancy. The vibrancy of the music is due in part to the notes themselves but also to the fact that both Nair and Danna's enthusiasm helped "jazz-up" the players in the recording studio.[40] Of course, this is not to deny the importance of the melodic material itself, which is based on *Raga Kalyan*. The choice of this mode is significant because in India it is associated with feelings of harmony and joyfulness. Its distinctive sharpened fourth degree (A♯), on which Danna constantly focuses, adds a delightful piquancy (in Western terms the mode is equivalent to Lydian E). Danna's *Baraat* music is a powerful metaphor for the film's central themes, where conflicts between tradition, modernity, and globalization in contemporary India are played out through the life-affirming Punjabi characters.[41]

As his career has progressed, Danna has found it increasingly important to support musicians in their home environment, the people who are still making music on the soil of their homeland. This is partly in response to the ethical factors outlined above, but also because Danna believes that there is a palpable difference in the quality that the music possesses.

> I do as much research as I can. I respect the culture and the music by doing that research, by trying to understand the place of that music in that culture: what its meanings are, what its strengths are; respecting those musicians by actually hiring them and paying them money. I've consciously gone to countries like Armenia, for instance, and brought funds to musicians there that otherwise would have ended up in Los Angeles or some other urban center.[42]

The male voice choir in *Ararat* (2002), for example, was recorded in a fifth-century church in the holy city of Etchmiadzin, the center of the Armenian apostolic faith.[43] The recording took place at night by candlelight because the church had no electricity and as a result candles can be heard "spluttering in the background."[44] The music could easily have been recorded in a Hollywood studio with session musicians and "some fake reverberation, and maybe it would sound pretty well the same."[45] But it was meaningful to Danna that the music was performed by Armenians in Armenia and was "bouncing off of 1500-year-old stone."[46] Egoyan initially held that this approach was impractical given the tight budget, but was later extremely grateful as it was a "huge part of the emotional journey" that he and Danna made.[47] It is symbolic that the music is the only component of *Ararat* that physically came from Armenia. However hermetic and intellectual these decisions may seem, and however consciously or subconsciously they may be perceived by an audience, they do imbue Danna's scores with a unique sensibility and multiple meanings.

Claudia Gorbman observes: "In the 1980s, as exotic ethnic musics became raw materials to pass through the mills of global media commodifications and consumption by Western markets, a world music soundtrack began to stand for a style in itself, defining the film audience as much as the film itself."[48] It is undoubtedly true that Danna's use of world music is a central stylistic feature that has defined him mainly as a composer of art film. However, his musical choices do not stem from a political aggression towards the mainstream, but rather he feels that the emotional range of the language of Western cinema music is limited. As Jonathan Bellman reminds us: "Musical exoticism above all seeks to state the otherwise unstatable."[49] Danna revels in the music of other cultures because it allows him to say more, access greater emotional range, and to create many layers of signification. Nair believes that Danna's music is unconditionally distinct from "half-arsed world music; take a bit of this, take a bit of that."[50] He is not simply influenced by the exotic, it is a vital component of his compositional language. While this approach may be thought of as being exploitative or superficial, Egoyan argues that this is not the case: "I think it is as deep as a Westerner can go."[51] Indeed, Danna's compositional approach suggests a shift away from a model of the exotic within Western music to challenge exactly what is "exotic" or "Western" in music.

Early Music, Referentialism

Just as Danna feels able to use any global musical language, so he believes that music from any historical period may provide an intelligent scoring option. His desire to liberate world music from the restraints of geographical location is matched by the use of historical musical forms and styles that do not necessarily anchor the film to a particular era. This approach allows for considerable freedom in the spatiotemporal conventions of film scoring practice, such as the (historically inaccurate) use of early Baroque music for period drama set in the late eighteenth century. As Russell Lack explains, "certain instrumental sounds become synonymous with certain cultures and certain eras. This becomes a kind of stylistic shorthand which cinema audiences absorb and accept without even realizing it."[52] I have outlined elsewhere some of the affinities between Baroque music and film scoring, but Danna takes this affection to an extreme and seeks every opportunity to incorporate early music elements into his scores.[53]

Based on Michel Marc Bouchard's play *Les Fleurettes*, John Greyson's *Lilies* (1996) is a revenge fantasy that deals with the intricate subject of repressed homosexuality and Catholicism. A bishop (Bilodeau) is called to a prison in 1952 to hear the confession of a dying inmate (Doucet) only to be held captive and forced to watch a re-enactment of events that took place forty years earlier when he and the prisoner were involved in a homosexual *ménage à trois*. All of the characters, regardless of gender, are played by the male inmates as they create the play within the film. The sumptuous homoerotic narrative, including kitsch performances of the masochistic saga of Saint Sebastian, drag, social prejudice, and denied love make the film a fascinating example of New Queer Cinema.[54] The confession at the core of the film is not that of the prisoner but of the bishop who admits to having brought about the death of the young man (Vallier) for which the prisoner was convicted. Drawing on the liturgical references and the death that fuels the revenge central to the narrative structure, Danna's score is based upon the Requiem mass. The Renaissance-like polyphonic choral writing (for boy soprano, counter-tenor, two tenors, and bass) represents the gamut of masculine vocal production.[55] The choral music is largely unaccompanied, but there are occasional glimpses of a trumpet in B♭, cello (acting as a viol), and organ. Instrumental postludes, based on the *cantus firmus* of the previous choral piece are occasionally provided by the solo cello.[56]

Figure 2.9 shows the structure of Danna's mass which loosely adheres to the structure of the traditional Requiem, but there are some sections taken from the Ordinary mass such as the Gloria and the Alleluia. In addition, the structural location of the Dies Irae and Lux Aeterna would normally be exchanged. However, the placement of Danna's material is designed to reflect the dramatic events. For example, the Lux Aeterna (let perpetual light shine upon them) is heard as Doucet strikes a match, filling the screen with flame, leading to a flashback sequence accompanied by the young Bilodeau's statement: "Babylon the Great, city of sin, and lust, I saw the Saint set fire to the fallen city." Later the Dies Irae (Day of wrath; that day will dissolve the world into glowing ashes) is used when the enraged Bilodeau sets fire to Doucet's bedroom, an act that eventually brings about Vallier's death. Contained within the Alleluia is the hidden tenor text "Justus germinabit sicut lilium: et florebit in aeternum ante Dominum" (The just shall spring like the lily: and shall flourish forever before the Lord). This music accompanies Vallier's mother as she wanders through the forest where she will eventually ask her son to kill her (Figure 2.10). Lilies become increasingly associated with her and she explains their metaphorical significance as symbols of "virginity and innocence, symbol of the French monarchy, cruel emblem branded into the flesh of prisoners convicted of infamous crimes." In this case the Latin text not only provides a somewhat oblique referential commentary on the narrative action, but also makes a moral judgment on the characters' actions through the film's central lily imagery.

While Danna's construction of the mass does not adhere to typical formal considerations, equally it can be seen as a means of imposing an external structure on a film that draws from experimental cinema tradition and has a free-flowing narrative arc. In this sense, the music helps to bind the enigmatic story together.

The advantage of using a recognizable historical style as a compositional starting point is that there are formal conventions which can be outwardly perceived but which do not necessarily need to be followed rigorously. Indeed, as Royal Brown observes, "film music

Kyrie

Gloria

Gloria (postlude)

Lux Aeterna

Alleluia: Justus Germinabit

Sanctus (interlude)

Ave Verum Corpus

Benedictus

In Paradisum

Pie Jesu

Dies Irae

Dies Irae 2 (postlude)

Libera Me

Figure 2.9: *Lilies*. Requiem Structure.

tends to borrow from classical music's freedom to manipulate without usually borrowing from its traditional restraints."[57] Danna's score gains all the advantages of historical referentialism while still maintaining his own compositional preferences; it is clearly "not meant to be a pastiche."[58] Although church modes form the basis of the melodic construction, there is an extremely liberal treatment of the "rules" of *musica ficta*.[59] The vacillating voice-leading and random bass entry in the Alleluia (Figure 2.10), or the dark chromaticism of the Dies Irae, all serve to make the music more dramatically potent. Judged as exercises in species counterpoint the score has many weaknesses, but as dramatic constructs for a contemporary audience the music gains from the weight of tradition without being beholden to it. Of course, one consequence of this approach is that the music cannot completely displace the stylistic framework that encases it otherwise the referential benefits are minimized. Danna explains that the concept required a "recognizable sacred, ecclesiastical quality, and it could not go too far away from that as far as dissonance or twentieth-century techniques were concerned."[60] In addition, quick changes in mood or color are harder to achieve within this framework and consequently the close matching of physical gesture or dramatic points of emphasis are not a feature of this score. The music makes clear its alliance to the image, then, by starting and ending cues on bold physical gestures or hard cuts and through general appropriateness of mood, rather than by close reflection of the moment by moment action. Within this framework the overarching Requiem structure provides vital unity of material and helps enhance the film's structural development.

Figure 2.10: *Lilies*. Alleluia, "Justus Germinabit."
© 1996, reproduced by permission of Triptych Media Inc.

Danna's decision to write a pseudo-Medieval score for *The Sweet Hereafter* (1997) also appears to have been an instinctive and comfortable idea: "If you want to get across the idea of a tiny, tight, very homogenized community. . . Medieval music is a nice place to start."[61] When a recognized historical style is used within a non-period film, the audience is immediately forced to question its dramatic function and referential meaning, because it is an approach that challenges accepted film scoring convention. A sense of novelty can, consequently, be a significant contributor to any layers of signification that the director or composer wish to create. Egoyan himself acknowledges this, but also highlights how this method can help foreground a range of meanings that would otherwise remain buried in the narrative. In *The Sweet Hereafter* the use of early music has very specific associations, because "to hear those Medieval instruments suddenly paints the whole film as a Grimm fairytale."[62] Implicit in this description is the notion that a historical musical score used in a modern context, through complicity and distance, can create a sense of timelessness. The juxtaposition can suggest that human conflicts rise above the ages and any single event. Early music in this context elevates the story beyond its parochial confines to something that provides a wider perspective on the human condition.

The Sweet Hereafter is about a small, close-knit community and the effects of a tragic school bus accident in which most of the town's children are drowned. A city lawyer arrives promising to win compensation by launching a class action suit against anyone who can be blamed. As he investigates the crash the overwhelming grief, tension, and tragedy that cannot be assuaged by the desire for money becomes increasingly apparent. A central motif woven into the film is Robert Browning's poem "The Pied Piper of Hamelin," sections of which are recited both diegetically and as voice-over by Nicole.[63] Just as in the poem, she is the sole, lame survivor who is left behind when all of the other children have departed (in her case she is paralyzed from the waist down following the accident). Many other parallels between the poem and film exist, but the principle difference is that the film's townsfolk have committed no collective wrong and there is no convenient guilty party.

Figure 2.11: *The Sweet Hereafter*. Thin Ice.
© 1997, reproduced by permission of Mychael Danna and Ego Film Arts.

The Pied Piper legend, with its small Medieval community and mysterious musical outsider, clearly provided the conceptual weight for Danna's score. A distinctive consort of early instruments consisting of recorders, crumhorn, shawm, sackbut, lute, vielles, and percussion is used. In addition, Danna features a Persian *ney* flute as a representation of the poem's magical pipe music. The score for *The Sweet Hereafter*, therefore, combines two of Danna's musical passions: early music and exotic music. As Danna explains he loves writing period music, "but I think it's more challenging to try and mix-up period-style music with other things and take it somewhere where it's not necessarily supposed to be."[64] Figure 2.11 shows Danna's musical material just before the school bus crashes. The distinctive juxtaposition of the capricious *ney*, with its rogue A♭, pitted against the period ensemble's solid, *organum*-like G minor is a portent of impending danger.[65]

A similar type of early/world music syncretism can be found in Danna's score for Ang Lee's short film *Chosen* (2001). Here the score juxtaposes Baroque and Tibetan musical influences, but the concept on this occasion was provided by the director, not the composer. *Chosen* is one of eight internet films commissioned by German car manufacturer BMW as part of a series entitled *The Hire*. Following market research showing that approximately eighty-five percent of purchasers used the internet before buying a BMW car, the company created an integrated web and television advertising strategy building on BMW's distinctive brand in an attempt to make a greater impression in the saturated luxury car market. Directors such as John Woo, Wong Kar-Wai, John Frankenheimer, Tony Scott, and Guy Ritchie were invited to produce short, downloadable films with the same central premise: the main character would help people through difficult circumstances by the skillful driving of a BMW car. The driver used in all eight films was actor Clive Owen, but the real star was the BMW brand. Each director was given complete creative control over content and direction, freedom far beyond boundaries of the Hollywood system and BMW's normal expectations of a traditional advertisement. However, paying for television airtime for eight eight-minute films would have been prohibitively expensive, so television trailers were designed to encourage potential purchasers to go to the BMW Films web site. After the required registration, viewers could watch streamed versions of the films or download the BMW Film Player, which provided further brand information. A DVD with slightly longer versions of the films could also be purchased. It remains one of the boldest and most successful marketing campaigns of the early noughties.[66]

Chosen is a loosely veiled allegory of the fourteenth Dalai Lama's escape to India and of the Tibetan government in exile.[67] A young Buddhist boy arrives at a New York dock and is met by his driver in order to be taken to a secret location. The boy gives the driver a tiny metal case, telling him not to open it until later. As they are about to leave the docks, an armed gang sets upon the driver and the boy. In the ensuing car chase the driver's ear is grazed by a gunshot that narrowly misses his head, but the boy is unharmed. After escaping from the docks the boy is taken to a suburban house where he is greeted by a Buddhist monk. The driver's suspicions are aroused by the unorthodox footwear that the monk wears and after further investigation he realizes that the monk is an imposter, dressed in the apparel of one of his hostages. The driver intervenes in time to save the boy from receiving a fatal injection. As the driver leaves the house, he opens the metal case given to him by the boy. It contains a Band-Aid which the driver places on his injured ear.

Lee's instinct was that Baroque music would be an appropriate aural metaphor for the "beautiful German machine"[68] that he was marketing, and consequently the temp track for the film was Bach's Double Concerto for two violins (BWV 1043).[69] This decision raises some interesting questions about the perceived dramatic functions of Baroque music and the scoring of action sequences. Baroque music, and particularly Bach, could be seen to communicate notions of German precision, control, speed, accuracy, and dynamism, but equally its association as refined, high-culture music makes it an unconventional method of scoring an extended car chase. As James Welsh observes, action-adventure films are "testosterone movies designed to match the interest of juvenile audiences—far-fetched, overstated, male-driven, often cartoonish, depending mainly on special-effects wizardry and hyped-up soundtracks."[70] One of the functions of the Baroque music in *Chosen* is to distinguish it from what some scholars have termed the "dick flick."[71] This is not to suggest that the film represents feminine issues or preferences, it still subscribes to many features of macho action movies, but the music is part of an intricate scheme to appeal to the supposedly more discerning, largely middle-aged, upper-middle-class, and male BMW demographic. Of course, there are other reasons for using Baroque music. Lee explains that after working on the detailed fight scenes in *Crouching Tiger, Hidden Dragon* (2000) he "fell in love with choreography."[72] The movement of cars within *Chosen* has an idiosyncratic balletic quality, and the Baroque music highlights this structural aesthetic as much as it generates adrenaline.

Danna explains that trying to replace the temp score was an extremely humbling experience, because Bach is the "closest thing to God."[73] However, despite the daunting process Danna agreed with the decision to use Baroque music which is "effortlessly emotional and . . . everything works together beautifully. It's an obvious metaphor for the lovely BMW product."[74] Danna worked with the Toronto-based period ensemble Tafelmusik to create the score. However, Lee also wanted to represent the boy through recognizable Tibetan musical gestures. Danna's solution to this challenge was to use the ensemble to allude to

Tibetan musical characteristics at specific dramatic moments. In the Buddhist liturgy instrumental sections are played by a wind and percussion ensemble of between eight and twelve players; the winds always play in pairs. One of the most recognizable sounds is created by two deep-sounding brass instruments named *dung*. These instruments, of various lengths and sizes, play gruff, overlapping pedals, dichordal ostinati, and two-note calls. Danna recreated this by working very closely with the horn players in order to emulate the distinctive sound quality. Although the performers use natural horns with a variety of crooks for most of the piece, they were also required to play modern horns in a "growly, hummy, Tibetan style" as imitation of the *dung*.[75] This effect is first heard when the driver waits on the dock as the boat arrives. So abstruse and deformed is the sound that on first hearing it could easily be confused for a ship's horn, an interesting example of music as sound design.

Danna's detailed understanding of the period instruments allowed him to exploit the ensemble to its full potential, as the leader of Tafelmusik, Jeanne Lamon, explains, "unlike some other composers, he was not trying to get us to play as if we were modern instruments. He used what we do best to his ends."[76] However, Danna was also not afraid to challenge the performers to play extreme dynamics and long sustained lines which are not traditionally associated with Baroque music. The *Chosen* score contains numerous features of Baroque style, particularly its gestural structure and orchestration. The ensemble consists of treble recorder, oboe, bassoon, two horns, solo violin, solo cello, strings, and continuo. The idea of the double concerto for violin and cello, developed from the temp track, allows Danna to generate *concertante* and *ripieno* textural contrasts. The music is also rhythmically vibrant with constant sixteenth-note patterns maintaining a sense of forward propulsion. However, the most striking feature is the overarching harmonic structure with its constant and sudden gear shifts. The beginning of the chase sequence, for example, is based within a Vivaldiesque E minor framework. The music often jumps erratically away from E minor to C minor or Eb minor, for example, but always returns to the tonic. The shifting harmony has a number of purposes. It mimics the unpredictable excitement of the chase but also generates an underlying sense of stability and security that the BMW car represents. It is interesting to note that the orchestration, performance style, gestural, and rhythmic structures all lead to a convincing representation of Baroque music, yet the simple use of strident harmonic changes with disjunctive voice-leading transforms the work beyond a skillful pastiche into something that sounds much more contemporary.

Influence of Popular Music

It has already been noted that popular music traditions were as important to Danna's musical development as his conventional art music education, if not more so. He played in bands, went on tour, and his fascination with music technology grew out of an involvement in progressive rock music. Consequently, an understanding and appreciation of popular music styles and techniques is more meaningful to Danna than many composers whose background is solely the Western art music tradition. While Danna's aesthetic should not be confused with film composers who have come exclusively from rock or pop backgrounds (such as Peter Gabriel, Mark Knopfler, Stewart Copeland, or Eric Clapton), the influence of popular music is nonetheless manifested in his compositional style and technique. Occasionally, Danna writes and produces pop songs for use in film soundtracks, but the influence is also apparent in his favoring of rhythmic textures, focus on synthesized timbres, and even harmonic language.

In *The Sweet Hereafter* the screenplay required the main character, Nicole, to be part of a band. In the narrative design of the film this represents her desire to escape small town life by becoming a famous rock star. Danna's approach to the task reveals a fascinating collaborative process with actress Sarah Polley. Together they created the Sam Dent Band, who are observed rehearsing for a concert at the town's harvest fair. Polley wrote lyrics and Danna wrote the music for two songs "Boy" and "Dog Track Drizzle," and some of the songs are also used nondiegetically in the film. Danna also made arrangements of the songs "One More Color" by Jane Siberry and "Courage" by The Tragically Hip. Both artists have cult followings in Canada, but are less well known elsewhere. The decision to create cover versions of local artists demonstrates both a detailed knowledge of the Toronto music scene and gives the Sam Dent Band regional credibility. Any middle-rung Canadian group would know these two artists and the two songs that are used, but the song selection also goes beyond mere local flavor.[77] As Nicole is the lead singer for the band, the lyrics reflect her hidden desires, thoughts, and actions. The overwhelmingly aspirational third verse of "One More Color," for example, equates effort with ultimate achievement and is contrasted with a sense of reconciled acceptance in the chorus (Figure 2.12). Like Siberry's, Polley's voice is light and pure, and the folk influence is represented in the line-up of the band: vocals, electric bass, cello, acoustic and electric guitars, pedal steel guitar, harmonium, and drum-kit.[78] The use of cello and pedal steel guitars adds a parochial, country-folk quality to the ensemble.

One More Color

Speak a little softer,
Work a little harder,
Shoot less with more care.
Sing a little sweeter,
And love a little longer,
And soon you will be there.

Here—all we have here is sky,
All the sky is is blue,
All that blue is is one more color now.

Figure 2.12: ©1985, Wing-It Music.
"One More Color" words and music by Jane Siberry.
Lyrics reprinted by permission of Jane Siberry and Wing-It Music.

The song "Courage" was originally an up-tempo rock song, but it was transformed into a slower and more contemplative arrangement, and both versions are used in the film. Nicole listens to the Sam Dent Band arrangement on her personal stereo while traveling on the school bus. The Tragically Hip original is heard just before she prepares to give a vital deposition. As the sole survivor of a tragic bus crash, the lyric summarizes the challenge that faces Nicole and the particular course of action which she must take: "Courage, it couldn't come at a worse time."

In his book *Rock: The Primary Text*, Allan Moore argues that contrary to critical belief "rock is rich in harmonic formulae."[79] The principal reason that he feels obliged to make this defense is that Classical "functional" harmonic models have often been used to analyze rock music, an imposition that uses the wrong tools for the job. Moore argues that in rock music the distinction between "functional" and "non-functional" harmony is neutral, that is "non-functional" harmony "does not entail the assumption of a lack of quality."[80] What I wish to suggest is that this kind of harmonic language—the tendency to treat harmonies as indivisible units, the importance of modality in defining harmonic structure, and particularly the centrality of parallel chordal movement—are equally vital to Danna's music language. This is not to suggest that Danna is unconcerned with functional harmony or that he consciously writes rock riffs, but rather the harmonic patterns of popular music styles infuse his harmonic language. It could also be suggested, by extension, that this is a feature of a good deal of contemporary North American film scoring.[81]

One of the principle motives created by Danna for the Anthony Hopkins vehicle *Hearts in Atlantis* (Hicks, 2001), for example, is a three-chord progression often heard on the piano. Moving in contrary motion the three consecutive major chords—B♭, A♭, and G, with a passing note F♮ between the last two chords—are clearly based in the Phrygian G mode. In *Girl Interrupted* (Mangold, 1999) Danna creates an acoustic-folk inspired score that incorporates the Toronto Glass Orchestra, a four-piece ensemble performing on blown, bowed, rubbed, and struck glass. The frailty of the music provides an appropriate aural metaphor for the fragile young women in the 1960s mental institution around which the film is based. When the character Susanna Kaysen (Winona Ryder) is first transported to the institution, chord progressions based on Mixolydian E create productive tension between G♯s and G♮s and the dominant and suspended chords do not resolve functionally, for example: E^7 I G^9 I D^7 I E I and I E^{sus4} I G^{maj7}I D I C I.

The influence described above can be found even in the most incongruous places. In *Vanity Fair* Danna composed a drawing-room song for the character Becky Sharp (Reese Witherspoon) to perform at a pivotal dramatic moment. "Now Sleeps the Crimson Petal," based on the Tennyson poem, has many well-observed historical and stylistic features such as the fortepiano performance and A = 430 tuning.[82] However, the song is also extremely harmonically adventurous for the period, generating an unconventional and dramatically potent version of an 1830s domestic song. The song is heard when Becky has been invited to a party at Lord Steyne's house. She is snubbed and ignored by the women, but is eventually befriended by Lady Steyne who pities her and invites her to sing. The sequence, therefore, marks the moment that Becky has the opportunity to enter into society, and the means of achieving this is through her musical performance. Harmonically, however, the song tells a different story indicating the underlying truth that is not witnessed on screen. The song features consistent use of first inversion chords so that there is rarely a strong resolution, and there are recurrent shifts between mediant harmonies. The final cadential section—"So fold thyself, my dearest, thou, and slip/Into my bosom and be lost in me"—demonstrates a dark harmonic descent through C♯m, A, C, B, Am to a final tonic chord of G♯m. The message is clear, just at the point that Becky Sharp appears to have made her entrance into society, the dark descending harmony in fact signals her inevitable downfall.

Conclusion

It is challenging to determine the boundaries of Danna's compositional style because of the broad range of work he has produced. The sheer variety of techniques at his disposal would seem to imply a lack of focus or clear direction. However, this would be to judge Danna's work by the criteria of a different age. Danna is able to use style itself as a compositional weapon to be deployed according to the requirements of each particular film and, thus, he explores the freedom provided by the postmodern condition. The work he produces does not suffer from a lack of identity, because he remains stylistically consistent within each particular project and because he ascribes real importance to conceptual and structural frameworks. The sincerity with which this stylistic diversity is applied—there is no tongue-in-cheek referentialism—suggests that Danna's approach is always about a genuine celebration and exploration that is at the service of the film.

Chapter 3

Locating *The Ice Storm*

There's a reason why people do things, and it isn't a director's job to judge them; that's up to the audience. Actors should provoke thoughts and emotions—that's what movies are about, not telling audiences how to feel.[1]

One of the particular challenges of Ang Lee's filmmaking, as the above comment indicates, is his directorial objectivity. Lee does not consider it his obligation to maneuver and manipulate, but would rather an audience create the film's meaning in their own minds. Inevitably, this philosophy of transferred authorial responsibility manifests itself in a carefully controlled and emotionally restrained filmic language. As Peter Matthews explains there is "something exemplary about a film-maker whose camera isn't always going lickety-split—and who pays the viewer the high compliment of an attention span."[2] Nowhere is this discipline more evident in Lee's work than in *The Ice Storm*, where subtly observed human situations require constant reinterpretation of characters' relationships, motives, and actions. But the obvious risk in such an approach is that the audience may not care enough about the material to want to become engaged with it. In this sense, Matthews's use of the word "exemplary," implying worthiness rather than worth, highlights one of the criticisms leveled at *The Ice Storm*. While critics did not deny the beautiful and striking qualities of the film, some commentators found it as emotionally cold as its title. Robert Sklar, for example, expressed frustration at what he believed the film could and should have been: "Film can show a fiction that makes the past appear to live again, not as in *The Ice Storm*, hold it at arms' length and say, this frozen image is as close as we can get."[3] Other writers viewed the film as a mini-masterwork claiming that it was "cinema at its most immaculate,"[4] or in the case of Gene Siskel championing it as the best film of 1997.[5] Furthermore, the benefit of hindsight later allowed some commentators to emphasize the long-term impact and importance of *The Ice Storm*. Ellen Cheshire, for example, believed that the film was "a far more telling attack on the excesses and failures of American suburbia than Sam Mendes' slick and showier *American Beauty*."[6] The dichotomies already illustrated here are perhaps best summed up by David Thomson's comment that *The Ice Storm* "was a critical triumph that hardly anyone had the stomach for."[7] This division of opinion would seem to be based entirely upon Lee's restrained directorial strategy. Those that did not—perhaps could not—engage with this approach concluded that the film was detached, brittle, or barren. Those that did engage, experienced a powerful and subtle narrative.

The refinement and cognizance of approach in *The Ice Storm* seems remarkable when one considers Lee's background. In 1973, the year in which the film is set, he was nineteen and had just moved to Taiwan's capital city, Taipei, to study drama at the Academy of Art. He had grown up in a middle-class household and knew virtually nothing about Western culture or society until he went to study in America at the University of Illinois in 1978. Lee had no reference points for post-sexual-revolution, "me generation" America. He had not experienced the Vietnam protests, nor witnessed the national turmoil surrounding the Watergate scandal. Yet it is perhaps this very distance that allowed him to delve into the American psyche with incisive awareness, because it is "easier to cut in to the core of expression as an outsider."[8] The dispassionate confidence Lee was able to bring to the process of making *The Ice Storm* may have been more difficult for an American director who had grown up in a suburban, WASP environment.[9] Indeed, at least one reviewer acknowledged the lack of nostalgic reverie which made the film more painful to watch, creating a "fairly desolating experience for people of my class and generation because it makes the flotsam of our living memories seem so completely *dead*."[10] Lee's *Ice Storm*, therefore, refuses to accommodate sentimental memories at the expense of its grim societal assessment. It is a bleak story about the disintegration of the American nuclear family and moral confusion at a pivotal point in the internal history of a nation. As the film's producer and scriptwriter James Schamus noted, the film is able to "sober up even the most rose-tinted observer," because "the seventies, except for the people *born* during them . . . tend not to elicit much allegiance from the people who lived through them."[11]

We shall return to the filmmakers' principles of emotional restraint below and in chapters 4 and 5, because they have significant implications for the shape and structure of the soundtrack. The remainder of this chapter will provide critical readings of some of *The Ice Storm*'s important narrative, structural, and aesthetic elements, as well as relevant production contexts. These features will help locate *The Ice Storm* within contemporary filmmaking practice and will provide an understanding of the durability of its significance as a filmic text.

Indiewood

The Hollywood film industry has been described by Janet Wasko as a "three-tier society" with the major studios at the top, smaller or less influential production and/or distribution companies in the middle, and smaller, often struggling "independent" distributors and production companies at the bottom.[12] On initial inspection, *The Ice Storm* would seem to reside in the last of these three categories, exhibiting many of the features of independent production. For example, it expresses the director's personal vision rather than an industrial notion of box office success. Furthermore, producers Ted Hope and James Schamus, and their then production company, Good Machine, had a long history of involvement in independent film production.[13] However, as Emanuel Levy reminds us, there is a great lack of clarity in the definition of the term "independent" as well as a problematic relationship between independent films and Hollywood.[14] Many critics observe that commercial cinema is so pervasive that even modes and strategies of filmmaking that attempt to develop alternative approaches cannot help but be affected by Hollywood's dominance. While anti-mainstream sentiment may be manifested clearly in the aesthetic approaches of many independent films and filmmakers, the economics of mass distribution and marketing mean that, of necessity, independent films run "parallel to Hollywood" rather than against it.[15] Consequently, the popular notion of the independent film as a low-to-no-budget project with a fresh, quirky spirit—and without commercial compromises—is also evolving. Schamus highlights the challenges that filmmakers face in the contemporary climate of American feature film production:

> the decision to make feature-length narrative films puts you in an economic sphere of activity that by necessity is going to be dominated by Hollywood. Dominated not only economically, but also ideologically. I look at what we do and no matter how aesthetically daring, and bold, and provocative and new and original, we're really committed to doing work with a very narrow bandwidth of aesthetic and political activity.[16]

The acknowledgment that both the economics and philosophy of supposed independent production have become imitations of Hollywood on a smaller scale has significant implications for our understanding of *The Ice Storm.* Given that the film had a comparatively large budget of eighteen million dollars, questions are immediately raised about the nature of its independence and the nature of contemporary Hollywood film production. Is a film's budget an appropriate defining factor of independent status? If independent films are produced within a profit-oriented system, how are their artistic boundaries altered and what alternative, if any, do they provide to the mainstream? The fact that a film such as *The Ice Storm* draws from independent filmmaking aesthetics, as well as Hollywood's financial and distribution clout, is an attempt to draw the best elements from both worlds. *The Ice Storm* can, therefore, be considered an example of a mode of filmmaking that has been increasingly referred to as Indiewood.

Fox Searchlight Pictures, which was established in 1994 as the independent arm of Twentieth Century Fox, financed *The Ice Storm.* Along with other Hollywood majors, such "specialty" divisions allow studios to reach a bifurcated and specifically targeted audience while providing significant financial support to independent filmmakers. The filmmakers, in turn, must identify a conspicuous potential audience. The specialty divisions also function as a testing ground and form of talent spotting, allowing a progression to be made from successful low-budget to bigger-budget projects. The lower-budget projects often provide filmmaking teams more artistic latitude because the studios' financial burden is not as onerous. Ang Lee explains that this balance was particularly well judged on *The Ice Storm,* enabling him to work with considerable autonomy yet also with enough financial support to achieve his artistic aims.

> I have the luxury of having money, but I can still be creative, which I think is every independent director's dream. You don't have to be cheap to be independent. It's best to keep a balance. Too much money ruins creative freedom; too little money makes the movie suffer too.[17]

Indiewood, therefore, strikes a delicate balance between filmmakers creating the films they want to make and studios acquiring movies that they can market and sell. *The Ice Storm* seemed to create a harmonious balance between studio expectation and its director's vision. As Matthews observes, the film is "perhaps too lapidary and elliptical to succeed with a huge audience—it may be the nearest equivalent in contemporary US cinema to a traditional art movie."[18] Certainly, the film has many features that would normally be identified with art film, such as a casual rather than a causal narrative structure, a lack of character objective, and an emotional bleakness that contrasts heavily with U.S. cinema's consistent emotional optimism. However, Matthews also sees an inherent conservatism in *The Ice Storm* that prevents it from extending its reach as far as that of "traditional" art film.[19] For example, he compares some elements of *The Ice Storm* to the work of the Japanese filmmaker Yasujiro Ozu, but recognizes that the film is not able to go as far in the framework in which it was constructed. The difficulty, as Matthews understands it, is that the film is only a near equivalent to an art film and not an art movie per se. There is certainly some truth in this statement, but it is something of which Ang Lee was clearly aware when making *The Ice Storm*, which he wanted to be "both provocative and conservative at the same time."[20] In this sense the effectiveness of the film's Indiewood structure helps to reinforce the filmmaker's aims and messages. *The Ice Storm* is not, as Matthews suggests, an inferior kind of art film, but a different construct, which illustrates the potential for broadening boundaries within the studio system.

Schamus realizes the profound importance of the successful integration of the independent film movement into the structures of global media conglomerates. It is a process that has brought significant benefits to American filmmakers and has produced some of the most exciting work from the 1990s onwards. However, he also explains: "I am ridiculously jaded on the topic of independence and don't find the category of particular interest. . . . I think independent means that everybody got to make the movie they wanted to make."[21]

Plot Summary

The year is 1973 and the Nixon Watergate scandal unfolds in the background as the inhabitants of New Canaan, Connecticut, celebrate Thanksgiving. Two middle-class families, the Carvers and the Hoods, live outwardly enviable, suburban lifestyles, but the surface sheen conceals a struggle for purpose and self-awareness, and the aimless pursuit of satisfaction. All of the characters are mistrustful, insecure, unhappy, and hide their true feelings.

Ben and Elena Hood have perfected the skill of non-communication and their marriage is collapsing. At Ben's insistence they have dropped out of couples' therapy. Elena searches for solutions in self-help books, but her desperation is manifested in impulsive acts of petty crime. Ben has also found a way to bypass reality and finds relief in an adulterous affair with his sultry neighbor, Janey Carver. Janey's workaholic husband, Jim, is frequently away on business so she seeks excitement elsewhere.

The Hood's sixteen-year-old son, Paul, has left home to go to college. He experiments with drugs with his roommate, Francis, and is trying desperately to impress an alluring rich girl, Libbets. The Hood's fourteen-year-old daughter, Wendy, rebels constantly against her youth, experimenting sexually with the Carvers' eldest son, Mikey. She is also beginning to realize the sexual power she can wield and uses this to tease Mikey's younger brother, Sandy. The Carver brothers also exhibit growing pains. Mikey seems to be engaged in a unique, spaced-out vision of the world, while Sandy is developing into a pyromaniac, taking curious pleasure in exploding his old toys.

As the eponymous meteorological event builds up around the characters, the film draws to a climax. The day after Thanksgiving the Hoods and the Carvers attend a key party. The husbands' car keys are placed in a bowl and drawn out randomly by the women at the end of the evening in a sexual lottery. The men and women line up on opposite sides of the room and, as the keys are selected, newly paired-off couples leave to spend the night together. Before the party Ben admitted, as far as he was able, to having an affair. Consequently, Elena is convinced that Janey and Ben have made an arrangement to leave together. However, Janey picks the keys belonging to the son of one of their friends and Ben, who is by now drunk and disoriented, tries to stop her leaving. Elena's suspicions are confirmed and Ben passes out in the bathroom. Only Elena and Jim remain at the party, numbed by the events that have just taken place. Hurt, abandoned, and isolated Elena offers herself to Jim. Their pain is not assuaged by the extremely brief and embarrassing sexual encounter that takes place on the front seat of his car.

Meanwhile, Paul is in New York at a party that he understood to be only for two. However, to his surprise he discovers his roommate, Francis, has already tried to seduce Libbets. In an attempt to loosen Francis's grip on the object of his affection, Paul offers him some past-their-sell-by-date sleeping pills, raided from the household medicine cabinet, suggesting that they are somewhat more risky and hallucinatory than they actually are. Unfortunately, Libbets also takes one of the pills and before passing out declares that her affection for Paul extends to thinking of him only as a brother. Rejected, he rushes to catch the last train home, but the train is stopped mid-journey by the powerful ice storm.

Bored at home on her own, Wendy decides to visit Mikey. However, she finds Sandy alone in the Carver household, because Mikey has decided to investigate the ice storm. Wendy gets into bed with Sandy, unsure of her reasons for doing so. In the midst of the ice storm, Mikey's freedom and exploration of nature is cut short as he is electrocuted by a severed power line. Mikey dies. Ben finds Mikey's body on the side of the road and takes him back to the Carvers' house. Elena and Jim have just arrived, Janey is already asleep, and Wendy and Sandy have just emerged from bed. United by the tragic events and as reality hits them, the two families let down their guard and for the first time exhibit true emotion. The Hood family collects Paul from the station; Ben breaks down and cries with his family surrounding him.

Novel/Shooting Script/Film

Space does not permit a detailed study of the journey from Moody's novel—through Schamus's shooting script—to Lee's final filmic text. Furthermore, Schamus outlines his reinterpretation of the novel and many of the differences between screenplay and film in the published shooting script.[22] However, some general observations about alterations and revisions indicate the tactics employed by the filmmakers as the meaning of the "text" became more clear to them. Some scenes, such as Ben and Elena's therapy sessions, were not shot simply because time was running out and attention became focused on what was essential and what was expendable. Given that the first cut of the film was over two-and-a-half hours in length, other scenes were, with good reason, removed during the editing process. Before any of this took place, there was already considerable pruning from novel to shooting script.

On the final page of Moody's book the third-person narrator, who has been omnisciently recounting the story, suddenly reveals themself as one of the novel's characters; an unexpected shift from third-person to first-person narration. Of course, this device forces the reader to question the accuracy of the omniscience and the partiality of what has just been read. How is it possible for this narrator to know some of the things they have described? How can they take an impersonal viewpoint when their personal experience is involved? This fruitful tension, as Schamus sees it, is extremely powerful because it frames the novel as "an act of remembering, a search for meaning and truth."[23] However, filmically this is a device that does not often translate well and negotiating cinematic space via a first-person narrator, camera eye, or I-camera can be fraught with difficulties. Consequently, and despite some notable examples to the contrary, cinema tends to favor third-person narrative. This is particularly true where there would be doubts about the omniscience of the narrator. Schamus explains the challenge:

in adapting the novel for the screen, we were faced with an
immediate technical problem: Could we find some kind of filmic
equivalent to the novel's powerful literary devices, one that retained
at least some hint of the book's emotional and philosophical
grandeur? The answer, unsurprisingly, was no.[24]

However, first-person narration does insinuate itself in Paul's voice-
overs that appear at various points in the film. His last voice-over, more
knowing and impartial than the others, is heard after Mikey's death and
helps the audience to "recuperate somewhat from the shock of the
killing as well as to fold the emotional registers of the shock into one
primary consciousness."[25] The objectivity it provides creates a greater
sense of magnitude and philosophical meaning to the localized events.
However, it is also a device that does not overtly draw attention to itself
in the manner of the I-camera in *Peeping Tom* (Powell, 1960), for
example. Schamus's compromise in the film version of *The Ice Storm*
pays homage to Moody's text without losing filmic subtlety.

As one would expect, the novel's interior character motivation and
development were economically truncated in the film, but there was
also a considerable reduction of the novel's humor and social satire.
Technically, both of these procedures had the effect making a more
honed and dramatic filmic structure. However, Matthews understands
this as an attempt to create a "deliberate monotony of mood" that
reifies the period into an "inert zone for melancholy contemplation."[26]
That contemplative atmosphere would, therefore, seem to have a
number of purposes. First, it represents the filmmakers' anxiety about
lampooning the 1970s. The film of *The Ice Storm*, though containing a
great deal of humor, does not want its audience to simply laugh at the
clothes, social conduct, and mores of the characters, but to appreciate
these as a sociohistorical document of a critical period and its affect on
the American psyche. Ang Lee explains that, in the research process for
the film, the production team read many novels, self-help books, and
watched numerous movies from the early seventies.

Rather than approach the period as one of "kitsch" this process led to
a tremendous respect and humility. It turned out that there were many
truths buried inside the pop psychology and sometimes painfully
naïve self-help philosophies of the day, and that we two decades later
have much to learn from this "embarrassing" past.[27]

Second, the film's lack of explanation of character motivation helps to
create a greater sense of ambiguity. This ambiguity arises because the
characters themselves do not really understand their own motivations;
they are all sleepwalking through their lives. But whereas Moody can

describe explicitly a lack of self-knowledge, the film cannot do this to the same extent without resorting to dialogue. For example, Moody recounts one of Wendy Hood's random, promiscuous sexual acts as follows: "At a slumber party after her birthday, earlier in this very month, she had put her tongue in Debby Armitage's vagina. It happened suddenly, as if she hadn't been responsible for it somehow."[28] To hear the film character Wendy Hood rationalize that: "I put my tongue in Debby Armitage's vagina, but I didn't feel responsible for it somehow," would require a forced dramatic situation or a voice-over narration. Both of these devices would seem unnecessarily heavy-handed and moralistic, and would make a lack of self-awareness an intellectual focal point rather than an emotional one. The filmmakers take the view that hearing a character explaining that they feel lonely, for example, is not as powerful as watching them *being* lonely. Consequently, the approach in *The Ice Storm* is to turn "voice into action."[29] This brings us back to Ang Lee's comment that opened this chapter, where he articulates strategies that allow the actors to create meaning, not to impose meaning upon them or the audience by being prescriptive. A number of critics note this as a deliberate, brave, and effective filmic device. Janet Maslin, for example, understands that "Lee daringly chooses to keep his story's motivational mysteries unexplained, leaving this richly observed film open to the viewer's assessments."[30] Matthews likewise observes that "the film-makers choose indirection: the semi-opaque surfaces of character and environment are scrupulously respected and the audience is invited to draw what inferences it will."[31] Paradoxically therefore, the reduction of motivational explanation in the film of *The Ice Storm* generates greater emotional intensity and range of meaning, because it requires the audience to fill in the gaps that are deliberately created.

Existential Nihilism

Thomas Hibbs understands *The Ice Storm* as a film that "immerses the audience in a nihilistic world."[32] Exploring this assertion is problematic because a great deal of confusion and contradiction surrounds the term nihilism and its various philosophical strands. It is useful, then, to outline some of the major concepts briefly here before further examining their relevance to *The Ice Storm*.

When Nietzsche declared that "God is dead. God remains dead, and we have killed him," the statement had a profound influence on Western Christian thinking.[33] Throughout the 1880s, Nietzsche explored the hypothesis that man must find a new mode of being given the demise of God. Nietzsche argued that the effects of this pursuit would eventually destroy all religious, moral, and metaphysical convictions, and precipitate the greatest crisis in human history. Without moral fabric in the universe, existence would have no value, nothing would have meaning, and nothing could be known or communicated. In the absence of God and divine repercussions, everything would be permitted. Man could exercise his new freedom, proving that he had replaced God, by inflicting death on himself and others. Nihilistic ideas about the eradication of values and epistemological breakdown gathered momentum during the twentieth century and preoccupied philosophers, artists, and social analysts. Indeed, some writers believe that one of the most horrific and graphic realizations of nihilistic thinking was the Nazi reign of terror and the Holocaust.[34]

Following the Second World War, widespread feelings of despair led to the development and popularization of a muted and refined form of nihilism, known as existentialism, which is frequently associated with the philosophy of Jean-Paul Sartre.[35] Existentialism put a "positive" spin on the ruinous potential of nihilism by emphasizing free will and choice, and seemed to provide a framework for making rational decisions in an irrational world. However, as Sartre and others explained, the challenge of freedom is responsibility. Because individuals are free to choose their own path, existentialists argued, they must accept the risk and responsibility of their actions no matter how difficult. The individual's confrontation with nothingness and with the impossibility of finding ultimate justification for the choices they make, as well as the understanding that they are entirely responsible for their actions, causes what has been described variously as dread (Kierkegaard), angst (Heidegger), or nausea (Sartre). Because few decisions can be made without negative consequences, individuals become overwhelmed by anxiety. According to the existentialist writers, attempting to deny freedom and responsibility in order to escape from this anxiety is self-deceiving; a condition to which mankind is particularly prone (Sartre's term for this is bad faith). Existential nihilism then is, as Karen Carr describes, "the feeling of emptiness and pointlessness that follows from the judgment, 'Life has no meaning.'"[36] It is this meaningless and barren existence, and the confusion that surrounds it, that pervades the film.

Hibbs believes that *The Ice Storm* "depicts the living death of its characters,"[37] whose "despair is so deep they fail to recognize it."[38] All of the characters are bored, alienated, and passionless. They do not fully understand their own thoughts and actions. The cumulative effect of their inability or lack of willingness to communicate creates cocooned people. For example, Elena ends one of the many arguments she has with Ben with the statement: "Please have the decency to at least not tell me what I'm thinking." This highlights her desperation and fear, as well as her avoidance of the truth. Despite the fact that the characters live in family units there is little reference to or contact with each other. The complete lack of involvement in each other's lives "paints a portrait of the loneliness and suffering they all experience."[39]

Prior to one of Janey and Ben's adulterous sessions, Ben indicates that Elena may be suspicious and asks Janey if she has noticed anything:

Janey: Have I noticed anything? I'm not married to her Benjamin, you are. I think you've probably a better vantage point from which to observe her.

Ben: Yeah, but—I've been working a lot lately and—No, that's not it. I guess we've just been on the verge of saying something, saying something to each other. On the verge . . .

Ben does not seem to realize the absurdity of asking his lover whether she is aware of his own wife's suspicion, and he is confused about what or how he should communicate, or indeed what communication is. The characters in *The Ice Storm* are always "on the verge" of saying or doing something, but never quite manage to do so. They all pursue some kind of further meaning in their lives, but either do not know what that is or cannot find a way of reaching it. Elena's self-denial, for example, is all consuming and she tries desperately to find purpose in self-help books. Interestingly, and as if to articulate the existential agenda, one of the texts that Elena scans at a local book fair is a well-worn version of Sartre's *Being and Nothingness*. It also becomes apparent that she has investigated an alternative religion, but has never been "much of a joiner." After seeing her daughter riding a bicycle in town, Elena also craves youthful freedom—or childish innocence—a sensation which she describes to Wendy: "Well, you looked very free when I saw you. As if I were seeing my own memories of being a girl." Consequently, Elena finds an old bicycle and her ensuing ride through the town has a momentary atmosphere of reminiscent purity, but it leads her to the pharmacy where, for no apparent reason, she attempts to steal some lipstick and is caught shoplifting. None of the approaches she takes lead to a solution, and she has given up hope that her husband can provide the succor she needs.

The outwardly permissive, post-sexual-revolution society in which the characters live seems to allow ample freedom but, in keeping with Sartre's concept of bad faith, this freedom is not exploited without regret, discomfort, and anxiety. While the characters can discuss watching the pornographic film *Deep Throat* (Damiano, 1972) openly and casually, engage in the key party's sexual pick-and-mix, or have affairs with their neighbor, the individual moral distress is in constant evidence. When neither instinct nor social tradition direct the characters toward what they ought to do, they soon find themselves in an existential void where they do not even know what they want to do. Ben and Janey's adultery is not a dangerous act of rebellion or liberated passion, but is as methodical and enervating as their respective marriages. After one of their mid-afternoon sessions, Ben lies next to Janey and rambles jealously about the golfing prowess of a work colleague. Her reply indicates the lack of fulfillment both her marriage and the affair bring her: "Ben, you're boring me. I have a husband, I don't particularly feel the need for another." Rather than acts of passion, purely mechanical sex acts are witnessed. They are so boring, cold, commonplace, and devoid of love that Hibbs believes they represent the finest contemporary expression of the "banality of evil."[40] The pursuit of sexual pleasure is entirely self-defeating.

Even the children are engaged in passionless and perfunctory sexual experimentation. On one occasion when Wendy and Mikey "fool around," Wendy wears a grotesque Nixon mask, promising to touch Mikey's genitals; "but that's as far as it goes." What should be an intimate act of sexual discovery for both teenagers is thoroughly de-personalized and devalued; Wendy can only engage by covering her face, disengaging her mind, and alienating herself from the experience. Curiously, erotic contact with her own boyfriend does not seem to excite her as much as manipulating his younger brother. She initiates an "I'll show you mine if you show me yours" encounter with Sandy which terrifies him; he is still too young and too naïve to deal with this kind of sexual intimacy. Later, during the ice storm itself, Wendy plies him with vodka and gets into bed with him. He is someone she can control and exploit with ease, and she laughs at his lack of knowledge and experience although she does not have significantly more experience herself. Almost as if citing a biology textbook, she asks him if he has "ever had a nocturnal emission?" Sandy has no idea what this means and Wendy mocks his innocence: "They haven't told you about this stuff yet? Oh what planet are you living on?" Sandy is completely infatuated with Wendy, but her curiosity appears to extend only to studying him as a non-threatening male specimen. Her lack of emotional involvement is degrading to both of them.

In the New Canaan society, even religion seems to have lost its way. When Elena first encounters the Reverend Philip Edwards at the book fair she may be somewhat suspicious about his intentions towards her. But when he appears at the key party, her misgivings about him seem to be confirmed.

Elena: You're here . . . I'm a bit surprised.

Philip: Sometimes the shepherd needs the company of the sheep.

Elena: I'm going to try hard *not* to understand the implications of that.

The implications are of a predatory preacher taking advantage of his position and other people's vulnerability, although this is never made explicit. Certainly, there is the strong suggestion that Reverend Edwards is attracted to Elena and would seduce her if he had the opportunity. The film's presentation of the destruction of a society's moral fabric is so comprehensive that even the symbols of institutional religion are shown as corrupted, collapsing, and struggling to understand their purpose.

The children, as has already been seen, present some of the clearest evidence for an existential nihilist agenda in *The Ice Storm*. Sandy, for example, has an obsessive focus on destruction. He relishes blowing up his old toys and, when his mother chastises him for doing so, he obliterates a flowering bush with a whip. He also threatens to fly a remote-controlled plane, packed with explosives, into an English class and blow it up. Later, with Wendy's help, he hangs his G.I. Joe army doll.

Sandy: Check this out. He's supposed to say all sorts of stuff, but he's kind of malfunctioned.

He pulls the tag on the doll, and G.I. Joe emits a plastic macho voice.

G.I. Joe: Mayday! Mayday! Get this message back to base!

Sandy: Same thing. Again and again.

Wendy takes the doll and yanks the cord.

G.I. Joe: Mayday! Mayday! Get this message back to base!

Sandy: It's gonna get a lot colder tonight, I predict. Probably a blackout. Do you have candles in your house? I know where the candles are, and I know where every emergency exit is on this floor.

During the course of his monologue, as Wendy looks on, Sandy calmly ties a noose for his doll.

Sandy: This knot's called a hangman's noose. Let's hang him.

Copyright © 1997 by Fox Searchlight Pictures, Inc.

The act of hanging G.I. Joe is framed by moments of quasi-philosophical contemplation about means of escape and repetitiveness. Sandy's fears and concerns are represented through play, and he uses G.I. Joe's incantation to punctuate and emphasize his own anxieties. It is a scene that creates a sensation of cyclical monotony that is only broken by an act of violence, albeit mock violence.

Sandy's brother Mikey also has existential inclinations. For example, in one scene he reads a paper about molecules in front of his classmates. Mikey explains that molecules connect human beings to the outside world from their bodies; a potentially liberating discovery of a connection between man and nature. However, at the same time he is terrified by what he has unearthed. He identifies the fact that smells are constructed from molecules that have been shed from certain objects: "So, when you smell something bad, it's like in a way you're eating it." Mikey's solution to this dilemma is to try to avoid smelling bad odors, just as he would avoid eating everything in the world around him. He is concerned that the vile smells he describes can be internalized and pollute the body, "so the next time you go to the bathroom after someone else has been there, remember what kinds of molecules you are in fact eating." This unusual and profoundly depressing interpretation provides Mikey's peers with a challenging question: if the world is literally full of excreta how can we stop it from becoming part of us? Mikey's answer is to strive for purity, and this is why he will go out to explore the cold ice storm where the frozen molecules become inert. He believes that there will be nothing in the air to breathe into your body, "the molecules have stopped. It's clean."

Paul Hood's voice-over privileges his position and the importance of his internal thoughts in the narrative structure. Consequently, he provides a philosophical locus for the audience in his attempts to understand his own life and the events around him. Paul is a deep-thinker and extrapolates broad conclusions from *The Fantastic Four* comic books that he reads avidly. We do not know if Paul agrees with Libbets's interpretation of the Dostoevsky novel *Notes from*

Underground (a required read for their English class) as an existential text, but the existential nihilist dilemma is certainly debated in his voice-overs.[41] For example, Paul's attempt to understand the relevance and significance of the negative zone, a place where the Fantastic Four often find themselves, is a description of what is, in effect, an existential vacuum.

> **Paul (voice-over):** It seems to me that everyone exists partially on a negative zone level; some people more than others. In your life its kind of like you dip in and out of it. A place where things don't quite work out the way they should. But for some people there is something about the negative zone that tempts them and they end up going in, going in all the way.

> Copyright © 1997 by Fox Searchlight Pictures, Inc.

Paul's introspection appears to describe accurately the "paralysis of life" in the society around him.[42] To a greater or lesser extent, everyone is affected by a world where things do not work out as they should. The challenge, as Paul sees it, is to try and understand how to negotiate this space; he is asking fundamental questions about how he should live his life. It is an attitude that, unlike the other characters, displays an active attempt to negotiate the problems raised by the existential agenda, rather than displaying a radical indifference to life. Following the death of Mikey, another voice-over confirms Paul's interpretation: "When you think about it, it's not easy to keep from just wandering out of life. It's like someone is always leaving the door open to the next world, and if you aren't paying attention, you could just walk through it." The irony of using the comic book device to allow a sixteen-year-old to articulate philosophically complicated issues forms part of the film's strategy to show that the children in *The Ice Storm* understand just as much, if not more, than the adults. Comic books provide clear parameters for exploring right and wrong and in some senses they provide for young people a more explicit moral code than they can appreciate through conventional forms of religion. As James Schamus argues: "Comic books both say profound things about American culture and are, in fact, as profound a piece of American culture as you can come up with."[43]

While the film is unquestionably bleak it also contains a great deal of dark humor because the characters are observed at a distance, a distance that is reinforced by Paul's voice-overs. The audience, therefore, is provided with "a perspective that the denizens of that world lack."[44] If Ang Lee does not see it as a director's job to judge the film's characters, then the audience is challenged to form opinions about the protagonists' actions and the events that have taken place.

Family and Absent Fathers

Ang Lee has referred to himself as a director "who does family dramas," and his obsession with domestic environments, familial relationships, the generation gap, and the role of the father figure can be seen throughout his work.[45] By placing a microscope against the family unit, Lee is able to make detailed explorations of the challenges faced from a variety of different perspectives. He has referred to his first three feature films—*Pushing Hands* (1992), *The Wedding Banquet* (1993), and *Eat Drink Man Woman* (1994)—as the "father knows best" trilogy, where the focus is on imposing patriarchs and the effect they have on their families around them.[46] Ironically, the fathers in these films frequently do not know best, and the role of the mother is either absent or subordinate. However, in *Sense and Sensibility* (1995) and *Ride With the Devil* (1999) it is the death of the father figure that creates the dramatic situations to which the characters must respond. The former requires Elinor to assume responsibility as the head of the Dashwood family in an eighteenth-century patriarchal society, whereas the latter forces Jack Bull Chiles to join the Southern Bushwackers in order to avenge his father's murder. Despite the potential dangers, the children in *Crouching Tiger, Hidden Dragon* (2000) are as keen to rebel against authority as the adults are to instruct them. Even in *The Hulk* (2003), Lee flaunts dominant action-adventure conventions by centralizing the narrative consequences and tensions that arise from the children's interaction with their parents. In *Brokeback Mountain* (2005) the complex, sexual, and romantic relationship between two men in the American West eventually brings about the deterioration of a marriage and the separation of a family.

This recurrent focus on the family is understood by Sheng-Mei Ma as a particular Eastern cultural influence drawn from the religious traditions of Confucianism. Ma explains that Confucian cosmology is founded on family mores that revolve around a patriarch. Fulfilling one's role in family relationships is seen as the way to full human development. Ma also highlights the fact that the Mandarin term "*Chia-t'ing Pei-hsi-chu* (family tragicomedy) with its suggestions of *Chi-t'ing Lun-li* (family ethics)" forms the backbone of Lee's work.[47] Indeed, Lee acknowledges the importance of the family and, in particular, the role of the father in his films.

Because Chinese society is a patriarchal society, I have always thought the father figure has bigger meaning than just the parent—it's the symbol of how tradition works. And in my first three movies, I used my father as a model.[48]

As the firstborn son, Lee faced the pressure to acquiesce to his parents' wishes in ways that his younger brother and two sisters did not. He was expected to follow his father into a teaching career, but his interest in creative arts and lack of academic achievement was a great source of disappointment to his family.[49] The fact that so many of the young characters in Lee's films try to break free from conformist obligations and are challenged by issues of filial allegiance can be traced back to his relationship with his own parents, particularly his father. While Lee acknowledges the very personal nature of his exploration of blood relationships, he also believes that these belie larger societal meanings. The family, as he understands it, is "the seed of society" and consequently provides the best way to examine wider civilization: "It is the unit that makes a society that you can see, it is a miniature."[50] The recurrence of themes relating to marriage and wedding ceremonies in his films, for example, illustrates an ultimate faith in the family despite its inherent conflicts. The examination of people responding to testing situations is a means of working through some of the challenges that both family and society pose. The mass appeal and success of Lee's films is, in part, due to the fact that these issues are globally relevant; family tensions and disputes occur the world over. Despite the widely divergent genres and styles of filmmaking used by Lee, familial themes unite and remain the dramatic locus of all his films.

Considering the framework outlined above, *The Ice Storm* provides a fascinating example of Lee's work because its families are entirely dysfunctional. In his other films, the family unit is either disrupted physically, or its various members hold different views with regard to tradition, which causes conflict. The tensions emanate from strongly held and argued beliefs or external constraints. However, in *The Ice Storm*, the family units are not in conflict but are completely confused and failing. The lack of interaction highlights the vulnerability of the American family after the turmoil of the 1960s threw moral certainty into question. Lee explains that the characters in *The Ice Storm* "do not know what to do, they've lost confidence in role models, and ways of behaving, and they are kind of scared, and they want to be conservative, they want to be good. That irony to me was very attractive."[51] The characters maintain the trappings of family without really understanding how they should function and relate to each other, and this provided Lee with a powerful dramatic situation to explore.

The Hood family's dislocation begins to present itself through one of *The Ice Storm*'s central narrative constructs, the Thanksgiving holiday. This annual, national celebration provides an opportunity for families to be reunited. The fact that Paul has returned from college means that the entire Hood family is gathered together. Ben's chest swells with pride as he observes his family in front of him. He relishes the position as head of the household, even asserting his dominance by explaining that there will be no hysteria or yelling this year with "grandpa not here . . . although we miss him." Somewhat carried away with the occasion, Ben tries to enhance the sense of tradition: "So let's do it right and, Wendy, why don't you say grace? You used to love to say grace, remember?" Wendy looks as if this is the last thing she would like to do. A little surprised at Ben's request, everybody bows their head, but Wendy's acerbic prayer does not harmonize with her father's enthusiasm.

> **Wendy:** Dear Lord, thank you for this Thanksgiving holiday, and for all the material possessions that we have and enjoy, and for letting us white people kill all the Indians . . .
>
> Everyone looks up.
>
> **Wendy:** . . . and steal their tribal lands and stuff ourselves like pigs . . .
>
> Mutterings and groans: "Wendy!" "For Christ's sake" etc.
>
> **Wendy:** . . . while children in Africa and Asia are napalmed and—
>
> **Ben:** Jesus! All right, enough!
>
> Copyright © 1997 by Fox Searchlight Pictures, Inc.

Wendy's tirade could be viewed simply as that of a disaffected, anarchic teenager, but her diatribe simultaneously manages to destroy the unity of the family, belittle her father's pride, and ridicule the societal meaning of Thanksgiving. Her view concurs with writers who have highlighted some of the hypocrisies and inaccuracies on which the Thanksgiving story is founded, and who suggest that the first 1621 celebration did not display the alleged, mythical harmony between Pilgrims and Indians.[52] As such, Wendy clearly believes that the whole concept of Thanksgiving is based on a lie, and she also draws other issues into her outburst such as the materialism of society and war, in order to show her resentment. By denigrating the expression of national values that Thanksgiving represents, Wendy chooses to highlight the hypocrisy of her own family and of American society generally.

In one of the film's most painfully comic scenes of parental confusion, Janey Carver attempts to reprimand Wendy for having taken advantage of Sandy. Janey demonstrates an adult responsibility that Wendy's own parents seem unable to provide and, therefore, could be viewed as a source of sorely needed moral, parental guidance. However, she fails so miserably at the task that its value is severely limited.

> **Janey:** Wendy, a person's body is his temple. This body is your first and last possession. Now as your own parents have probably told you, in adolescence our bodies tend to betray us. That's why, in Samoa and in other developing nations, adolescents are sent out into the woods, unarmed, and they don't come back until they've learned a thing or two. Do you understand?

> Copyright © 1997 by Fox Searchlight Pictures, Inc.

The likelihood that Wendy, or anyone else, could understand Janey's vague recollection of Margaret Mead's anthropological study of adolescence in Samoa is extremely slight.[53] The incoherent babble confirms that Janey is just as confused as Wendy, but her position as an adult seems to compel her to try and act responsibly. It is one of the film's supremely ironic devices that Janey should find herself scolding Wendy for sexual impropriety, while at the same time being involved in an extramarital affair with Wendy's father. The hypocrisy of the situation merely compounds parental failure and the wearing down of family values.

As with Lee's other films, the family is explored through the role of the father figure. In *The Ice Storm* fatherhood is shown as being in a profound crisis. Schamus observes that in the early 1970s in America "the patriarchal order was re-configuring itself" and societal freedom meant that that there was "no patriarchal injunction."[54] It is not so much a case of father knows best, therefore, as father knows nothing—or father does not count. Lee explores this issue in a number of different ways. Unlike *Ride With the Devil* and *Sense and Sensibility* the father figures are not dead—at least not literally—but their absence or inability is frequently highlighted. For example, after returning from a three-day business trip, Jim is pleased to see his two sons and expects to find them equally pleased to see him. Standing at the doorway to their bedroom, he greets them: "Hey Guys, I'm back." Honestly confused, Mikey replies, "You were gone?" The children neither feel nor notice his absence, because it does not upset the normal run of their lives; the insignificance of the father figure is personified. Later when Janey scolds Sandy for blowing up his toys, she seems to acknowledge this breakdown in the patriarchal order. Sandy asks his mother if she is going to tell his father about his dangerous pyrotechnic destruction, but Janey thinks that this would be pointless: "Would it matter?"

Although he is more physically present than Jim, Ben is an equally hapless patriarch. Confused about his role in society, he can no longer "live up to the image he has of himself as a respected and revered father and breadwinner."[55] We witness him on his journey to work and in a board meeting looking dazed and distant, as if he were a lost child. However, he is concerned to be *seen* as a man in control, as somebody who fulfils traditionally perceived fatherly functions, even though he rarely displays them in reality. Whenever Ben feels that he is being particularly strong or in control, he draws attention to himself as if to validate his purpose and justify his position. Inevitably, this occurs when he attempts to discipline his daughter. For example, as he is about to scold Wendy for using the telephone late at night, he asks his wife to watch him in action (in reality we see his inaction). His reprimand, "Get to sleep young lady, I mean it!" is of little consequence. Wendy's typically bellicose response is to call her father a fascist. Schamus observes that when parents are forced to say "I mean it," they have lost control and do not "have any power whatever."[56] Ben's characteristic use of language for disciplining his daughter includes the recurrent phrases "I mean it" and "young lady," which fail to disguise the fact that he is putting on an act. When he catches his daughter in a compromising situation with Mikey, he gives the children the strongest castigation he can muster, but Wendy's belligerent response is simply to say, "forget all the stern-dad stuff"; they are both aware of the masquerade. However, later Ben will present himself to his wife as the savior of his daughter's virginity, having arrived just in time: "I really let him have it, and she came home peacefully." There is clearly a conflict between the image Ben would like to portray and the person he really is. This is also evident in a cringe-worthy discussion about masturbation that he has with his son on a drive home from the station.

> **Ben:** Well . . . um . . . on the self abuse front—and this is important—uh, I don't think it's advisable to do it in the shower—it wastes water and electricity and because we all expect you to be doing it there in any case—and, not onto the linen. Well anyway, if you're worried about anything, just feel free to ask, and, uh, we can look it up.
>
> **Paul:** Dad, you know I'm sixteen?
>
> **Ben:** All the more reason for this little heart-to-heart.

The car pulls into the drive

Ben: Paul . . . uh, I was wondering, um . . . could you do me a favor and pretend I never said any of that?

The important factor here is that Ben is aware of the embarrassing idiocy of what he has just said. Although he is failing as a father, he is always trying to do the right thing and does occasionally have redeeming moments. For example, on the walk home after scolding Wendy, he explains that he is not especially cross, but that he simply thinks Mikey is not the right boy for her. Ben believes that insight into whether relationships will be successful develops as you grow older. Wendy is somewhat taken aback by her father's display of genuine emotion and concern and it is the only moment in the film where she reciprocates with respect for his experience and opinion. One of the challenges of being a parent, as Lee understands it, is that "sometimes the things children need to hear most are the things parents find hardest to say, and *vice versa*. When that happens we resort to ritual."[57] But on this occasion Ben does not resort to ritual, he engages with Wendy reinforcing the familial bond. As they continue to walk home through the cold, drizzling rain he offers to carry his daughter home (Figure 3.1). It is a moment of true intimacy and affection where she seems like a child and he seems like her father.

There is one other father figure referenced by the film, the "father" of the nation, Richard Nixon. Remembering that Ang Lee views the patriarch as a symbol of tradition and the family as a microcosm of society, parallels can be drawn between Ben and Jim's domestic uncertainties and Nixon's national fragility. In 1973, the Watergate scandal revealed that Nixon had "feet of clay,"[58] eventually leading to his resignation in 1974. He remains the only U.S. president ever to have resigned from office. *The Ice Storm* raises the question that if the president can not be trusted "what hope do Jim and Ben have at their level?"[59] Archive footage of Nixon maintaining his innocence appears throughout the film, as if to provide a civil mirror image to the characters' domestic failings. Wendy takes great interest in the events and has already found Nixon guilty, claiming that he is a liar and "should be shot." Ben's attempt to defend the president: "Hey, drop the political assassination stuff," highlights a deep-rooted desire to trust in the establishment. Ben wants to believe in the institutions of society and the family, but the Watergate scandal is an affront to the way he needs to understand the world. It is one more example of the crisis of fatherhood that the film represents and there appear to be no easy solutions at personal, domestic, social, or national levels.

Figure 3.1: *The Ice Storm.* Ben Carries Wendy Home.
Reproduced by permission of Twentieth Century Fox and Studio Canal Image.

As has already been seen, Paul is the only character who has some kind of self-awareness, and his opening voice-over shows him to be conscious of the vulnerability of the family. In this monologue he describes a typical predicament faced by *The Fantastic Four* where the evil Annihilus (or perhaps *a nihilist*) has turned the son of one of the heroes into a human atomic bomb. This situation forces the superhero family to face their most difficult challenge, one that threatens to tear them apart. Paul draws parallels between the family of superheroes and his own family unit, and highlights the paradox that "the more power they [The Fantastic Four] had the more harm they could do to each other without even knowing it." This destructive tendency is exhibited consistently and painfully throughout *The Ice Storm*, where characters are oblivious to the harm they cause each other. However, Paul also explains that a family is "like your own personal anti-matter," a void from which you emerge and will return to when you die. The paradox, as he sees it, is that the "closer you're drawn back in, the deeper into the void you go." His identification of the inseparability and permanence of family seems to contrast heavily with the individualism displayed by the characters throughout the narrative. However, the final sequence, which has been previewed in the film's opening flash-forward, shows the whole Hood family waiting for Paul at the train station as he returns from his delayed journey. It is to Paul an unexpected and touching act of family union. The gaunt and shocked faces of his mother, father, and sister show for the first time the realization of the importance of their relationship to each other and its ultimate fragility. Mikey's death has woken the characters from their individual trances. It is a scene that Matthews understands as a powerful summation of the film's moral position with regard to its characters. Despite the various disasters that have taken place, the film returns to the human need for the comfort, support, and power of the family.

> It speaks of the family as an archetype, essentially unchanged by the fluctuations of time unvarying in its strength, its weakness, its cruelty. We can't understand this image, and perhaps for that reason, can never forget it: the family simply *is*.[60]

The Ice Storm, therefore, presents a fundamental paradox in the characters' isolation from each other. Although they are trapped in themselves, "their lives are inextricably bound up with one another."[61] Hibbs's understanding of the message this sends to the audience is unequivocal: "Individualism depletes rather than enriches the self."[62]

Nature as Character

The Ice Storm's human characters, their actions and motivations, have been the focus of attention thus far, but the prominence of the eponymous meteorological event is also extremely significant. The film contrasts its various crisis-laden and confused father figures with an incisive Mother Nature. But in *The Ice Storm*, the storm itself has much greater meaning than the purely event-based narratives of films such as *Earthquake* (Donaldson, 1974), *Twister* (de Bont, 1996), *Volcano* (Jackson, 1997), *Dante's Peak* (Donaldson, 1997), or *The Day After Tomorrow* (Emmerich, 2004). The disaster-movie genre demonstrates mankind's battle against an unpredictable and uncontrollable force. It brings the best out of people, showing them at their most ingenious, heroic, altruistic, and often reinforces a shallow message about self-sacrifice and human unity. Although some people invariably die, mankind is seen as stronger for having survived the worst that nature can unleash. However, *The Ice Storm* does not display the same kind of apocalyptic scale and there is no active battle. Ang Lee explains that he sometimes thought of *The Ice Storm* as "a disaster movie, except that the disaster hits home."[63] The ice storm's effect on the characters is profound, providing them with a painful wake-up call that challenges them to reconsider their lives and actions. Lee believes the film is "not about a natural disaster, but a human-nature disaster tied to a specific place and time."[64] In this regard, the storm is crucial to the film's resolution and the audience is invited to draw parallels between the natural disaster and family/relationship disasters that take place. Therefore, the ice storm is more than just a powerful force that the characters must endure. It is simultaneously a metaphor for the human drama and an integral part of the human drama. These factors, coupled with its lifelike presentation, indicate that the ice storm can be understood as a character in its own right. While storms are used consistently as metaphorical devices in films to illustrate underlying dramatic tensions or portent, rarely is their presence as significant as in *The Ice Storm*. This is an approach that is unmistakably Asian in outlook.

The Confucian understanding of nature is based on a central belief in what Wei-Ming Tu refers to as the *continuity of being*,[65] where "all of the parts of the entire cosmos belong to one organic whole and . . . all interact as participants in one spontaneously self-generating life process."[66] The vital force known as *ch'i* is a basic energy that is everywhere and connects all things. Since all forms of being (rocks, rivers, plants, animals, humans) have *ch'i* everything is understood as flowing together, organically connected and interdependent. Lee's understanding of man's relationship with nature concurs with this kind of thinking.[67]

> For me nature is an active force, something you have to fear and respect. That's related to how I grew up. It's probably different from an American perspective. But honestly, I can't tell anymore which part of me is American and which is Oriental.[68]

Lee's identification of nature as an "active force" supports the concept of the ice storm as a character, albeit an enigmatic one. He understands that a Western viewer may not fully appreciate nature's role and its connection to man within the film, although his unique position as somebody who has experienced both East and West allows him to transcend such polarities. Furthermore, this position provides the director with the insight and ability to reflect and comment on various aspects of Western and Eastern culture from a fresh perspective, causing us to reconsider our own perceptions. For example, the film's stance with regard to nature provides an interesting corollary to the existential nihilist agenda that was examined earlier. The Confucian understanding of the universe as spontaneously self-generating, without a God or external will to life, is in direct contrast to Judeo-Christian beliefs, but is not at all dissimilar to existential nihilism. Both

Confucianism and existential nihilism reject notions of original sin, inherent evil, and the dependence on a savior. However, unlike existential nihilism, Confucianism emphasizes the harmony between man and nature; harmony that man can enjoy also being harmony that man helps to create. This is a cycle of repayment in which the force of nature equally plays its part.

This philosophical outlook is in stark contrast to the plastic, artificial world in which the characters in *The Ice Storm* live. Although their homes are in the middle of a beautiful Connecticut forest, they are hardly aware of any connection to nature. The various shots of these houses in the midst of the natural forest seem to be designed to enhance this sense of dislocation (Figure 3.2).

Figure 3.2: *The Ice Storm*. Forest/House Dislocation.
Reproduced by permission of Twentieth Century Fox and Studio Canal Image.

However, if the film makes a comment on the characters' lack of engagement with nature, Mikey's death presents us with a dilemma. The irony is that he is the only character who shows an awareness of, curiosity about, and respect for his connection to nature. His death could easily have been avoided if his fascination had not taken him outside into the storm. In terms of Western narrative filmmaking, this is problematic because Mikey does not deserve his fate. Our understanding of this tragic event, therefore, is fundamental to an appreciation of nature's role in the film. Some writers believe that the appearance of the ice storm is directly induced by the characters' behavior, so that nature is seen as a malevolent, punishing force. For example, Smith observes that "when the actions of the adults are at their most negative, destroying the social fabric of the New Canaan community, the natural forces reach their most positive with devastating consequences."[69] Indeed, this type of interpretation is shared by the composer. The Western concept of nature exacting a form of retribution, or as a corrective force, is emphasized by disaster movies and narrative theory's focus on cause and effect, or "causal networks"[70] to use Noël Carroll's words. In line with Eastern philosophy, however, I am inclined to see the ice storm as a much less aggressive natural force. Its beautiful and delicate representation seems to request contemplation rather than outright fear. The fact that the Confucian vision of nature as a force that is not judgmental or discriminatory emphasizes the notion that Mikey's death is simply part of a life continuum, often referred to as the great transformation. As Tu explains, "the great transformation of which nature is the concrete manifestation is the result of concord rather than discord and convergence rather than divergence."[71] Mikey's wide-eyed fascination with the storm suggests an elated freedom and ultimate union with nature. However sad the death is, to my mind it is not an act of retribution or a direct punishment. The ice storm certainly has a profound effect, but it does not correct the characters' collective wrongs, it simply acts as part of an impersonal natural law. As Ang Lee explains, "whatever the surface patterns you might see reflected there, the customs and morals, and hopes, and loves of the characters are infused, and overturned, and re-established by the force of nature that the storm represents."[72]

Visual Style

Before focusing on the sound of *The Ice Storm* (in chapters 4 and 5), it will be useful to examine the visual style of the film. Lee's early work has often been criticized for its lack of stylistic coherence; some commentators perceived him as a director "whom one would not necessarily regard as a stylist."[73] As if to preempt this kind of criticism, from *The Ice Storm* onwards he became more overtly conscious of stylistic structures, devices, and goals in his films, and also emphasized this awareness in press conferences and interviews. In terms of style, therefore, *The Ice Storm* is a milestone and many writers recognized the increasing maturity and confidence in approach. With specific reference to *The Ice Storm*, for example, Matthews noted that "of the younger directors currently working in Hollywood, Lee has perhaps the most fully articulated technique. He just doesn't beat his chest as much."[74] The strategies employed in production design, costume, cinematography, and framing, therefore, are carefully controlled to enhance the film's narrative themes, already outlined throughout this chapter.

According to Lee, the film's stylistic structure is delineated in two clear sections. For most of the film, the mise-en-scéne is heavily influenced by the Photorealist art movement, whereas the final section relies more on a "sort of impressionism," because "the ice storm and the force of nature suggested that."[75] We shall presently examine the significance of Photorealism to the filmic text, but the more "Impressionist" stylistic influences may have arisen long before principal photography began, after a stroke of good fortune. The second unit had taken a water truck and hoses into Connecticut on successive evening shoots in the hope that it might turn cold enough to record footage of actual ice on the streets and trees. However, on one of these nights, the crew encountered a real ice storm, the only one to hit the area in more than thirty years. Schamus recalls that there was remarkable footage, but that it "soon turned into a snowstorm, and we couldn't use most of what we filmed."[76] Snow was later digitally removed from some of this material. However, the second unit's success in shooting a real ice storm was a challenge to the cinematographer Frederick Elmes. He compared actual close-up shots of ice on branches to a variety of other simulated textures. The fact that ice is both a reflective surface and "acts as a lens in that it captures detail and light behind it" suggested the intricacy of the "crystal wonderland," that Elmes was trying to create.[77] The crew eventually discovered that transparent hair gel provided an appropriate refractive and glassy atmosphere when sprayed onto roads and other surfaces. The Impressionist influence is, therefore, manifested in Elmes's attempt to capture the transient effects of light and color in various outdoor scenes. The film's subtle stylistic shift from Photorealist to Impressionist influence differentiates between the natural and manmade environments, but also matches the physical, metaphorical, and emotional freezing, and subsequent thawing caused by the impact of the storm.

Photorealism is a style of painting that was instigated in the late 1960s, in which people, objects, and scenes are depicted with such naturalism that the compositions resemble photographs. The movement was centered in both New York and the West Coast of the United States, and it is particularly associated with artists such as Ralph Goings and Richard Estes. Their meticulously detailed and "realistic" depictions evolved as a reaction against Surrealism and Pop Art. Although the paintings resemble photographs, the representation of a supposed reality is continually questioned. Usually concentrating on

mundane subject matter, each Photorealist artist had particular
preferences and obsessions. Goings, for example, tended to paint trucks
and diners, whereas Estes specialized in street scenes with elaborate
reflections in the glass of shop windows (Figure 3.3).

Figure 3.3: *Thom McAn.* 1974, oil on canvas, 36 x 48".
© Richard Estes, courtesy Marlborough Gallery, New York.

Elmes explains that the production team studied many Photorealist
paintings from the 1970s, and by further following the chain of artistic
influence also "looked at the work of still photographers who were
imitating the photorealist painters at the time."[78] The appeal of this
design strategy seems to have been the use of reflections and
translucent, blurred textures that could represent both the surface gloss
and the confusion and complexity of the characters' emotional
situation, creating simultaneously metaphorical and sensory attributes.
Ellen Cheshire even understands the use of windows and mirrors as
symbols of the "self-made prisons that the characters find themselves
in."[79] Fundamentally, this transparency and translucence is a stylistic
connection to the film's central ice metaphor, and consequently
foreshadows the ice storm itself. The blue-toned whites that give the
film its chilly ghostliness also emphasize this. Lee observes that the
Photorealist aesthetic allowed for an acutely objective view of the

environment and the characters, and he highlights some of the technical approaches that were employed in order to achieve this.

> [It] required higher contrast, a lot of reflective material such as glass and metals, and a lot of defocused subjects and negative space in the compositions to distract the audience and force them to become more analytical.[80]

There are a number of significant comments embedded within this statement. The identification of the creation of negative space in the composition of shots seems to be a visual analog for the negative zone that appears in *The Fantastic Four* comics. Accordingly, the existential nihilist motif that the negative zone represents embraces visual as well as verbal, emotional, and intellectual levels. In terms of framing, the blurred and confused space that surrounds the characters often enhances the sense of isolation and helps to convey their lack of communication. Elmes carried out extensive tests with identical close-ups of actors' faces using a variety of different lenses in order to create a spatial strategy. He explains that the tests clarified "how the combination of the focal length and camera distance [would] affect the geography of a performer's face and the relationship to the background."[81] Furthermore reflections, the use of shallow depth of field, and deliberately blurred focus are all designed to compel the audience to contemplate these stylistic devices and their relationship to the characters. An excellent example of this occurs when Ben wanders aimlessly about the glassy confines of the Carver household after Janey has suddenly abandoned him in the middle of one of their afternoon sessions (Figure 3.4). Lee explains that he wanted the house to be "open to nature, but give the feeling of being exposed."[82] Thus, Ben is seen virtually naked, surrounded by reflections of nature, which open out onto actual images of the woodland itself. The conflict between interior and exterior, reality and its image, is the landscape of Ben's vulnerability and bewilderment. As Lizzie Francke observes, the film displays a rare "ability to communicate via the spatial relationships between the characters and the things around them."[83]

Although Peter Matthews understands that the film's aesthetic approach creates an atmosphere that is "unaccountably *off*,"[84] he also has considerable reservations about the technique: "What's the point of a movie that imitates a painting imitating a photograph?"[85] The purpose of this aesthetic strategy and its application in *The Ice Storm* is precisely to question the reality of what is seen and experienced by the characters. The film provides an ethereal representation of the commonplace, because the filmmakers wish to hint at the false truths that litter the New Canaan society; reality dissolves into its own appearance. Matthews perfectly well understands this, but does not view it as an effective dramatic device, explaining that the film displays an "agnosticism about the past," and that "by means of *triple distancing*, it empties the 70s of drama, urgency or threat and stages it as pure *pastness*."[86] Robert Sklar also supports this analysis, claiming that despite the design team's recreation of a world filled with period objects it feels "harrowingly empty." The effect is "like an old photograph, in which we see evidence of past lives though the people are no longer living."[87] I do not disagree with the descriptions that these two critics provide, but rather than understanding the issues they highlight as indictments of the film's dramatic weaknesses, I am inclined to interpret these factors as a confirmation of the emotional and aesthetic significance of the film. It is precisely this emptiness, objective distance, and vacillation that is fundamental to the film's mood, aims, and structure.

Figure 3.4: *The Ice Storm*. Isolation in Reflective Surfaces.
Reproduced by permission of Twentieth Century Fox and Studio Canal Image.

As Ang Lee explains, art direction and cinematography normally work to support the actors, but in *The Ice Storm* they are designed to "represent an obstacle to humanity."[88] The film does not present overt urgency, threat, or conventional causal dramatic structures in any aspect of its narrative. Understandably, this also applies to its cinematography and production design. The story is not propelled forwards with neoformalist aesthetic structures, as is the case in many mainstream films, because the characters themselves lack any goals or direction. The Photorealist aesthetic, therefore, helps articulate the film's desire to make the audience an active contributor, rather than a mere consumer of a preexistent meaning. Matthews's and Sklar's analyses of *The Ice Storm* arguably place too great an emphasis on the centrality of narrative agency and the importance of visual style in narrative terms, at the expense of the viewer's ability to choose to engage with a variety of cinematic pleasures. *The Ice Storm* succeeds in provoking its audience to engage with it, rather than limiting the interpretive choices they can make. The film is engaged in the deliberate construction of plural meanings.

Chapter 4

Evolution of the Score

> For we are interested in art as an occasion for communication with others as well as a source of aesthetic pleasure. And to the extent that communication or communion is among the leading purposes of art, authorial intention must always figure in interpretation, at least as a constraint on whatever other purposes we seek.[1]

For more than fifty years the relationship between authorial intention and the interpretation of artworks has been fiercely debated. Many scholars have argued that a focus on intention restricts the imagination and limits the artwork as a source of interpretative pleasure. For writers such as Wimsatt and Beardsley, for instance, it is an error to assume that a text means what its author(s) intended it to mean; rather meaning can be derived solely from close readings of the text.[2] This concern for the independence of the reader has led to the belief that authorial intention is somehow external to the artwork. However, our goal as a cinematic audience is to attempt to understand what is being expressed, and the collaborative process of filmmaking is about the struggle to communicate that meaning. When we interpret an artwork we attempt to determine the author(s)' intentions as they are evinced in the work of art itself. An understanding of process, therefore, can aid our communication or communion with the text. Rather than closing down meaning, understanding intention can unlock meaning and support interpretation. As Noël Carroll's comment above suggests, there is no convincing rationale for ignoring intention, particularly when examining contemporary filmmaking, where numerous collaborators contribute towards a shared vision of how a work might be interpreted. It would, in fact, be irresponsible to disregard potential source materials that might illuminate authorial intentions and approaches. To this end, the final two chapters will deal respectively with the evolution of the score and the completed soundtrack itself.

Of course, there are inherent challenges with this methodological
approach. Artists may not fully understand the psychological process
by which ideas occur to them. They may be unable to objectify their
own instinctive methods and intentions, nor remember afterwards
exactly how they constructed their work. They may even choose to
revise their memory in order to make their process seem more rational
and coherent than it actually was, or they may reproduce "the banalities
of publicity interviews" and fail to provide genuine detail or critical
insight.[3] Conversely, film musicologists have been reluctant to engage
in the examination of both process and product, perhaps because of a
fear that any discoveries may distort or problematize academic
arguments. But this debate is one of the most potentially fertile and
fascinating areas for development in second-generation film music
studies. It is important to engage our interpretive abilities in the context
of a genuine conversation, or as Carroll puts it, "the problem of
aberrant authorial pronouncements need not drive us toward anti-
intentionalism."[4] To explore contemporary film scoring practice
thoroughly, the technological and political influences experienced by a
composer—and how these intersect with creative and aesthetic
concerns—must be recognized. This type of study allows an
appreciation of the unity and the conception of a work, not solely in
terms of the integrity of the thought process, but also as the result of a
set of responses by the composer to the interaction of sometimes
contradictory compositional instincts, aesthetic values, and external
influences.

In order to understand the evolution of *The Ice Storm* score,
therefore, a range of different source materials will be examined. These
will include interviews, e-mails, faxes, handwritten notes, postproduction
schedules, sketches, and audio and computer sequencer files.[5]
Sequencer files provide a particularly interesting methodological
challenge as the data they hold cannot easily be represented in a book.
Screen captures or "transcriptions" of sequencer files hardly begin to
demonstrate their multiple layers of information, and there is no
obvious solution to the challenge of presenting this material. However,
it is necessary to attempt to do so because these are the resources that
Danna uses. Sequencer files, for example, provide a valuable insight
into the composer's methods and thought processes. They can also
clarify the working period through files listing the date and time they
were initially saved and last modified. In comparison, it is impossible
to verify the working time frame with Beethoven's sketchbooks, for
example.[6] Unlike paper sketches, sequencer files represent
compositional materials that have normally been played in through a
MIDI keyboard, the direct translation of a musical idea to a material

sound. Consequently, they can bear witness to a composer's instinctive, physical response to a particular compositional challenge, thereby capturing raw compositional ideas. Equally, sequencer files can help chart the developmental process of a work as musical concepts are shaped by external influences and become more formalized and goal-oriented.

While outlining the framework for the ensuing discussion, it is useful to highlight one further important issue. The title of this book would suggest that the score is the work of only one person. While it is clear that the focus is on Mychael Danna's music for the film, we are also concerned with other aspects of the soundtrack such as the sound design, the role of the music supervisor, the editors, the director, the use of preexistent music tracks, and how these various aspects interact with each other. More than any other art form, film is a collaborative medium involving hundreds of different people at different stages. Danna's score is not his sole creation although it can, of course, be understood as a development within his general body of work. At the heart of this analysis, therefore, are the same potential pitfalls and concerns that are frequently leveled at *auteur* theory.[7] What follows is an examination of the score for the film in relation to its social, historical, technological, and political production contexts.

Workstation Set-up

Our understanding of Danna's decision making process is profoundly affected by his composition workstation set-up, and it in turn impacts upon his compositional style. While developers of music hardware and software react quickly to compositional trends and practices, compositional choices can also be affected by the technology available to the composer. It is standard practice for composers to produce detailed "mock-ups" of their cues for the director and other production members. This is a process that helps minimize the imaginative leap required by the production team from an aural representation of the music to the finished product. Understandably, composers tend to use their most convincing and effective samples or synthesized sounds when creating these materials, even if they will later be replaced by real instruments in a recording session. It is extremely time-consuming to create realistic orchestral mock-ups and, as film composers generally face considerable time pressures, it becomes vital to create convincing sounds as quickly as possible. Because certain textures and instruments are easier to mock-up than others, it could be argued that the instrumentation and orchestration of contemporary film scores have been profoundly affected by the technical resources available to composers. The avoidance of contrapuntal textures and the prevalence of homophonic scoring (especially in string writing) is a possible consequence of some of these technical factors and may eventually be understood as a specific feature of post-1990s film scoring practice. Likewise, the widespread use of sequencers as a tool for composition and click-tracks for recording purposes has led to somewhat constrained rhythmic regularity in film music performances.[8]

Figure 4.1 profiles Danna's workstation set-up as revealed by the Environment page from his Logic sequencing software from July 1996. The Environment page shows the various instruments that comprised Danna's studio set-up as well as their connections.

Workstation Core
Power Macintosh, running e-magic Logic v. 3.5
Yamaha CBX-D5 Digital Recorder/Audio Interface
Opcode Studio 4 MIDI Interface
Tascam DA-88 Digital Multitrack Recorder
Mackie 2408 Analog Mixing Desk

Controller Keyboards
Roland A-80 Controller Keyboard
Roland FP-8 Electric Piano

Sound Modules
Roland JD-800 Synthesizer
Roland D-50 Synthesizer
Yamaha TX-7 Synthesizer
Alesis D-4 Drum Module
Sequential Circuits Prophet 2002

Samplers
Roland S-750 Sampler
Roland S-760 Sampler

Effects Unit
Lexicon LXP-5 Multi Effects Processor

Figure 4.1: Danna's Workstation Set-up for *The Ice Storm*, July 1996.

Danna's workstation was fairly typical for a film composer working in the mid-1990s. The emphasis was on outboard hardware rather than the later trend for software synthesizers and samplers. The workstation core consisted of a Power Macintosh computer running Logic sequencing software. An audio interface and a multitrack recorder allowed Danna to output his compositions into a physical audio format. A variety of sound-generating sources were available. Two controller keyboards, with their own internal sound banks, allowed compositional ideas to be played into the computer sequencer via a MIDI interface. There was also a range of MIDI synthesizers each containing numerous patches, that is, sounds, colors, and textures. Synthesizers use electronic circuits (oscillators) to generate sounds, which often lack the complexity of acoustic instruments' harmonic and inharmonic overtone structures. In compensation, Danna used two hardware samplers that, unlike synthesizers, recorded sound digitally and successfully reproduced the sounds of acoustic instruments. Danna also used a Lexicon audio effects processor that allowed audio output to be treated with reverberation or delay effects.

The Ice Storm sequencer files also reveal that Danna consistently used the internal banks of the Roland JD-800 for his string sounds. However, he preferred to use samples for the woodwind instruments, which were loaded into the Roland S-750 and S-760 samplers.

Unsteady Beginning

When Mychael Danna began work on the score for *The Ice Storm* in July 1996, the process of picture editing was far from complete. It is common for the edit to change somewhat while a composer is writing the score, but structurally *The Ice Storm* was transformed more than any other film on which Danna has worked.[9] The postproduction calendar suggests that a locked picture, that is the final edit, would be available from September 19th 1996, but faxes from the production office reveal that Danna attended a screening of the director's ninth cut and a spotting session as late as September 26th.[10] A spotting session is a meeting in which the director, composer, editor, and music supervisor determine exactly where the scoring for the film will be placed. Given that, by his own admission, Ang Lee completed eighteen different edits of at least one scene from the film, it is reasonable to assume that even by the end of September the picture edit was latched rather than locked.[11] The orchestral recording sessions took place on October 30th and 31st, and the masters were delivered on November 3rd. It is clear, therefore, that for most of the four months in which the music was developed the edit was evolving constantly, and that Danna had only one month of relative stability in which to complete the score. It is not clear how long the postproduction sound mix lasted, but Danna's score master tapes formed part of this final mix.

The radical reorganization of the edit appears to have been undertaken because there was a lack of agreement about how the film was working. Lee had complete faith in the material—no reshoots were carried out for example—but thought that that the correct rhythm and emotional register had not been pinpointed, and that the process of re-editing would help locate the emotional center of the film. According to the picture editor, Tim Squyres, the challenge centered on the fact that the film was not plot-driven.

> There is not a real narrative drive to it. There is emotional drive, but not narrative drive, so when you move things around they all work. . . . very often there is nothing obviously wrong with that move, or if you take a scene out. But in *The Ice Storm* that scene, while not necessary in a narrative sense, might resonate with something forty-five minutes later in an abstract way. We screened the film many times and we never had any consensus among ourselves—let alone an audience—about what was wrong and what was right, and how to fix it, and what we should leave alone. It was just such an abstract film that it was very hard to ever make a decision and see the results and say: "Ah yes, we got that right."[12]

The most significant transformation, according to Danna, was a shift from a heavy quality throughout to an almost comedic, "light and snappy" mood for the first two-thirds of the film.[13] Danna recalls attending a September screening and "suddenly finding it very funny, when it had not been funny before."[14] However, Squyres recalls removing jokes and comedic scenes from the edit. Squyres does not perceive these recollections as contradictory, but rather as a function of the fact that the film was simply working more effectively. The different versions of the edit no longer survive, but it appears that the "relentless restructuring" had the effect of transforming the narrative and emotional arc of the film.[15]

It is undoubtedly true that the composer faced a significant creative and technical challenge due to the constant reshaping of the edit, but it is also important to establish that the score could not have developed into what it eventually became without taking this iterative journey. Since the music grew from the process of uncovering the emotional center of the film, the composer and production team were constantly forced to reevaluate the precise purpose and nature of the score. The music grew organically from detailed collaboration, rather than as a response to a finished visual product. This process had a profound effect on the expressive register of the score and on the film as a whole.

The Sequencer Files

Danna's sequencer files provide us with valuable information about his approaches to scoring *The Ice Storm* and also illustrate the journey that the music took as the project developed. Table 4.1 represents all of the sequencer materials that Danna produced. Within nine different folders, exactly 103 files or music cues were generated. Ninety of these are sketches or drafts.[16] The folders highlight the overarching chronological development of the score from initial ideas to final locked picture. Where folders are named VERSION 6, VERSION 13, and so on, this relates to the specific edit of the film on which Danna was working at a particular time. The fact that there seem to be some missing folders—one through to five for example—is not because they have been deleted, but because Danna did not work specifically on these early edits of the picture. It appears that Danna began to work closely to picture on VERSION 6 of the edit and that he did not write music for every single re-edited version of the film thereafter.

It is possible to determine when each sequencer file was first created and last modified, and important to explore what information this metadata provides us with and how it should be examined. In broad terms it offers an indication of when, and for what period of time, Danna worked on a particular cue or group of cues. For example, one of Danna's first concept sketches, Test 3, was created on July 10th at 16:00 and last modified on July 15th at 01:12. It is a reasonable assumption that a file was last modified because Danna was satisfied with it, or was progressing on to the composition of a new version. However, this does not mean that Danna spent all of these five days working on this piece of music. The backup files (which are saved automatically at regular intervals) show, in this particular case, that Danna modified the cue on July 10th, 11th, 14th, and 15th. He did not physically work on the cue on Friday 12th or Saturday 13th. The time between a file's first creation and its last modification is not, therefore, an exact record of a working period. Likewise, the metadata cannot account for ideas that Danna may have been developing before they were saved or ideas he may have deleted because he was unhappy with them.

Some of the information contained within this metadata also gives cause for skepticism as there are a number of obvious contradictions and anomalies. Some files seem to be created and completed on the same day at exactly the same time. For example, NYC ICE STORM MIDI FILES: Jenny come home1 is both created and last modified on August 30th at 14:14. This is not because Danna is an extremely fast composer, but rather because he copied an existing file from another folder and saved it under a new name in order to begin revising it. In this case, the file eventually became From ICE Janey and was completed on September 2nd. Likewise, in VERSION 13 all fourteen cues were created on September 9th, a remarkably productive day's work. However, Danna did not start from scratch with each new revision of a cue; rather the files were copied from previous version(s) and then developed. It is thus clear that careful logging and structuring of the work in progress and meticulous version control were important organizational and developmental tools for the composer.

Some metadata is hard to reconcile. For example, VERSION 6: V6 1M6 was created on September 7th and modified on November 7th. Given that the finished master recordings were delivered on November 3rd, this seems unusual. Why would Danna modify a sequencer file after the score recording has already been completed? Examination of the backup files for this particular cue indicate that Danna worked on it between September 7th and 9th, but for some unknown reason he returned to it two months later. We could assume that Danna intended to modify some aspect of the cue to assist with the final mixing process, which was taking place at this time. However, it seems unlikely that he would return to a relatively early version of this cue if that were the case. Furthermore, direct comparison of versions of the cue saved respectively on September 9th and November 7th reveal that they are in fact identical. A more likely explanation, therefore, is simply that Danna chose to listen to this sequence in November and from force of habit saved it when he had finished. Just because a file has been "modified" on a particular date does not mean that it has been modified significantly, if at all.

All of Danna's sequencer files as they were saved in their respective folders are listed in Table 4.1. Within each folder, the files are presented in chronological order from when they were first created. It could be argued that a chronological order defined by when files were last modified would be equally valuable. Certainly an awareness of both sets of dates is necessary in order to draw useful conclusions from these materials. It is apparent, for example, that there was not a great deal of compositional activity during August, or rather very few files were created or saved. This is understandable given the re-organization of the edit. Of course, compositional process is not only about the physical act of creation. Discussions with the production team, individual research, analysis of the rough cut(s), reading the screenplay, and listening to appropriate musical models all formed part of the development of ideas.[17] These aspects can not be captured by sequencer files which reflect the physical nature of process.

EARLY VERSIONS

File Name	Created	Time	Modified	Time
Test 1	07/10/96	10:47	07/11/16	15:44
Test 2		11:28		17:46
Test 3		16:00	07/15/96	01:12
Test 5		16:37	07/11/96	16:59
Test 4		16:52	07/10/96	18:49
Redemption Theme1	07/25/96	08:15	07/26/96	19:29
From Last Cue NYC8/30	09/02/96	15:42	09/04/96	16:20
From Janey NYC8/30		17:02	09/05/96	12:28
From Carry NYC8/30		20:48	09/02/96	22:59
Carry 9/3	09/03/96	09:01	09/03/96	15:09

NYC ICE STORM MIDI FILES

File Name	Created	Time	Modified	Time
Jenny come home1	08/30/96	14:14	08/30/96	14:14
Ice Last Cue Stand Midi File		15:04		15:05
ICE Jenny com hm1.2		16:29		16:29
Cary1.1Stand Midi File		18:18		18:18
From ICE Last Cue Stand Midi File	08/31/96	11:02	08/31/96	15:07
From ICE Janey		15:11	09/02/96	17:01
V7 End Try 1	09/09/96	09:40	09/10/96	12:12
V7 End Try 2		09:42		12:11

VERSION 6

File Name	Created	Time	Modified	Time
V6 Last Cue NYC8/30	09/04/96	16:27	09/08/96	21:06
V6 1M1		23:00	09/10/96	10:54
V6 1M3		23:25	09/09/96	10:45
V6 6M1	09/09/96	12:29	09/05/96	12:29
V6 1M4	09/07/96	12:56	09/09/96	11:26
V6 1M5		16:55	09/08/96	10:41
V6 1M6		15:15	11/07/96	20:23
V6 3M3	09/08/96	18:25	09/10/96	11:27
V6 6M4		21:06	09/08/96	21:06

VERSION 8

File Name	Created	Time	Modified	Time
V8 1M3	09/09/96	11:52	09/10/96	10:58
V8 1M4		11:58		11:21
V8 3M3		16:48		11:36
V8 6M1		17:34	09/09/96	00:13
V8 6M4	09/15/96	01:11	10/26/96	21:24
V8 1M5	09/17/96	11:16	09/17/96	11:26
V8 6M3		13:07	09/18/96	15:48

Table 4.1: *The Ice Storm*. Danna's Sequencer Files, 1996.

VERSION 10				
File Name	Created	Time	Modified	Time
1M12	09/30/96	15:07	10/06/96	15:07
2M1		20:45		15:17
2M2		23:37		15:24
2M6	10/01/96	11:37		15:36
1M1		20:17	10/04/96	17:53
3M6		21:57		14:18
3M2	10/02/96	16:26	10/04/96	21:00
6M1		20:52		21:11
test 1	10/03/97	21:48		21:07
test 2		21:52		21:07
5M2	10/04/96	14:40		21:11
6MA		15:12		21:10

VERSION 12				
File Name	Created	Time	Modified	Time
6M4C	10/05/96	17:01	10/09/96	00:39
3M2		22:10	10/08/96	19:19
1M1	10/06/96	09:50		17:27
6M1		15:40		15:33
2M2		15:24	10/07/96	16:36
3M6		15:40	10/08/96	19:52
1M12		15:41	10/06/96	15:41
2M1		15:41	10/07/96	16:18
2M6		15:41	10/08/96	19:02
5MJaney&Jim		22:22	10/06/96	23:13
V83M6	10/07/96	14:04	10/08/96	19:39
3M4		19:20		19:26
3M7		21:09		14:34
6Mbathroom	10/08/96	00:19		16:22
1M9	10/08/96	17:59		18:37
6Mbathroom#2	10/08/96	22:14	10/09/96	13:19
Reel6 test	10/08/96	23:21		01:03

VERSION 13				
File Name	Created	Time	Modified	Time
1M1	10/09/96	12:43	10/17/96	00:31
1M9		13:23	10/15/96	18:59
2M1		14:17	10/18/96	20:18
2M2		14:24	10/09/96	14:27
2M6		14:40		15:00
3M2		15:29		15:29
3M4		15:34		15:40
V83M6		15:44		15:51
3M6		16:03		16:09
3M7		16:14	10/15/96	22:27

Table 4.1, cont.

VERSION 13 (Continued)				
File Name	**Created**	**Time**	**Modified**	**Time**
6Mbathroom#2	10/09/96	16:46	10/11/96	01:57
V8 6M1		16:51	10/09/96	17:00
Reel6 test		17:21	10/11/96	01:59
6M4C		17:29	10/10/96	17:15

VERSION 16				
File Name	**Created**	**Time**	**Modified**	**Time**
3M4	10/15/96	21:43	10/21/96	09:47
V8 3M6		22:05	10/19/96	12:27
3M7		22:28	10/22/96	18:44
6Mbathroom#2		22:38	10/16/96	20:37
6M1	10/16/96	11:40	10/19/96	17:53
1M1	10/17/96	08:21	10/23/96	16:20
1M9		08:25		14:57
2M1		08:38	10/22/96	18:37
2M2		08:42	10/18/96	11:50
3M2	10/19/96	11:08	10/22/96	22:27
2M6		14:52	10/21/96	09:49
3MRoaming		18:24	10/22/96	16:45
6MBowl	10/20/96	09:52	10/23/96	13:29

LOCKED				
File Name	**Created**	**Time**	**Modified**	**Time**
6Mbathroom#2	10/15/96	22:38	10/25/96	20:48
3MRoaming	10/19/96	18:24	10/28/96	22:05
6MBowl	10/20/96	09:52		22:56
1MTrain	10/23/96	14:57	10/25/96	16:41
2MBike		17:07		17:24
2MWalk		17:25		17:46
2MShoplift		17:30		18:14
3MPickUp P		18:46		19:25
3MDinner		19:34		19:55
3MDrive		19:36	10/23/96	19:36
3MToes		19:35		19:35
6MJaney		19:58		23:55
1M1	10/25/96	10:14	10/28/96	18:16

Table 4.1, cont.

EARLY VERSIONS	NYC ICE STORM MIDI FILES	VERSION 6	VERSION 8	VERSION 10
		V6 1M1		1M1
		V6 1M3	V8 1M3	
		V6 1M4	V8 1M4	
		V6 1M5	V8 1M5	
		V6 1M6		
				1M12
				2M1
				2M2
				2M6
				3M2
		V6 3M3	V8 3M3	
				3M6
				5M2
				6MA
From Janey NYC8/30	Jenny come home1 ICE Jenny com hm1.2 From ICE Janey	V6 6M1	V8 6M1	6M1
From Last Cue NYC8/30	Ice Last Cue Stand Midi File From ICE Last Cue Stand Midi File	V6 Last Cue NYC8/30 V6 6M4	V8 6M3 V8 6M4	
Test 1				
Test 2				
Test 3				
Test 4				
Test 5				
Redemption Theme1				
	V7 End Try 1			
	V7 End Try 2			
From Carry NYC8/30 Carry 9/3	Caryl.1Stand Midi File			
				Test 1
				Test 2

Table 4.2: *The Ice Storm*. Cue Interrelationships.

Danna employs conventional film scoring nomenclature to identify his cues. They are classified initially according to the reel in which they belong and subsequently by their chronological location within that reel. For example, 1M2 would identify reel one, music cue two.[18] However, owing to the elaborate nature of the working process and the evolution of the edit, the individual sequencer files are often labeled in different ways making it difficult to see how they relate to each other. It is not immediately apparent, for example, that VERSION 10: 6MA, VERSION 16: 6M1, and LOCKED: 6MJaney are developments of the same cue. Table 4.2, therefore, demonstrates the interrelationship between various versions of the cues showing the structural development of the music from initial concept sketches to completion. The columns show the respective chronological versions of the edit while the rows show the causal relationship between materials. The

VERSION 12	VERSION 13	VERSION 16	LOCKED	PUBLISHING CUE SHEET
1M1	1M1	1M1	1M1	1M1 "Opening"
1M9 1M12	1M9	1M9	1MTrain	1M8 "Train"
2M1	2M1	2M1	2MBike	2M2A "Bike Kiss" 2M2B "Bike Kiss (cont.)"
2M2	2M2	2M2	2MWalk	2M3 "Walk"
2M6	2M6	2M6	2MShoplift	2M6 "Shoplift"
3M2	3M2	3M2	3MPickUp P	3M1 "Pick Up Paul"
3M4	3M4	3M4	3MDinner	3M3 "Dinner"
		3MRoaming	3MRoaming	3M4 "Roaming"
V8 3M6 3M6	V8 3M6 3M6	V8 3M6	3MToes	3M5 "Toes Cold"
3M7	3M7	3M7	3MDrive	3M6 "Drive"
5MJaney&Jim				
6MBathroom 6Mbathroom#2	6Mbathroom#2	6Mbathroom#2	6Mbathroom#2	6M1 "Bathroom"
6M1	V8 6M1	6M1	6MJaney	6M2 "Janey"
6M4C	6M4C	6MBowl	6MBowl	6M4 "Bowl"
Reel 6 test	Reel 6 test			

Table 4.2, cont.

last column, PUBLISHING CUE SHEET, lists the names of tracks as they were finally registered by the music supervisor.[19] The music itself is not altered or developed between the LOCKED version and the PUBLISHING CUE SHEET version, the cues are simply relabeled by the music supervisor in order to accommodate and acknowledge (in chronological terms) the preexistent pop music tracks that also form part of the soundtrack. We shall be referring to this nomenclature and the preexistent music tracks used in the film in chapter 5, thus the information is included here in order to facilitate cross-referencing.

The bottom half of the table contains concept sketches and cues that cannot clearly be related to specific narrative sequences within the film or to other cues. It is clear that many of Danna's initial ideas do not lead directly to material that appears in the finished film. Unsurprisingly, as the scoring process develops and the conceptual framework becomes more secure, less material is discarded. The cues also become more homogenous in terms of style, instrumentation, and orchestration.[20]

Initial Ideas

Danna's initial concept sketches (created on July 10th 1996) were not written specifically to picture, but were an attempt to articulate the territory that the score would eventually cover. These initial ideas are not as polished as later cues, but are useful in demonstrating instinctive compositional approaches. In line with the film's existential nihilistic agenda, already highlighted in chapter 3, Danna attempted to emphasize the barren, alienated, and passionless existence of the central characters. The cues Test 1 though to Test 4 are developed from the same basic harmonic and melodic cell (Figure 4.2). Harmonically, the material is in D minor, particularly because of the C♯ leading note and an implied tonic/dominant relationship. However, the security of this supposed tonality is disturbed by the use of the tritone (between B♮ and F♮), which adds a distinctive color to the A major harmony underneath.

Figure 4.2: Test 1–Test 4, Basic Thematic Material.
Reproduced by permission of Mychael Danna.

Figure 4.3: Test 1 (transcribed from sequencer file).
Reproduced by permission of Mychael Danna.

In Test 1 the thematic material is given to the piano in a repetitive, cyclical, triple-time accompaniment pattern with the melody presented on the downbeat of each new bar (Figure 4.3). Above this Danna creates a florid improvisation with characteristic triplet mordents, based on the mode of the 4th degree: (d–e–f) G–A–B♭–C♯–D–E–F–G. The overwhelming impression is of a cue that sounds stereotypically Middle Eastern, particularly because of the augmented 2nd interval between B♭ and C♯. However, the recurrent B♮s in both bass and melody lines disrupt the modality creating a quirky, awkward atmosphere. Given that the whole cue is treated with a great deal of reverberation, a distant, emotionally isolated mood is created. The piano material is later reinforced by a dark, synthesizer pad (Roland JD-800: Black Hole), which provides harmonic support through a spacious texture. It is important to note that this synthesizer pad is not intended to be an imitation or mock-up of a live instrument, the chosen sound is used precisely because of its synthetic, analog quality.

A number of scoring concepts are defined within this cue: the mixture of "live" and synthesized materials, conflicting modality, Middle Eastern influences, and use of reverberation as a narrative device. The conflation of ideas presented here should not be surprising given the proximity of Danna's work on *Kama Sutra*, which immediately preceded *The Ice Storm*, and *Exotica* which had attracted the production team to the composer in the first instance. Indeed, the main thematic material for *Exotica* (see chapter 2, Figure 2.6) is strikingly similar to Test 1. There is correspondence between the simple piano accompaniment pattern, the modal (sometimes harmonically conflicting) improvisatory features, and the use of electronica in combination with live instruments which is a central feature of the *Exotica* score (e.g., *shehnai* and synthesizers). In terms of compositional process two issues arise from this observation. First is the notion of the baggage that a composer brings with them from their previous films. Beyond recurrent features of compositional style or method, when a composer begins a new project there will be an inevitable tendency to rely on prior experience, at least initially. This is especially true because of the severe time pressures—which do not always allow opportunities for experimentation or failure—that contemporary film composers face. Second, the nature of the industry is such that a composer is often brought onto a film because of their previous credits. Both James Schamus (producer) and Alex Steyermark (music supervisor) have suggested that the production team wanted to work with Danna precisely because they were great admirers of Egoyan's films and thought *Exotica* was a innovative score.[21] The production team's enthusiasm for specific previous works is often revealed during initial meetings. This may steer the composer towards particular methods or approaches and is consequently an influence on authorial intention. The use of temp tracks also contributes towards this phenomenon.

Figure 4.4: Test 3 (transcribed from sequencer file).
Reproduced by permission of Mychael Danna.

Test 3 further develops the thematic material by creating a 6/8 rhythmic syncopation against the basic 3/4 pattern. Danna discards the modal, improvised passage but retains the synthesizer pad which more frequently punctuates the repetitive piano material and contributes to the general sense of unrest. A feature of the wave envelope of the Black Hole pad is a *crescendo* from silence when a note is struck and a long decay after a note is released. The transcription from the sequencer file would suggest hard entries and exits, but the synthesizer pad notes are, in fact, more carefully dovetailed into the texture than the score would suggest. This effect is compounded by the wash of reverberation that covers the entire cue. Danna also develops the conflict between the B♭ and B♮ (Figure 4.4). This conflict seems relatively unsystematic in Test 1, but in Test 3 it is more carefully controlled. Measure 8, for example, contains a particularly uncomfortable dissonance, with a B♭ in the left hand pitted against a B♮ in the right hand. This could be a simple mistake as Danna played the music into his sequencer, but the fact that the same clash recurs later in the piece suggests a deliberate attempt to create unease. This music is unsettled and bleak as Danna endeavors to capture the mood of the early edits of the film.

Figure 4.5: Test 4 (transcribed from sequencer file).
Reproduced by permission of Mychael Danna.

Test 2 and Test 4 remain within the same D minor framework but are much more reminiscent of the ambient electronica that Danna composed during the 1980s. The piano is not used in either of these cues and only synthesized textures are employed. Given that there is no suggestion that these synthesized sounds were due to be replaced at a later stage with real instruments, we can begin to define a central feature of Danna's initial scoring ideas. Clearly synthesized timbres as a means of articulating dramatic tension were integral to the initial concept of the score. The use of the Yamaha TX-7 as one of the

generating sound sources within these two cues is worthy of note, as it
was rather dated by the mid-1990s. The distinctive cold sound quality
of the instrument is generated through FM synthesis.[22]

In Test 4 (Figure 4.5) the TX-7 is used to help reinforce the bass
texture with a low, rumbling Pain patch. The Jet Strings pad has a
characteristic "whooshing," sweeping quality which is due to the
application of a flanging effect.[23] Danna doubles the Jet Strings in order
to create a thicker texture as the piece progresses. Above these textures
a piercing, thin Hi-Voltage sample adds to the ugly and uncomfortable
synthesized soundworld. The cue is almost Herrmannesque in its
dramatic and oppressive intensity, emphasized by the continuous,
relentless repetition of the basic four-measure pattern and recurrence of
the tritone.

Unlike the sketches examined so far, Test 5 does not use the basic
thematic material. It is a texturally shifting, synthesized drone based on
D minor with an uncomfortable low pulsing E♭ (TX-7: Ugly) creating a
constant harmonic clash. A variety of distorted, buzzing noises also
contribute to the dark, evolving texture.

The recurrent use of synthesizer materials throughout these first
five cues reveals an interesting conceptual framework. There have been
some notable examples of purely synthesized film scores, although this
is still a relatively rare occurrence. In films such as *Blade Runner*
(Scott, 1982) or *The Terminator* (Cameron, 1984) the synthesized
music is used to help represent some of the futuristic aspects of their
narratives. But in both films issues surrounding what it means to be
human and the representation of artificial humanity (replicants or
cyborgs, respectively) are explored. In Kubrick's *A Clockwork Orange*
(1971) the sociopathic central character endures bouts of experimental
aversion therapy in order to be cured from a propensity towards
extreme violence. However, this brainwashing eradicates a basic
human characteristic, the ability to exercise freedom of choice. Again,
the score is entirely synthesized, highlighting the human/inhuman,
organic/inorganic dialectic that is at the heart of the film. In *Witness*
(Weir, 1985) a young Amish boy is the sole eyewitness to a murder
while traveling with his mother. A hardened detective is assigned to
protect the boy and his mother, and they go into hiding when the killers
pursue them. The film is an honest study of the Pennsylvanian Amish,
who reject many of the features of modern society, through the eyes of
an outsider suddenly introduced into their world. The synthesized
score, in this case, appears to enhance the preternatural, transcendental
world of the Amish community. It is clear, therefore, in all of these
examples that a certain type of analog synthesizer score tends to be

associated with recurrent concepts of a lack of humanity, emotional and/or physical isolation, and artificiality.

Danna explains that an appropriate aural metaphor for the emotionally barren, "plastic" central characters in *The Ice Storm* appeared to be a heavily synthesized score, "something very *Switched-on Bach*–ish."[24] Wendy Carlos's seminal reinterpretation and re-orchestration of well-known Bach works for the Moog synthesizer, *Switched-on Bach*, was first released in 1968 and quickly sold more than one million copies. It influenced rock and pop musicians such as the Byrds, the Doors, and the Beatles who all used the Moog as part of a search for a new sound palette. The Minimoog released in 1970 was the first mass-produced, portable synthesizer and led to an explosion of interest in electronic music, something that had previously only been the domain of electroacoustic composers.[25] Therefore, the Moog synthesizer and *Switched-on Bach* are powerful and evocative musical icons of their age, part of the cultural currency of the early 1970s. Given that the film is set during this era, the instrumental resources are a valuable historical and cultural locator.

The influence of 1970s synthesized sounds is also apparent in VERSION 6 and VERSION 8. Three isolated cues appear within each of these versions of the edit and in terms of emotional content the material is diametrically opposed to Danna's initial ideas. Funk and Latin jazz styles are fused to create a light, ironic, and corny mood. VERSION 6: V6 1M3 features a rhythm section consisting of agogos, timbales, cuica, shakers, cabassa, and industrial percussion. A sampled Fender Rhodes keyboard and a fretless bass guitar play clipped, syncopated patterns that alternate with excessive *glissandi* to create an irreverent quality (Figure 4.6). The Fender Rhodes was used in jazz-fusion styles throughout the 1970s, so it is clear that Danna references this in his historical and stylistic pastiche.[26]

In VERSION 8: V8 1M4 the same material appears in a slightly slower arrangement. Danna adds a "cheesy" introduction based around the chord sequence: B–B^{maj7}–B^7–E/B–Em–B–D♭m–G♭–Em. The first three chords help generate a descending semi-tone pattern (B–B♭–A) that moves over a dominant pedal B, there are direct shifts between major and minor, and the instrumentation contributes to the deliberately saccharine quality. Eventually these cues were replaced with pre-existent tracks that were genuine historical and sociocultural locators while Danna attempted to find other ways through the score.

In terms of Danna's initial thought processes, two distinct approaches to using synthesized materials are witnessed. The first uses synthesized music with a parodic quality as a historical locator and consequently pokes fun at the central characters. The second approach uses the artificial quality of synthesized sound itself to highlight emotional dislocation by mirroring the false lifestyle of the characters. In both cases Danna attempts to use timbre as a fundamental articulator of the character-based, narrative themes.

Figure 4.6: V6 1M3, Latin Funk (transcribed from sequencer file).
Reproduced by permission of Mychael Danna.

Plastic to Organic: The Call of the Land

The score had initially attempted to mirror the artificiality of the characters' lifestyles through the use of a synthesized sound palette, but just as the edit changed focus so the scoring strategy evolved into a radically different approach. This could be described as a transformation from a "plastic" to an "organic" score.

Steyermark explains that the first month of scoring had been very difficult, the signature sound for the film had yet to be discovered, and Danna had completed a number of sketches that were "not quite on target."[27] Ang Lee wanted the music to have a brittle quality reflecting the fact that "it is winter, there is a lot of ice, people are cold, and the personalities are cold."[28] The concept of emotional and physical coldness was something that Danna had already attempted in his initial sketches, so a reevaluation was necessary. In order for the score to function effectively it would need to express more than could already be seen on the screen. A breakthrough came by approaching the representation of the characters from a radically different perspective. As Danna explains, the people in *The Ice Storm* have

> tried to break any connection with tradition, with the past, with nature. Nevertheless, those things are still there and are strong and have a more profound influence on them than they care to acknowledge. I remember attending one of the screenings and watching a scene where the father is walking through the woods and seeing these goofy, prefab, geodesic-shaped 1970s houses, and they are in the middle of beautiful Connecticut forest. I remember thinking about the strange contrast between how they live in this forest and how a couple of hundred years before—and for thousands of years before—native people would have been living in that forest, and the different ways they would have been interacting, behaving, and living, and eating, and cooking. Then it occurred to me that it might be interesting to suggest that with the music.[29]

Danna's sideways analysis of the film is particularly striking. Rather than creating a direct musical representation of emotional dislocation, the approach outlined above suggests dislocation through an opposition with environment. It is a mode of scoring that is concerned with subtext rather than representational commentary. It is also an approach that refocuses the narrative on nature and consequently on the eponymous meteorological event at the heart of the film. In order to realize this concept, Danna chose to incorporate two distinct and seemingly contradictory instrumental resources into his compositional materials, a Native American flute and a gamelan ensemble.[30]

Given the rationale already outlined, the Native American flute appears to be an intelligent and logical instrumental resource. It could be made from materials found within the Connecticut forest where years earlier Native Americans lived in harmony with nature. The film is set around the Thanksgiving festival, and the lack of connection with nature and tradition is highlighted in the central narrative; Wendy's prayer/rant at the dinner table is one example of this. Danna played examples of Native American flute recordings to Ang Lee who was fascinated by the concept, believing that it could emphasize many of the film's central themes because the sound was "like the call of the land."[31]

It is interesting to note that the process of creating and recording the Native American flute element of the score required a collaborative compositional process that seemed highly appropriate for the newly developed scoring concept. The flautist, a Native American named Dan Cecil Hill, did not read musical notation. The challenge, therefore, was to find a means of communicating ideas and to generate useful materials through discussion and improvisation. It was an approach that involved the music supervisor, composer, performer, and director.

> He [Dan Cecil Hill] works through the sounds of animals and birds, and if you want to talk emotion with him you can but then he will relate that to the scream of an eagle yearling or something like that. So for him it is specific—different birds, eagles, different animals and sounds of nature—that is how he relates to music and sound, and he would not necessarily play the same thing twice, so it was all improvised, some of it to picture, most of it to our direction.[32]

The flute was recorded directly into Danna's Logic sequencer and was later edited in order to create the completed cues.[33] Lee was actively involved throughout this recording and editing processes. Working with the flautist, therefore, required the foresight to generate a variety of materials that could be assembled at a later stage. While this approach may have been relatively uncommon in film scoring practice in the mid-nineties, the parallels with other filmmaking processes are clear—numerous versions of a particular scene are shot then edited together afterwards. The fact that no specialist musical language was required to direct the flautist may have enabled Lee to contribute extensively to the creative music-making process. A number of commentators note that Lee is not particularly verbose or descriptive and that his direction is often cryptic. Danna explains: "He does a lot of listening and he is very quiet, but there will always be something that he picks up on."[34] The material engagement with the scoring process seems particularly suited to Lee's directorial style and was important for the composer, because it allowed Danna to have a direct understanding of Lee's wishes, even though the director might not articulate them verbally. Danna also exploited this methodology in other aspects of the compositional process. For example, a deerskin drum and *nautch* bells feature in the finished score and in some cases they are performed by Ang Lee himself (see Figure 4.7).[35] The fact that Danna labels some of these audio materials Ang Lee Recording Star suggests the close collaborative process between director and composer in the development of scoring ideas which contribute to the integration of music into the larger narrative and conceptual framework of the film.

Figure 4.7: Ang Lee Recording Deerskin Drum, Danna at the Computer, 10/07/96. Reproduced by permission of Mychael Danna.

The Native American flute and percussion appeared to fulfill a central requirement of the score. However, justifying the decision to use a gamelan ensemble was more challenging, particularly because it clearly belonged to another culture and location, and Danna had initial difficulty in persuading the production team that it would be dramatically appropriate. The gamelan could be understood as a direct aural analog to the visuals, the inspiration coming from numerous shots of glittering ice and of ice melting. However, on closer reflection

Danna also believed there were deeper philosophical and subtextual meanings that were relevant.

> Gamelan is played in a social setting, in a culture that is very much connected to its natural surroundings and certainly works at living, literally, in concert with nature. So it [the gamelan] works sensually and it works philosophically. It gives a paradoxical message about an instrument that is played by a completely opposite society—same species—but with a very different way of relating to nature and relating to each other. Just that idea of a fractured setting and music coming from a place that is so much more integrated with itself seemed to strike a really beautiful paradox.[36]

In order to demonstrate the soundworld that could be created, Danna played examples of gamelan music to Lee who remained unconvinced. This highlights an interesting separation between a composer's musical concept and what can be demonstrated to members of the production team through preexisting musical examples. Gamelan music is often jarring, with constant changes of tempi, yet Danna's concept was more "minimalist and soothing" than the music extracts he was able to play.[37] According to Danna, the production team found it difficult to grasp the concept because of the specificity of the music that they heard. Danna's approach to persuading the director shows both political acuity and determination of purpose.

> I talked Ang into it in a physically sensual way. I know he is very visually oriented . . . so I asked him to fly up [to Toronto], because I knew when he saw these instruments he would fall in love with them, and he did. We had them all set up and they are gorgeous, beautifully decorated, and the history of them probably being cooking pots turned upside down—Ang loves cooking—the construction of them and the sound of them. I had him come in and already he was loving it, and then I asked the ensemble to play a very simple pattern. I did not even write it, I just said: "Right you play D♭, you play E♭, and you play A♭, just give me straight quarter notes at 80 BPM," and Ang was saying: "OK, now I see what you mean."[38]

It is interesting to note, despite Danna's conviction about using this type of ensemble, that he had not worked with gamelan before and needed to learn more about the instruments. A fax received from percussionist Mark Duggan of the Toronto-based Evergreen Club gamelan ensemble illustrates the instruments that were available to Danna and their ranges (Figure 4.8).[39]

Evergreen Club Instrument Information

Figure 4.8: Fax, Mark Duggan to Danna, 10/07/96 (transcribed), p. 2 of 2.
Reproduced by permission of Mychael Danna.

The fax was sent on October 7th, relatively late in the composition schedule. By this stage Danna was already working on VERSION 12. However, the sequencer files reveal that Danna had composed gamelan material long before this date. Unsurprisingly, Danna's compositional materials become more secure in relation to the gamelan after receiving this fax, especially in relation to the particular tuning of the Evergreen Club ensemble. Duggan also reports that Danna came to see the instruments several times and discussed which "sounds and mallets might work best."[40] Given the unique nature of each gamelan ensemble, Danna altered some of his compositional ideas in order to accommodate the particular instruments he was writing for.

A typical gamelan ensemble will usually have two sets of instruments with different tunings, *pélog* and *sléndro*. *Pélog* is a seven-note tuning system and *sléndro* is a five-note tuning system. In each system three five-note melodic modes may be constructed. The fax reveals that the Evergreen Club gamelan set is Sundanese (from West Java) as it is slightly smaller in size than other types of gamelan and uses the *degung* mode, which is a pentatonic subset derived from the parent *pélog* scale. In fact, the Sundanese gamelan is often called gamelan *degung*, a unique type used exclusively for listening and ritual, rather than for various forms of theatre or dancing. The fax also reveals that the main pitches available to Danna approximated to C–Db–Eb–G– Ab, and that he was able to write for the ensemble in Western notation rather than traditional cipher notation.[41]

The use of the *degung* mode directs the composer towards using particular harmonic language, especially as the intention was to combine the gamelan with other Western instruments in a tonal context. However, the implementation of the *degung* mode appears to have been a necessity rather than a choice, as the Evergreen Club did not own a complete gamelan set in 1996. The additional *sléndro* tuning was not available to the composer even if he had wanted to use it.

The notion of combining gamelan with other Western instruments raises a further challenging issue. The tuning of a gamelan is not equally tempered so, in Western terms, some notes within the mode can sound extremely sharp or flat. Historically, Javanese tradition dictated that the design and tuning of old and sacred gamelan sets could not be copied, so each ensemble has an individual identity and sound quality. For example, Duggan explains that in particular the Evergreen Club's low *bonang* were often sharp.[42] Danna also reports that, aside from discrepancies with individual pitches, the gamelan set was approximately a quarter-tone flat in relation to the Western instruments. Given this context, the combination of gamelan and orchestra seems particularly challenging.

Remarkably, Danna recalls undertaking minimal retuning of the recorded gamelan master tapes. The only adjustment made was an approximately thirty cent sharpening of the gamelan—just under a third of a semitone—in order to bring it up to concert pitch.[43] There are some aspects of this recollection that will be challenged in chapter 5.

Nonetheless, general pitch shifting of the audio files would still allow for individual sharp and/or flat note discrepancies within the various instruments of the ensemble. This created a particular quality and timbre that appealed to Danna, but the rest of the production team also needed to be convinced. Danna's demos were completed using equally tempered synthesized gamelan sounds. The production team did not hear the true tuning of the ensemble until the recording session itself; a fascinating if risky strategy.

> I used my equal tempered samples of the gamelan to get them used to the sound, but there were a lot of jaws dropping when we got to the session and they heard the actual tuning. People were quite shocked. . . . We recorded them first separately to click and then recorded the orchestra.[44]

Tyranny of the Temp Track?

It is common practice in contemporary film scoring for pre-existent music from films or recordings to be used during postproduction in place of a specifically composed score. These temp tracks are later usually replaced by the composer's score, although Kathryn Kalinak's famous comment about the "tyranny of the temp track" refers to the film *2001: A Space Odyssey* (Kubrick, 1968) where the composer's score was, in fact, rejected and the temp score favored.[45] Accordingly, Kalinak is scathing about the practice of using temp tracks in the filmmaking process. She acknowledges that they can be useful as a point of communication between the composer and the production team, but they can also "function as straitjacket, locking the composer into certain musical ideas, gestures, styles, and even melodies."[46] Temp tracks are used for three main reasons: assisting the picture editor especially in the creation of appropriate filmic pace and rhythm, focusing the ideas of the production team about the design of the score, and lastly for prerelease screenings, particularly audience test screenings and screenings for financiers. In *The Ice Storm* some of the temp track choices reveal interesting thought processes and collaborative approaches. One of the tracks used was a piece by Peter Gabriel entitled "Before Night Falls" from the film *The Last Temptation of Christ* (Scorsese, 1988). Gabriel's music is a postmodern fusion of Middle Eastern percussion, synthesized drones, and wind and string instruments. Gliding over a fast, repetitive sixteenth-note percussion pattern played by *sakat* (finger cymbals) and *darbukkah* (conical hand-drum), a Turkish *ney* flute melody is answered in canon by a delayed version of itself and an Indian violin, a dark synthesized drone sits low underneath. The music succeeds in achieving both a sense of forward, propulsive movement through the recurrent sixteenth-note pattern, but also a sense of gradual, spacious evolution from the slower-moving melody instruments. This music was used as temp for two scenes in *The Ice Storm*, the first where Ben walks home through the forest after having sex with Janey, the second where Elena is caught shoplifting at a local pharmacy. The two scenes do not seem to have much in common in terms of mood or pace—the first is much slower and more contemplative than the latter—though the use of the same music may have suggested a narrative link between the respective misdemeanors of the central married couple.[47] This music was not used at any other point in the film, however, which highlights a general functional weakness of temp tracks. Individual temp cues tend to function locally creating appropriate moods or highlighting specific emotions for particular scenes, but rarely are they able to reflect larger narrative concerns or structures. On most films, therefore, the composer must distill the relevant surface information from particular temp cues and locate this within their own larger conceptual and structural framework. Inspired by the "Before Night Falls" cue Danna might have distilled the notion of ethnic music in a nonethnic context, the postmodern amalgamation of various world music traditions and styles, the attempt to make a narrative link between Ben's adultery and Elena's thievery, the sense of forward-moving rhythm, and free-flowing woodwind. The eventual use of Native American flute, driving gamelan, and *nautch* bells certainly suggests the strong influence of the temp cue, and would seem to reinforce Kalinak's concern about a process that may restrict compositional creativity.

Steyermark, however, believes that temp tracks are a necessary "fact of life."[48] He also proposes a solution to the fact that composers often feel pressured into creating a pastiche of the temp.

> If you are going to temp the music for a movie then you should use music that is written by the composer that you are going to work with, because a lot of directors are not able to articulate what it is about their music that they actually like, but if they can show the composer who wrote that music what it is that they like, the composer can reverse engineer it from there.[49]

This method was, indeed, employed in *The Ice Storm*, where a number of cues Danna composed for previous film projects were used. Figure 4.9 shows a working draft of Steyermark's source and temporary music cue sheet for the third reel and part of the fourth reel of the film. Danna's handwritten notes—to the right of the printed text—provide useful information about his response to this temp material. In the third reel the two pieces used, "House Tour" and

"Archery," were both originally composed for Egoyan's film *The Adjuster* (1991).

REEL 3

3M1S   MIKEY FALLS OFF BIKE (hummimg) (0:26)
(SCORE)   IN: 0:31:02
             OUT: 0:57:00

3M2S   PICK-UP PAUL AT TRAIN STATION - (temp-Mychael Danna
(SCORE)   "Archery") (0:33)
             IN: 3:37:25   Wendy looking at messed bed
             OUT: 4:10:18 under Ben "how's school treating you?"

3M1   SKIPPING RECORD - (Humble Pie "DEATH MAY BE YOUR SANTA
             CLAUS") (1:17)
             IN: 6:34:13   cut to ext. Wendy's bedroom door
             OUT: 7:51:11 cut to stream

3M2BS BEN ROAMS CARVER HOUSE

3M3S   TOES COLD ? - (temp-Mychael Danna "House Tour") (0:39)
(SCORE)   IN: 16:42:15 after Ben "toes cold?"
             OUT: 17:22:00 under Ben "...dress for the Halford's now?"

3M4S   RAINY DRIVE TO HALFORD'S - (temp-M. Danna "Archery") (0:57)
(SCORE)   IN: 20:07:07 cut to Elena & Ben driving in car
             OUT: 21:04:00 under door opening to party

3M2   HALFORD PARTY 1 (Boz Scaggs "DINAH FLO" (0:48)
             IN: 20:58:28 door opening to party
             OUT: 21:46:13 CU bowl of keys (LFOA)

REEL 4

4M1   HALFORD PARTY 2 (Bobby Bloom "MONTEGO BAY") (2:22)
             IN: 2:25:13   cut to party as Elena enters
             OUT: 4:47:17 after Ben "don't bullshit me around!"

4M2   HALFORD PARTY 3 (Johnny Nash "STIR IT UP") (1:10)
             IN: 4:49:09   after Ben "waited around for half an hour"
             OUT: 5:59:20 cut to Paul on train

4M3   HALFORD PARTY 4 (Harry Nilsson "COCONUT") (1:17)
             IN: 7:39:14   cut to Elena sitting at party
             OUT: 8:56:07 cut to Paul in Libbits' bathroom

Figure 4.9: Source and Temp Music, 09/20/96, p. 3 of 5.
Reproduced by permission of Mychael Danna.

"Archery" was used for two sequences that involve driving: when Ben collects Paul from the train station and when Ben and Elena are on their way to the Halfords' party. Interestingly, the music shares many similarities with the "Before Night Falls" temp cue. There is a clear sense of momentum as Danna uses African percussion to create a recurrent ostinato pattern over which solo *duduk* plays a breathy, improvisatory melody; synthesized gestures also feature heavily. The

"House Tour" cue is very different in its mood and consists of a warm, reverberant, slow-moving synthesized pad with a sparse solo piano melody. This was used for the scene when Ben carries his daughter home after having caught her "fooling around" with Mikey.

Danna's handwritten notes suggest that the temp cues and discussion about them helped deepen his reading of the film. The comments "Neg Zone/Primitive" and "Primitive Drums" indicate an attempt to generate musical materials that symbolize the existential features of the narrative, the negative zone that Paul Hood constantly refers to. It is easy to understand how the rhythmic features present in both the "Archery" and "Before Night Falls" temp cues could contribute towards the concept of primitive percussion as representative of the negative zone. The word "Family" next to the "House Tour" cue suggests the structural and narrative importance of the tender moment when Ben carries Wendy home. The warmth of the temp cue highlights the emotional bond that is created between a father and his daughter, which is striking in a film where family members rarely connect with each other in any meaningful way. The words "Nature" and "Flute" are associated with a proposed new music cue that accompanies Ben as he roams the Carver household in his boxer shorts after an interrupted adultery session. The formation of the idea that solo flute could represent nature in contrast to the barren lives of the characters is witnessed here, although, at this stage Danna seems to consider the possibility of a Mayan influence rather than the Native American flute he later selected.

Film musicologists and composers have, understandably, focused on the negative aspects of temp tracks and frequently highlight their constraining characteristics. Burt, for example, notes: "I can't think of anything that would more inhibit a composer or more effectively dislodge his or her creative process."[50] It is interesting to note, therefore, that there were some positive benefits to using the temp track in *The Ice Storm*. It functioned as useful shorthand for discussion from which Danna was able to draw out important elements and shape them into a new distinctive musical language. Some of the instrumental resources that Danna chose were defined in response to the temp track. But most significantly, the temp track seems to have contributed to the conception of three fundamental building blocks on which the score eventually became constructed: Nature—Negative Zone—Family.

Nonetheless, there were occasions where the influence of Danna's own preexistent music constrained rather than unleashed his creativity. Temp music often ceases to be a source of inspiration when the production team becomes obsessed with its particular qualities and the composer is forced to imitate it. This challenge was experienced in one particular scene. The temp cue entitled "Memories, These Things Possess You" was originally written by Danna for Egoyan's film *Family Viewing* (1987) and was used for the scene where Janey returns home alone after the key party and falls asleep in the fetal position.

> I remember very clearly that I rewrote that piece dozens of times and I don't think Ang was ever convinced that it was as good as the temp piece, which was me. That was very frustrating. . . . He would just say: "No I don't feel anything, try it again."[51]

The struggle with this particular scene reveals some fascinating aspects about the development of the score and about the nature of communication and collaboration. The cue, eventually labeled 6M2 'Janey,' did indeed experience constant transformation (see Table 4.2). In fact, it was the only cue in the whole film for which Danna wrote music for each successive version of the edit, a period of transformation that lasted from August 31st until October 23rd.

The temp cue is a gentle 3/4 time piece for piano, oboe, and clarinet with occasional synthesized pad and *pizzicato* textures. The prominent features are the use of a modal melodic structure, harmonically static piano pedal, dovetailing contrapuntal phrases between the oboe and clarinet, and the avoidance of resolution.

The influence of this temp music on Danna's various attempts at the cue is clear. All versions use harmonically constant piano and/or gamelan accompaniment and recurrent triple time signatures. The pulse of the temp track is quarter-note 68 BPM. Danna starts his initial versions (EARLY VERSIONS until VERSION 6) slightly faster than this at quarter-note 75 BPM, but on VERSION 8: V8 6M1 he uses exactly the same tempo. Danna's subsequent versions slow to quarter-note 54 BPM but then return to quarter-note 68 BPM. After some wavering, therefore, the final versions of the cue are at exactly the same speed as the temp track. The clarinet features in all Danna's versions of the cue, but as work progressed he also added oboe and eventually flute.[52] The thematic material is frequently dovetailed, where a particular pitch is used as a pivot note and one instrument passes the melody onto the other. The fact that the music becomes increasingly contrapuntal as the cues develop suggests that this was an important element of the temp track that the production team wanted Danna to emulate. The evolution of the cues, therefore, demonstrates movement towards exactly the same speed, character, and mood as the temp track.

The chronological development of the main thematic material for the various versions of the cue, labeled A, B, and C, appears in Figure 4.10. There are, of course, numerous variations of each version with altered instrumentation, orchestration, register, dynamics, and so on. Danna's music is constantly updated, but on VERSION 13 he discards the modifications made in VERSIONS 10 and 12 and returns to the music that he composed in VERSION 8: V8 6M1. It is this material that is then developed into the finished cue. Given Danna's comments about working with Lee on this scene, it is likely that there were aspects of VERSIONS 10 and 12 with which the director was unhappy. Clearly some quality that was present in both the temp track and V8 6M1 was eluding Danna. As has already been noted, V8 6M1 shares the same tempo as the temp track, perhaps justifying the return to it.

However, the most striking feature of Danna's thematic material in comparison to the temp track is the pentatonic character of many of his different versions. Theme A is essentially an F♯ minor pentatonic melody and Theme C is a D minor pentatonic melody. However, the temp track's clarinet and oboe melody is constructed on the Dorian E mode (**E**–F♯–**G**–**A**–**B**–C♯–**D**–E). Contained within this mode are, of course, the notes of the pentatonic scale (in bold above). But the significant coloristic difference is the sharpened sixth degree (C♯) which gives the Dorian mode its distinctive quality. Theme B, however, does not have a pentatonic quality. It is in C minor with an emphasis on the ninth degree (D♮) and the melody instruments (oboe, clarinet, and later flute) are, in fact, in the Dorian mode based on C. Indeed, the melodic phrases in both clarinet and oboe frequently rest on the sharpened sixth degree (A♮) emphasizing this Dorian quality. Aside from the tempo, instrumentation, and contrapuntal characteristics, it appears that the feature from the temp track that particularly appealed to Lee was the use of the Dorian mode, although it may have been difficult for him to articulate this.

If Danna is to be believed, Lee's direction—"I don't feel anything"—offers little in the way of detailed musical guidance. Yet, Danna and other commentators also note that Lee was extremely supportive, demanding, and perfectionist in his approach. Steyermark explains that Lee spent a great deal of time standing over Danna's shoulder while he worked: "I'm sure it was like torture for him. But it was amazing, and the result was that Ang had the ability to push him further."[53] What the analysis above suggests is that, contrary to popular belief, directors do not necessarily lack musical sophistication or detailed listening skills, but rather lack the appropriate musical terminology to guide composers. It is unlikely that most directors could precisely identify a specific mode as the element of a cue that appealed to them. However, without this type of clue the composer may not be able to understand which particular features they have failed to exploit. Essentially, no appropriate shared language exists and as a result misunderstandings will continue to arise in the collaborative compositional process.[54] In fact, the lack of a useful shared language to describe the abstractions of music guarantees the continued use of the temp track as a means of facilitating conversation between composers and the production team.

Figure 4.10: Thematic Developments for 6M2 "Janey."
Reproduced by permission of Mychael Danna.

Orchestration

One of the least documented aspects of the film scoring process is the relationship between the composer and orchestrator(s). The journey from MIDI mock-up to full score is often shrouded in mystery and issues such as the division of labor and authorship are blurred, not least because the process varies radically between different collaborative partnerships.[55] Ideally, Danna would prefer to orchestrate all his own music, but the considerable time constraints and frequent requests for last-minute changes, particularly on big-budget projects, make this virtually impossible.

Danna claims that he is an "orchestrator's nightmare. I am everything that they find dull."[56] This comment can be understood in the context of his preference for simple, subdued orchestration and "primary colors."[57] One manifestation of this is the frequent use of single or solo woodwinds, rather than fuller orchestrations. Danna is also vehement that strings should play *senza vibrato*, a direction he reinforces repeatedly during recording sessions. This approach is employed in part to contain emotional excess, but it is also influenced by Danna's lifelong passion for Baroque music. A striking feature of eighteenth-century performance practice is the purity of sound and lack of vibrato, other than as an occasional ornament.

The Ice Storm was the first and only project on which Danna worked with orchestrator Jamie Hopkings, subsequently preferring a close working relationship with orchestrator/conductor Nicholas Dodd. Dodd explains some of the distinctive features of Danna's orchestration style.

> One note will do where several are normal. Melodies are strong. EVERYTHING IS WELL CONSIDERED. Anything remotely Romantic (7ths/9ths etc.) is not present. Woodwind solos are well documented. Do not expect textbook.[58]

The fact that Dodd draws attention to the detailed consideration given suggests that, for Danna, orchestration is not simply a process of adding color to his musical ideas. Rather the idiosyncrasies of Danna's orchestration are central features of his compositional style. In order to maintain these particular features, therefore, it is unsurprising that Danna's working process demonstrates a certain amount of control over the precise nature of the orchestration, even though some of this responsibility is relinquished due to time pressures.

Danna normally passes the sequencer files to the orchestrator who "translates" these into a conductor's score. This can be a challenging process as there are often considerable differences between the way music sounds, how it is represented within a sequencer, and how notation appears on a page. Performers interpret musical notation whereas sequencers reproduce sound in exact detail. The same aural effect may be achieved, but the process of creating scores for human performers involves second-guessing their likely interpretation of that notation. The orchestrator may also prepare parts or, more likely, will delegate this responsibility to a separate copyist (this was Martin Loomer on *The Ice Storm*).

As has already been seen, Danna produced detailed sequencer files for each cue in *The Ice Storm*. The final cues were then translated into score by Jamie Hopkings. Hopkings did not have any input into the size and nature of the ensemble, nor was he expected to add to anything beyond what was contained within the sequencer files. It appears as if his role as orchestrator was strictly technical rather than creative.

> Mychael seemed to know exactly what he wanted. I got a clear sense of this early on when having looked at one of my scores, he commented that I had doubled the cellos with bassoon—a doubling that was not in his sequence. You can hardly imagine a less controversial doubling, but he questioned it. He accepted it, and began to use this doubling in subsequent cues, but I took this as a message that he would be the one to decide such matters, and I was not to add such things on my own.[59]

Within this framework, therefore, the orchestrator's role was to create user-friendly notation and to consider the ease of playing for the performers. Much of the music in *The Ice Storm* is constructed around repetitive rhythmic patterns which often cut across regular bar structures and generate rhythmic and textural variety. This is particularly evident in cues that feature the gamelan ensemble. Hopkins recalls one cue "needed re-barring in order to make sense on the page" but because different instruments were playing odd phrase lengths he found it impossible for "every instrument to have a nice neat entry of their motif on beat one of a bar."[60] This concern for the performers was also evident in a cue that eventually became 2M6 "Shoplift" where

> Mychael had a clarinet line that was practically continuous, with nowhere for a real player to breathe. I recall trying to figure out which notes could be deleted without significant impact on the flow of things, and having to tell Mychael the part needed to be changed. This is just one of the traps of using MIDI for composition, though I should say that, in retrospect, Mychael is by far one of the more disciplined writers in this regard.[61]

The advantage of working with the sequencer is that it allows different sounds and textures to be auditioned and manipulated, but it is also easy to be seduced by the technology and compose music that may not be comfortably realized by performers. The sequencer "performs" the music convincingly on every occasion, so it can be easy to overlook aspects such as breathing or bowing.

On some occasions, however, the notation that the orchestrator produced was too detailed to be fit for purpose. Danna's music for the cues that eventually became 3M1 "Pick Up Paul" and 3M6 "Drive" involved a group of percussionists playing a 7/8 hand-drum groove. The composer had, of course, created a mock-up of these cues which Hopkings had transcribed "rather carefully, with accents, and ghost notes—probably a little overboard, but I was expecting Mychael would want to hear his own groove."[62] Danna was surprised that the notation was fastidiously written out, expecting to create the groove through discussion and improvisation with the performers during the recording session. In practice, most percussionists would rather improvise on cues when the music requires a certain looseness rather than reading detailed notation. Hopkings explains that "it took a while for it to stop sounding stiff."[63]

Sound Design

In discussing his initial reaction to Rick Moody's novel *The Ice Storm*—on which the film is based—Ang Lee identified the fundamental importance of sound to his conceptual filmmaking process.

> I also thought a great deal about the sounds that an ice storm would make, not just the howling of the wind and rain, but the sounds that come afterwards, as the entire world becomes covered in transparent crackling glass. It was these elemental feelings that brought me to *The Ice Storm*.[64]

The fact that the sounds Lee imagined formed part of an experiential reflection on the environment once again highlights the centrality of nature as a character in the narrative structure of the film. Directors are often perceived to be visually biased individuals who conjure striking images but not necessarily striking sounds. However, the comment above indicates that Lee had a clear concept for the sound and, according to Philip Stockton, the supervising sound editor, the director was also actively involved in its creation. Stockton explains that Lee would often indicate the kind of sounds he wanted by imitating them, noting that on one occasion he even vocalized a "whooshing" wind noise in the recording booth to achieve the desired effect. That wind sound can be heard in the finished film at the beginning of the scene where Mikey runs across an open field in the aftermath of the storm. This physical approach seems to be typical of Lee's directorial process.[65] It is clear that he worked closely with the sound design team, sometimes listening and reacting, sometimes generating spontaneous and instinctive ideas.

The extent to which there was an active collaboration between the composer and sound team, however, needs further investigation. Danna believes that the soundscape for *The Ice Storm* is a good example of a fusion between sound design and music because "there are places where you cannot tell who is doing what."[66] Certainly, some of the percussion instruments used by Danna were similar to the materials that the sound design team used. For example, both Stockton and Danna recall recording beads, wind chimes, and other "tinkling noises" as part of their respective soundworlds.[67] While the finished film may effectively blur the boundaries between sound design and music (and the extent to which this is true will be explored in chapter 5) this seems to have been mediated by the director rather than through a direct collaborative process between the composer and sound design team. Stockton describes a working method that is, in fact, typical of mainstream contemporary filmmaking practice where there is relatively little contact between the sound team and the composer prior to the final mix; there is minimal cross-referencing or mutual development of ideas. Given that the sound and music occupy the same aural space, the final mix frequently bears witness to clashes with regard to the focus, dynamics, presence, and location of respective aural elements. The reasons usually put forward for this working method, rather than a more consistently interactive engagement between sound and music, are pressures of time and simultaneous postproduction working periods. The drawback is that last-minute decisions often need to be taken in reaction to a particular challenge that is presented at the final mix.[68]

An important episode, described by Stockton, illustrates both the strengths and weaknesses of this type of approach.

> I remember once Mychael coming into the studio and doing an overdub live on the stage as we were putting in a cue. Ang wanted a different sound and Mychael had a synthesizer and he hooked it up right during the final mix and played something extra into the track.[69]

This refers to the cue that eventually became 2M2B "Bike Kiss" where Wendy and Mikey embrace, followed by a cut to Ben and Janey having sex. Squyres explains that the music was "preventing the next scene from being funny. It was not setting the scene up well because it was too emotional."[70] Danna had recorded two versions of the cue; the second version contained light woodwind figurations at the end in order to attempt to achieve the required levity. However, it was only at the dub that the decision to replace this with something else was finally taken. Danna added just a few synthesized string *pizzicato* notes using a Yamaha DX-7 on the dub stage in New York in an attempt to lighten the end of the scene. Danna explains that from his perspective it was far from ideal, because: "I would never use a DX-7 for pizz unless I had too (I did!)."[71] However, the necessity to find a quick solution to the problem that had arisen was required and rerecording real strings would have been time-consuming and expensive.

Two important and arguably contradictory concepts arise from the working method described above. First is the importance of serendipity in Lee's filmmaking process. Clearly Lee enjoys reacting to situations and developing ideas on the spot. Danna likewise explains that although conceiving ideas under extreme pressure (during the fifteen-minute break of an orchestral recording session for example) can be extremely stressful, and ideas can be weaker than when there is more time to develop them, those moments are an integral part of filmmaking and are when it becomes a "living, breathing, vital art."[72] Second is the notion of a mediated collaborative process, where respective elements of the soundscape are conceived independently and with relatively little reference to each other, except through the central figure of the director.

Process and Product: Whose Music?

Figure 4.11 shows the first page of a fax sent by Tim Squyres, the picture editor, to Danna on October 22nd 1996. The date would suggest that the comments are a response to the music for VERSION 16, near the end of the scoring process. Squyres's notes are, understandably at this late stage, extremely detailed and suggest among other things: altering balances between specific instruments at exact moments, changing aspects of the orchestration, making clearer melodic statements, confronting particular issues in relation to synchronization, and so on. Squyres also seems to act as a spokesperson for the director—"Ang prefers the beginning of the version from 10/09"—so once again a mediated collaborative process is witnessed. Even at this late stage the picture editor's input into the development of the music is vital. It is fitting to return to this idea because it is clear that the score might have been very different if the edit of the film had not undergone such a radical restructure in postproduction. Danna believes that one of the most positive features about the process of scoring *The Ice Storm* was that he attended numerous screenings. There was a consequent process of discovery, evaluation, and reevaluation, and the production team was constantly engaged in discussions about the purpose, nature, and function of the score. Although Ang Lee clearly steered the filmmaking process, numerous other contributors also influenced and affected the shape and structure of the music.

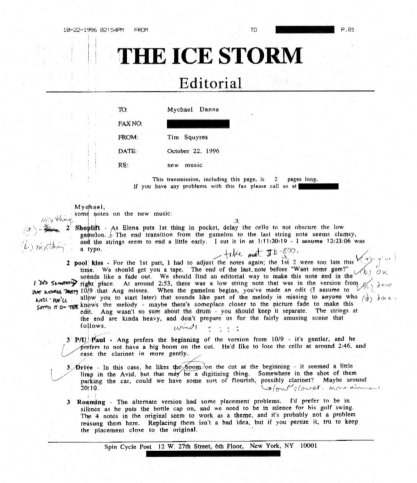

Figure 4.11: Fax from Tim Squyres to Mychael Danna, 10/22/96. Reproduced by permission of Mychael Danna and Tim Squyres.

This chapter has aimed to demonstrate how political structures and a network of collaborators interact with the creative compositional process. The fact that this aspect has been undervalued by film musicology has contributed to the idealistic and mythologized notion of the film composer as *auteur*. This is a misleading and purely academic construct because, as has been seen, the composer does not work in isolation from other members of the production team. The composer is only one of a number of people who influence the shape and structure of the score at every stage of the filmmaking process. We have witnessed, for example, the express influence and importance of the music supervisor, the picture editor, the performing musicians, the director, the producer, the orchestrator, and perhaps to a lesser extent in *The Ice Storm*, the sound design team, although clearly the sound mixer had a profound and unique influence on the final balance of Danna's music in relation to the soundtrack as a whole. Unfortunately, relevant materials for a detailed examination of this mixing process were not accessible; however it is likely that this will become a vital area for future study in film musicology. We have witnessed the influence of certain technical processes and procedures—creating and demonstrating compositional ideas with the sequencer, recording and editing, working with and responding to performers, and the temp track—all of which have steered the composition in particular directions. We have also witnessed the fact that artistic goals can frequently change, either through concerted action, persuasion, misdirection, limitation of resources, or accidental discovery. Indeed, what is most striking is the iterative nature of the scoring process in *The Ice Storm*, where different forms of communication and collaboration have profoundly affected the development of ideas. The music is in fact the sum of this process, and not the independent strand of the whole it might first appear to be.

Chapter 5

The Soundtrack

I think a very powerful sound is a huge group of strings, maybe sixty players, playing quietly with mutes, because you sense the power and you sense they could let rip, but that they are not. That is potential energy instead of kinetic energy.[1]

The idea of the dramatic power of restraint rather than overt expression—potential versus kinetic energy as Danna puts it—highlights not only an important feature of the composer's philosophical attitude towards film scoring, but also the fundamental characteristic of *The Ice Storm* soundtrack. Music and sound are never ostentatious, they rarely raise their voices above a whisper, and consistently withhold overt emotionality. Instead the soundtrack is subtle and controlled with carefully structured expressive moments. This quality is, of course, influenced by Ang Lee's directorial strategy and style, which avoids manipulation of the audience by generating the space and the opportunity to engage fully with the filmic text. Danna explains that the director "was emphatic that he wanted the emotion to be stored up and held back . . . held back . . . held back, but at specific moments there would be emotional release."[2] Likewise, the supervising sound editor, Philip Stockton, explains that the sound design for the film is "primarily invisible, it supports what is happening on the screen without distracting from the dialogue or the story."[3] The director and his collaborators generate openings between the film and the audience through a measured aural language.

In chapter 4 some of the iterative collaborative processes that led to the generation of that subtlety were explored. This provided an insight into the evolution of ideas as a network of collaborators honed the dramatic and emotional register of the film, and it also illustrated how the politics of filmmaking interacts with creativity. I argued that intention should not be divorced from interpretation and consequently that the score should not be studied in isolation from the external influences that are integral to its development. Likewise, the completed score is a component part of a larger whole and should not be examined without reference to the other elements of the soundtrack. This approach recalls what Rick Altman describes as *mise-en-bande* analysis, that is, a focus on the interaction of the various components that make up the soundtrack.[4] Altman creates a system of notation where relative volume levels of dialogue, sound-effects, and music are compared with each other on a timeline. This provides useful information about the soundtrack as an entity, but little analytical detail about the constituent elements, except volume. While the guiding principle of Altman's holistic methodology is convincing, it is somewhat limiting for our purpose, mainly because there are specific auditory moments and details that need to be examined, sometimes in isolation, in order to appreciate how they fit into a larger conceptual structure. In essence, my approach has the same basic aims as Altman, but is viewed from a somewhat less holistic angle. Therefore, I examine a variety of elements such as cultural referentialism, structure, development of thematic materials, space, orchestration, texture, tuning, rhythm, and pitch, in order to highlight the deliberate and consistent use of restraint as an aural strategy. For the sake of clarity in the ensuing analysis the term *score* refers to materials that Danna composed, *source music* refers to all preexistent music that is clearly located within the diegesis, and *sound design* refers to all recorded, edited, and manipulated sound effects.

Music Overview

A central feature of the structural design of a soundtrack is when and where music is located. Placement is a fundamental concern because music is used selectively and normally falls into a number of different functional categories. In *The Ice Storm* the music is clearly demarcated as either diegetic or nondiegetic. Danna's score and a re-arranged end title song by David Bowie are nondiegetic. All other music used in the film is taken from preexistent materials and is firmly located in the diegesis as source, television source, or musical performance. There is no blurring of boundaries between the diegetic and nondiegetic materials. The film is 113 minutes long and the music, in its various forms, lasts fifty-five minutes.[5] Adapted from the Publishing Cue Sheet, Table 5.1 represents all of the music that is heard in *The Ice Storm*.

Danna's twenty-five-minute score is peppered lightly throughout the film but is notably absent from the party sequences in reel 4, where preexistent tracks are used as source music instead. Danna's cues also tend to be short; many last less than one minute, especially in reels 2 and 3. The exceptions to this sparse approach are the opening and closing scenes. For instance, the final cue, 6M4 "Bowl," lasts an extraordinary nine-and-a-half minutes. It is rare in contemporary narrative cinema to find a single cue of this length and it is a structural approach that results in a deliberate weighting towards the end of the film. Indeed, more than half of Danna's score is heard in the final twenty minutes. If one of the principal functions of a score is its role as a signifier of emotion, as most film scholars suggest, then *The Ice Storm* demonstrates an emotional restraint that is only finally released at the end of the film.

Complicit in this structural organization is the use of the song, "I Can't Read", originally written by David Bowie and Reeves Gabrels for the *Tin Machine* album of 1989. The song was specifically reworked for the film by Bowie, but is used solely on the end credits and is not heard or referenced during the film narrative itself. It is also the only pop track in the entire film that is not credibly historically accurate. According to Steyermark, Bowie was Ang Lee's favorite artist of the 1970s, yet none of Bowie's music from the period, or that of his alter-ego, Ziggy Stardust, is used in the film.[6] The song, "I Can't Read," therefore, demonstrates restraint in the use of a 1970s icon as well as the importance of transforming and updating that iconography.

All of the other tracks used in the film are preexistent and the supposed technical apparatus of their production (reel-to-reel tape recorders, for example) is frequently visualized, situating the music unambiguously within the diegesis. The function of this source music is distinct from "I Can't Read" and the score. As it is theoretically owned by the characters, the source music acts primarily as a historical and sociocultural locator, particularly in scenes such as the Carvers' dinner party in reel 1 or the three different "party" locations of reel 4. If "nothing more infallibly classifies than tastes in music"[7] then the choices the characters have made about the music they wish to hear tells the audience how those characters should be perceived. But that perception depends on the audience's own experience. Kassabian defines this set of relationships as "affiliating identifications" where the knowledge and history possessed by the audience affects their interaction with the film.[8] Audience members who consumed music during the early 1970s, for example, will have a different relationship to the source music from younger perceivers, because people tend to "organize and evoke their memories in part through the practice of music consumption."[9] The same is true of the television extracts that punctuate the film. These extracts, and indeed television itself, are experienced exclusively by the younger child characters. Wendy avidly follows the Watergate scandal including Nixon's San Clemente news conference of August 22nd 1973. Mikey and Wendy watch *The Green Hornet* and Sandy watches *Time Tunnel*. Both series were first broadcast in the late 1960s and, because they were popular enough to be rerun frequently, had become part of the cultural fabric of the early 1970s.

It is interesting to note that approximately the same amount of source music as score is heard in the film, which highlights the importance of preexistent material to the narrative structure and conception of the soundtrack. Two library music tracks attempt to avoid specific affiliating identifications. "Rainbow Colors," an example of frivolous piped music, adds a mischievous atmosphere as it accompanies Wendy shoplifting from Varnum's pharmacy. "Monterey" is a blues-rock track that is located in Paul's college dormitory and can be heard underneath his telephone conversation with his family. This music is stylistically similar to 1970s "guitar hero" songs by Jimi Hendrix and others, but the important factor is that the track is purely instrumental. Attention is not diverted from the dialogue by song lyrics, or a distinctive vocal performer. It is also extremely unlikely that an audience would specifically recognize the track except as a typical genre of the period. However, it is interesting to note that the decision to use this piece was driven by financial as well as artistic concerns. Tim Squyres recalls the original intention to use an Emerson, Lake, and Palmer song for this sequence, but clearing the license was prohibitively expensive. Given the fact that the music is placed in the background, the decision was taken to use the library music track and save money.[10]

Sound Design Overview

Unlike music, sound design is normally heard continuously throughout a film. In *The Ice Storm*, as in most films, sound design is omitted only for the final credit sequence. Even where there are moments of "silence" there is rarely complete absence of sound. Since the use of music is selective, attention is automatically focused on particular narrative moments and, by logical extension, on the communicative function of the music. However, identifying specific sound design moments and their communicative function can be more challenging. A single isolated sound may be as dramatically potent and important as the sound design for a whole sequence. Subtle sound design might be just as telling as more exaggerated or stylized sound effects.

One obvious focal point in *The Ice Storm* is the sound of the storm itself. Just as source music tracks are given precedence in reel 4, sound design is foregrounded as the storm builds for most of reel 5 and the beginning of reel 6. There are consequently sixteen minutes at a dramatic high point—the climax of the key party, Mikey's journey into the storm, and Wendy and Sandy's encounter—where there is no music and sound design carries the narrative forward. The impact of the music when it does return in reel 6 is all the more keenly felt as a consequence. Phil Stockton, the supervising sound editor, explains that: "The storm gave us an opportunity to do more design work, and a lot of the rest of the film was pretty straightforward, themes going from A to B, natural backgrounds, and nothing very articulated or fancy."[11] This comment raises some interesting questions with regard to the study of sound design. The most striking feature is that Stockton distinguishes between sound design that he perceives to be purely technical and sound design that he perceives to be more creative. The corollary is that synchronous sound is understood as a craft procedure because it is inevitable and demanded by the picture track, and asynchronous sound is understood as more artistic because it is not expected or ordinary. This distinction between craft and art is also frequently articulated in sound design scholarship.[12] The duality is, of course, a gross over-simplification because every single sound that is recorded, created, or mixed conceals creative decisions that influence how a film will sound and sound design's relationship to the image track.

Walter Murch suggests that a soundtrack is comprised of elements that fall within a spectrum of encoded or embodied sound. According to Murch, the clearest example of encoded sound is speech, because sound is simply "a vehicle with which to deliver the code."[13] Conversely, Murch defines music as the clearest example of embodied sound because "it is sound *experienced directly*, without any code intervening between you and it. Naked. Whatever meaning there is in a piece of music is *embodied* in the sound itself."[14] For Murch, most sound design is located on a sliding scale somewhere between these two spectral extremes; like "sound-centaurs" they are part language, part music.[15] Some sounds are more encoded or linguistic (footsteps, door knocks) and some sounds are more embodied or musical (room tones, atmospheres).

In *The Ice Storm*, where subtlety of sound design is one of its salient features, there are a number of moments where the sound creates a fruitful tension within the spectrum that Murch describes. Of particular interest is how sound design relates to the character Mikey. In an early scene, we observe him playing football with his school

NARRATIVE	CUE TITLE	TIME
REEL 1		
Main titles, Paul on train	1M1 "Opening"	00:31–02:08
		02:47–04:39
College dormitory	1M2 "Dirty Love"	06:23–07:45
	1M3A "Monterey"	07:45–09:11
	1M3B "Monterey" (first interrupted use cont.)	09:23–09:56
Carvers' dinner party	1M4 *Samba Triste*	11:11–11:07
	1M5 "Two Part Invention in B♭ Minor"	11:07–11:46
	1M6 *Suavecito*	11:47–12:20
	1M7 "Sugar Sugar"	12:21–13:12
Ben's journey to work	1M8 "Train"	14:58–16:06
REEL 2		
Wendy rides bike and shoplifts from pharmacy	2M1 "Rainbow Colors"	18:44–19:09
Wendy and Mikey kiss	2M2A "Bike Kiss"	19:41–20:21
	2M2B "Bike Kiss" (cont.)	20:56–21:49
Ben walks home	2M3 "Walk"	22:59–23:40
Band practice	2M4 "The Morning After"	24:46–24:59
	2M5 "The Morning After"	29:16–29:46
Elena rides bike and shoplifts from pharmacy	2M6 "Shoplift"	29:47–32:02
Wendy and Mikey watch television	2M7 "The Green Hornet"	34:38–37:35
REEL 3		
Ben drives Paul home	3M1 "Pick Up Paul"	39:59–40:42
Paul and Wendy discuss their parents	3M2 "I Got A Name"	42:39–43:56
Thanksgiving meal	3M3 "Dinner"	45:23–45:46
Ben wanders semi-naked in the Carver household	3M4 "Roaming"	47:42–48:37
Ben carries Wendy home	3M5 "Toes Cold"	52:25–53:03
Ben and Elena drive to party	3M6 "Drive"	56:59–57:51
Arrival at Halfords' party	3M7 "Too Late to Turn Back Now"	57:51–58:39

Table 5.1: *The Ice Storm*. Music Cues

PERFORMED BY	WRITTEN BY	DURATION
The Ice Storm Orchestra.	Mychael Danna	01:37 01:52
Frank Zappa. Master: Rykodisc.	Frank Zappa	01:22
Music Library. Master: Audio Action.	Daniel Darrass, Christian Leroux, Rolando Tambin, Terry Lipton	01:26
As above	As above	00:33
Stan Getz and Charlie Byrd. Master: Verve Records.	Baden Powell, Billy Blanco	00:56
Wendy Carlos. Master: Sony Classical.	Johann Sebastian Bach	00:39
Malo. Master: Warner Bros. Records.	Richard Bean, Abel Zarate, Pablo Tellez	00:33
Wilson Pickett. Master: Atlantic Recording Corp.	Jeff Barry, Any Kim	00:51
The Ice Storm Orchestra.	Mychael Danna	01:08
Music Library. Master: Audio Action.	Philippe Lhommet, Jacques Mercier	00:25
The Ice Storm Orchestra.	Mychael Danna	00:42
The Ice Storm Orchestra.	Mychael Danna	00:53
The Ice Storm Orchestra.	Mychael Danna	00:41
Christina Ricci.	Al Kasha, Joel Hirschhorn	00:13
Cast.	Al Kasha, Joel Hirschhorn	00:30
The Ice Storm Orchestra.	Mychael Danna	02:15
TV Source. Master: George W. Trendle, Jr.	Billy May	02:57
The Ice Storm Orchestra.	Mychael Danna	00:43
Jim Croce. Master: SAJA Music Co.	Norman Gimbel, Charles Fox	01:17
The Ice Storm Orchestra.	Mychael Danna	00:23
The Ice Storm Orchestra.	Mychael Danna	00:55
The Ice Storm Orchestra.	Mychael Danna	00:38
The Ice Storm Orchestra.	Mychael Danna	00:52
Cornelius Brothers and Sister Rose. Master: EMI Records.	Eddie Cornelius	00:48

Table 5.1, cont.

NARRATIVE	CUE TITLE	TIME
REEL 4		
Halfords' party	4M1 "Montego Bay"	01:00:47–01:03:09
	4M2 *O Grande Amor*	01:03:09–01:04:19
	4M3 "Coconut"	01:06:02–01:07:17
Paul, Francis, and Libbets in New York	4M4 "Light Up or Leave Me Alone"	01:07:17–01:09:01
Halfords' party	4M5 "Help Me Make it Through the Night"	01:09:01–01:09:46
Wendy watches television	4M6 "Room 222"	01:09:46–01:09:55
Sandy watches television	4M7 "Keep America Beautiful" Advertisement	01:09:55–01:10:21
Paul, Francis, and Libbets in New York	4M8 "Mr. Big"	01:10:26–01:10:45
Sandy watches television	4M9 "Time Tunnel"	01:10:45–01:11:44
Halfords' party	4M10 "Compared to What"	01:11:44–01:11:56
Paul, Francis, and Libbets in New York	4M11 "Levon"	01:11:56–01:14:54
Television Carver household	4M12 "Time Tunnel"	01:15:19–01:16:12
REEL 5		
Halfords' party	5M1 "Night Lights"	01:16:14–01:17:24
REEL 6		
Elena says goodnight to Ben	6M1 "Bathroom"	01:33:31–01:35:06
Janey returns home	6M2 "Janey"	01:35:42–01:37:18
Aftermath of the storm	6M4 "Bowl"	01:39:58–01:49:20
End credits	6M5 "I Can't Read"	01:49:20–01:52:51

Table 5.1, cont.

PERFORMED BY	WRITTEN BY	DURATION
Bobby Bloom. Master: Polydor Records.	Bobby Bloom, Jeff Barry	02:22
Antonio Carlos Jobim. Master: Verve Records.	Antonio Carlos Jobim, Vinicius de Moraes	01:10
Harry Nilsson. Master: RCA Records.	Harry Nilsson	01:15
Traffic. Master: Island Records, Ltd.	Jim Capaldi	01:44
Sammi Smith. Master: Dominion Entertainment.	Kris Kristofferson	00:45
TV Source. Master: Twentieth Century Fox TV.	Jerry Goldmsith, Benny Golson	00:09
TV Source. Master: John W. Kazzi.	?	00:26
Free. Master: A&M Records, Inc./Island Records Ltd.	Andy Fraser, Simon Kirke, Paul Kossof, Paul Rodgers	00:19
TV Source. Master: Twentieth Century Fox TV	John Williams	00:59
Less McCann and Eddie Harris. Master: Atlantic Recording Corp.	Gene McDaniels	00:12
Elton John. Master: Mercury Records, Ltd.	Elton John, Bernie Taupin	02:58
TV Source. Master: Twentieth Century Fox TV.	John Williams	00:56
Gerry Mulligan. Master: Verve Records.	Gerry Mulligan	01:10
The Ice Storm Orchestra.	Mychael Danna	01:35
The Ice Storm Orchestra.	Mychael Danna	01:36
The Ice Storm Orchestra.	Mychael Danna	09:22
David Bowie. Master: Jones Music.	David Bowie, Reeves Gabrels	03:31

Table 5.1, cont.

friends. The quarterback sees Mikey running into a good position and throws the ball to him. Mikey makes no attempt to catch the ball and seems momentarily unaware of where he is. In slow motion, the ball falls towards him and drops by his side. One of his friends makes a pot-smoking gesture as if this explains his unusual behavior. The idea of using a "humming" motif for Mikey was explored during the postproduction process. Schamus explains that:

> The 'humming' motif which played prominently in the script as a kind of foreboding music of the spheres for which only Mikey's ears are available, was more or less removed by the final edit. Mikey's fate is foreshadowed strongly enough through Elijah Wood's performance—we didn't feel the need to prop it up with sound effects.[16]

Again this illustrates the notion of restraint, as layers were stripped away leaving a much more exposed sequence. Nonetheless, there are some sounds that foreshadow Mikey's fate in this football sequence. The faintest hint of an arcing electricity effect can be heard as the ball flies past him and falls to the ground. This sound is, of course, a premonition to Mikey's eventual death from electrocution. It is unlikely that an audience member would notice this unless their attention had been drawn to it, it functions subliminally. In Murch's schema the arcing electricity sound would normally be weighted towards an encoded categorization, but in this context the sound is not validated by a visual representation and is thus more ambiguous and embodied.

There are other moments when the sound design acts as a precursor. In a scene where Mikey and Sandy complete their homework an irregular, background "tinkling" can be heard. The sound continues while Jim speaks with/at his children, and Janey and Jim discuss Mikey on their waterbed. The waterbed is initially used as a comic device by the filmmakers. Janey is nearly thrown off the bed by the force of the wave as her husband sits down. There is an interesting juxtaposition here between the soft sound of undulating water and the harder, glassy, "tinkling" noises. Just before the cut to the next scene—where Mikey is giving a presentation about molecules to his classmates—the source of the tinkling is revealed as a set of wind chimes that live in the Carvers' garden.

These wind chimes are visualized on only one other occasion and again punctuate two scenes, generating the same thematic movement and structure—waterbed, wind chimes, Mikey—that was witnessed before. Janey has returned home from the key party alone in need of comfort. She curls up in the fetal position on the waterbed and the undulating sound of water reinforces a literal representation of the womb. The action then cuts to the wind chimes, which on this occasion are still and make no noise; ironically they are covered in ice. However, as Mikey stands in the middle of Silver Meadow, the icicles that have formed on the trees during the storm sway gently creating a natural, crystalline wind chime. This is supported by a mysterious groaning that sounds like an unusual environmental wind effect but is, in fact, manipulated whale song. The sound design here is more embodied than encoded and creates an atmosphere that amplifies Mikey's awe and fascination with the natural environment. He contemplates both the flowing visual movement and sound of the icy trees, and the audience is also invited to reflect on this moment of wonderment. It could even be suggested that sound design, particularly "tinkling" sound design, is a motif for Mikey and his connection with nature. The trajectory of this sequence reveals some interesting thematic transformations; a mother returns to the "womb" while her child wanders towards his death, and water turns to ice both aurally and visually. It also is clear that there is an exploration of water in a variety of states, from molecules through liquid to solid and back again, which creates multilayered symbolism throughout the film.

There is one sound design moment that stands out. This is the electrocution scene, constructed from a range of arcing electricity and buzzing sounds, which Stockton explains has an "almost cartoonish" quality.[17] This cartoonlike intensification may be linked conceptually to the film's references to *The Fantastic Four* comic books. Certainly, the hyperrealism employed here is distinguished from the emotional realism of much of the rest of the film, but it makes Mikey's death all the more shocking and powerful. Immediately before the power line snaps the texture of the soundscape is reduced and focuses only on Mikey's breathing. It is the equivalent of a visual zoom, drawing us close to Mikey before he breathes his last.

The Songs

It is interesting to note that many members of the production team would have been the same age as the children in *The Ice Storm* during the early 1970s. That perspective was useful in the process of selecting the source music. The concept of indistinct and involuntary recollection became important in defining the songs that were used. Schamus explains the methodology.

We did not want the greatest hits of the 1970s, we did not want everyone tapping their feet and going: "Oh yeah." What we wanted was that nauseous feeling that you get from a vague memory. Not that we picked songs that we did not like. We liked them all, but they were there to give a more ambient approach to source cues as a rule than otherwise. That is why the soundtrack album is funny because they are really not your favorite songs. They are good and you kind of remember them, but they were not the songs that you necessarily played, and you did not own the LP, but you heard them a lot. It was that kind of approach.[18]

Supporting this scheme, none of the Billboard top 100 number-one hits from the years 1970–1973 are used on the soundtrack. Squyres chose many of the songs during the early editing stage and explains that two important decisions were made with regard to these selections; there would be "no Motown," and no music would be chosen for its "camp value."[19] Squyres believed that Motown, although some of the best music of the early 1970s, was "not what the characters would be listening to."[20] Equally, there was no interest in choosing music that would ridicule the period.

The music supervisor, Steyermark, then took responsibility for the final selection of songs and for the copyright clearances. Ang Lee and James Schamus were very carefully involved in the discussions and decisions. Steyermark explains that he had whittled down the selection to three or four hundred tracks and would "send Ang songs every couple of days and with each one of those he wanted to have all the lyrics and a little biographical blurb about each artist to accompany the tape."[21] It is clear that the lyrics, social context, and historical accuracy were important defining features in the decision making process.

One of the principal functions of the songs is to define the musical tastes of the characters. There is, for example, a fundamental distinction between the music that the children listen to and the music the adults listen to. In an early scene, Frank Zappa's "Dirty Love" from the 1973 album *Overnite Sensation* plays in the background.[22] Zappa's music is often provocative, ironic, and contains biting social commentary and juvenile humor in equal measure. Zappa noted, "if one wants to be a real artist in the United States today and comment on our culture, one would be very far off the track if one did something delicate or sublime. This is not a noble, delicate, sublime country."[23] Indeed, the risqué lyrics of "Dirty Love" are far from noble or sublime, eventually building to a description of a poodle performing cunnilingus on somebody's mother. Consequently, the song would have received limited radio airplay. But censorship has always had the psychological effect of increasing the desirability of material, especially to certain youth subcultures. This music appealed to college teenagers— especially boys—precisely because it was lewd and would not be appreciated by their parents. It is unsurprising that the song is used in a scene where Francis and Paul are smoking cannabis in their dormitory and the hard rock sound supports the notion of youthful rebellion. The opening shot shows Francis packing cannabis into a bong. On the wall above his bed a sign reads "Authorized Dealer." He exudes confidence and enjoys comparing his "astonishing number of sexual conquests" to Paul's "pathetic virginity." The song supports his brash boasts; it is his music. However, it is also interesting to note how the lyrics—"Give me your dirty love, like you might surrender to a dragon in your dreams"—generate other meanings that are reframed by the dramatic situation. The powerful imagery of the dragon not only generates dark mythological references but also resonates with wider drug culture, as in the phrase "chasing the dragon." Within this context, the song is equally about a crude demand for sex and an enthusiasm for smoking pot. It is worth noting that in 1973, New York senator James Buckley wrote a report linking rock music to drug use and called for the record industry to eliminate drug-using or drug-endorsing rock musicians before the federal government took action. No action was taken, but the attitude exemplifies a long history of attempts to associate rock music with juvenile delinquency.[24]

Unlike scores that often provide a bridge across different scenes, pop tracks are frequently cut hard as the scene changes. This is a function of the fact that tracks are specifically located as source music. In the dormitory sequence, the song is uncomfortably ended in the middle of Zappa's tube-distortion-drenched guitar solo. The effect of this cut not only defines physical location but also personality. Paul leaves behind and is distinguished from Francis's predatory and dangerous influence.[25]

Further confirmation of this kind of musical distinction is provided by the fact that Paul owns the folk-influenced, soft rock album *I Got A Name* by Jim Croce.[26] The gentle title track from this album is used in a scene where Wendy and Paul discuss their parents' worsening marriage. Wendy has, in fact, borrowed the record from her brother so the song provides a link in terms of musical taste between the two teenagers. The record has also been damaged and becomes stuck. This narrative device is used to highlight that fact that Wendy has been exploring Paul's possessions despite his express request that she refrain "from entering the sacred precincts" of his room. However, the repetition inherent in the stuck record also acts as a metaphor for an inability to progress. The fact that the song stutters at the precise moment that Libbets is mentioned suggests that Paul's desire for a relationship with her may not be the success he hopes for.

Squyres explains that there was a great deal of discussion about the use of songs in a later scene in Libbets's apartment. Initially he chose three tracks from the Elton John album *Madman Across the Water* for the scenes in New York.[27] These songs included "Levon," which was the only song that remained at the end of the selection process. Some members of the production team argued that the teenagers would not have listened to Elton John. However, Squyres argued that "they were thinking of later Elton John. I remember that album was a cool album."[28] The discussion highlights the delicate balance required between songs to which the teenagers would conceivably listen and the overall strategy to generate a more ambient 1970s mood. The scenes in Libbets's apartment eventually featured three different tracks: "Light Up or Leave Me Alone" by Traffic, "Mr. Big" by Free, and "Levon" by Elton John.[29] The trajectory of the songs as the evening progresses is from hard rock to more thoughtful piano and vocal sound. This represents both a softening of Francis's dominance—Paul has tricked him into taking a sleeping pill—and provides an intimate backdrop as Paul attempts to seduce Libbets.

The adults, unlike the children, do not listen to music in private or intimate contexts. Music is used only during social gatherings. Therefore, the party sequences not only demonstrate the songs that the adult characters like, but also the music that they choose to play in front of their friends; musical taste on display. There is a general preference for jazz and Latin styles. For example, during the Carvers' dinner party "*Samba Triste*" performed by Stan Getz and "*Suavecito*" by Malo are heard. It is interesting to note that a great deal of the music used in relation to the adults has "exotic" characteristics. For example, as Ben and Elena return to the key party for the second time the song playing is "Montego Bay" by Bobby Bloom. This is arguably party music for middle-aged 1970s WASPs, which Squyres identifies as "almost hip, almost current, but not quite."[30] The energy and brightness of the song contrast starkly with the gathering storm outside. The songs are frequently used as a warm contrast to the bleak emotional content underneath, suggesting where the adults would rather be than where they actually are.

Harry Nilsson's "Coconut" taken from the album *Nilsson Schmilsson* provides a humorous backdrop for a scene where Reverend Edwards flirts with Elena during the party. The novelty calypso song, consisting of a single C^7 chord throughout, features three comically voiced characters, a narrator, a sister, and a doctor.[31] It is difficult to hear the lyrics on the soundtrack, but the different vocal layers and characters can be distinguished, and the song helps the audience to find humor at the expenses of the preacher. After Elena has snubbed Edwards he collects his keys from the bowl and leaves the party. With reference to the sexual lottery that is due to take place later in the evening, one of the male characters passing at this point cheekily comments: "I hope those weren't my keys." Melismatic vocal "wooohs" feature in the song at precisely this moment acting as a punchline that frames Edwards as the butt of the joke. Moments of synchronization such as this illustrate how the careful placement of the songs is used to underscore emotion and dramatic gesture.

When Ben confronts Janey during the party, for example, Antonio Carlos Jobim's "*O Grande Amor*" performed by Stan Getz and others is carefully edited to underscore the dialogue. Joao Gilberto's smoldering vocal performance is removed and only instrumental sections of the song are heard. Brief saxophone moments from the first part of the piece are edited into the piano solo section towards the end of the piece. It is this abridged amalgamation of the song that is used in the sequence. The saxophone gestures are carefully placed in the spaces between dialogue or at specific significant moments. For example, after a curt comment Janey pointedly looks away from Ben and hopes to end their argument. The moment is highlighted by a rising scalic saxophone motif featuring Getz's distinctive husky tone quality. This type of structural organization is exactly the same approach that composers would take if they were shaping their score around the conversation. However, the edited song has the advantage of a privileged location within the diegesis. An audience is arguably less conscious of its function as underscore than they would be of a composed score. The edited song is evocative but not intrusive; with great subtlety it is able to support the narrative action of the moment.

The use of different music in the respective locations helps maintain a multilayered narrative equally providing energy or repose as necessary. The progression of the songs throughout these scenes clarifies the passing of time and the different stages of the parties, as well as the mood and cultural values of those involved. Music is used almost continuously in reel 4, and the musical contrasts between the teenagers in New York, the children watching television, and the key party define the structural momentum. Given how much the organization of these scenes changed during the editing process, it is clear that the careful juxtaposition of different source music is central in generating structural coherence and narrative progression.

The Score

There are a number of striking features about Danna's score for *The Ice Storm*. Of particular interest to this analysis are the instrumental forces that are employed. The combination of chamber orchestra, Native American flute, and gamelan ensemble is not an obvious scoring strategy for a film set in 1970s suburban America. The deliberately oblique approach raises interesting questions with regard to the form and function of the music. Matthews suggests that its role is different from our expectation of mainstream narrative cinema scores, because the exotic instruments provide "just the minimalist touches needed to signify 'art'."[32] The fact that the instrumentation is used without an immediate and direct narrative justification forces the audience to search for meaning. The score generates its own "parallel emotional/aesthetic universe," as Brown might describe it, and consequently demands audience contemplation.[33] Unlike a great deal of film music, therefore, the score for *The Ice Storm* provokes the audience rather than acting purely as a generator of narrative affect.

Equally important to our understanding of the score is the idea of restraint. As has already been noted, this is evident in the use of comparatively little score and its structural placement in the film. However, restraint is also evident in the construction and use of the thematic material itself. The entire score is generated from only three themes, which relate to the larger philosophical issues at the heart of the film. The three themes, as was discovered in chapter 4, are: Nature, Negative Zone, and Family. There is no other score material and no isolated or orphaned cues. Furthermore, rather than being elaborately developed, the themes are stated simply and clearly. The harmonic language of the film is limited to three tonal centers: Db pentatonic/Bb minor pentatonic, Bb minor, and C minor. This limited harmonic palette may be explained, in part, by the gamelan ensemble and Native American flute pitches available to Danna, but this would not account for every cue and situation. It appears to be a deliberate strategy to generate stasis through limited harmonic transformation. Danna explains that "key structure through a film is very important" and is something with which he always experiments until the end of the scoring process.[34]

A fair amount of instrumental color is available in the resources that Danna uses, but restraint is in evidence here also. Single woodwinds are used sparingly and soloistically, and the chamber orchestra materials are dominated by the strings, frequently playing quietly and *senza vibrato*. There is no use of any brass or of any heavy percussion such as timpani or bass drum. Instead Danna chooses hand percussion such as shakers and an Indian deerskin drum. The gamelan ensemble is clearly a central feature of the score, but Danna rarely uses the full selection of instruments available to him. Frequently, one or two instruments are drawn from the ensemble to create smaller more intimate textures. There is not a single *tutti* anywhere in the score. The largest swell occurs only when the final credits are rolling and even this is not particularly expansive. The tonal and textural design of the score aims for intimacy by focusing the audience's ear towards subtle changes. Table 5.2 shows all of Danna's cues in the film. The fact that deliberate restraint is employed in the construction of the materials raises some methodological challenges. The score always relates to the larger conceptual and philosophical issues at the center of the film, and is not primarily concerned with moment-by-moment reflection. Rather than repeating what can already be seen on the screen the score aims to encapsulate the narrative. A chronological cue-by-cue analysis would inaccurately emphasize the reactive aspects of the score, such as the close matching of physical gesture, and would misrepresent its function. Therefore, each of the three themes that Danna used will be examined separately in order to highlight the potential for insight into the narrative which they provide. Drawing from examples throughout the film, the rich interpretative possibilities and coherence provided by these themes will be illustrated. However, because the score is weighted towards the end of the film, the final extraordinary cue will be examined separately. This approach will serve to illustrate how the three themes are structured to build towards an emotional and expressive release.

Nature

According to Danna *The Ice Storm* is "really about nature, and man's place in nature, working within that world and the consequences of working outside of it."[35] Therefore, the Nature theme helps foreground the environment as a central participant in the narrative. The characters' relationship to and their connection, or lack of connection, with nature is key. The theme is a wistful, flowing, free-timed melody for Native American flute, which was compiled from a selection of improvisations by the flautist Dan Cecil Hill, generated under Danna and Lee's direction. It is characteristically spontaneous as a consequence.

The construction of the melody emphasizes purity and simplicity through a limited use of pitch. Traditionally, Native American flutes are tuned to minor pentatonic scales although more modern instruments are able to play natural minor scales. The instrument used by the performer was a modern Bb flute, but Danna frequently restricts the material played to a pentatonic framework. Pentatonic scales have an interesting inherent duality because the pitches used in related minor and major versions are the same, but the tonal character is defined by the root note. Danna exploits this ambiguity as the theme frequently

TITLE	ENSEMBLE	THEMATIC MATERIAL	TIME SIGNATURE	TEMPO	TONAL CENTER
1M1 "Opening"	Native American flute, fl., ob., cl., bsn., 2 vibes (4 players), *nautch* bells, shaker, Indian deerskin drum, synthesized gamelan, strings (12, 12, 8, 6, 4)	nature family	free 6/4	free ♩ = 74	Db/Bb (pentatonic) Bbm
1M8 "Train"	fl., ob., cl., bsn., *peking, panerus, bonang, jenglong,* strings	negative zone	4/4	♩ = 122	Cm
2M2A "Bike Kiss"	Native American flute	nature	free	free	Db/Bb (pentatonic)
2M2B "Bike Kiss" (cont.)	Native American flute, ob., bsn., Indian deerskin drum, shaker, *bonang,* strings	nature negative zone	4/4	♩ = 75	Bbm
2M3 "Walk"	ob., cl., *bonang, jenglong,* shaker, *nautch* bells, strings	negative zone	2/4	♩ = 100	Bbm
2M6 "Shoplift"	fl., cor anglais, cl., bsn., egg shaker, *peking, panerus, bonang, gambang, jenglong*	negative zone	4/4, 3/4, 6/4, 5/4	♩ = 122	Cm
3M1 "Pick-Up Paul"	cl., bsn., shaker-rattle, hand drums (2 players), *peking, panerus, bonang, gambang,* strings	family	7/4	♩ = 120	Bbm
3M3 "Dinner"	piano, *bonang, panerus,* strings	negative zone	4/4	♩ = 100	Bbm
3M4 "Roaming"	Native American flute	nature	free	free	Db/Bb (pentatonic)
3M5 "Toes Cold"	cl., Indian deerskin drum, pno., strings	family	6/4	♩ = 72	Bbm
3M6 "Drive"	cl., hand drums (2 players), shakers, *kendang, peking, panerus, gambang,* strings (no basses)	negative zone	7/4	♩ = 122	Bbm
6M1 "Bathroom"	fl., bsn., *bonang,* strings	negative zone	3/4	♩ = 48	Cm
6M2 "Janey"	fl., ob., cl., pno., strings	family	6/4	♩ = 68	Bbm
6M4 "Bowl"	Native American flute, elk antlers, fl., ob., cl., bsn., *nautch* bells, Indian deerskin drum, 2 vibes (3 players), *peking, panerus, bonang, jenglong, gong,* synthesized gamelan, pno., solo vln., solo cello, strings	negative zone nature family	6/4, 5/4 free, 3/4 6/4	♩ = 71 ♩ = 48 ♩ = 72	Cm Bbm

Table. 5.2: *The Ice Storm.* Score Cues.

fluctuates between Db major and Bb minor pentatonic creating an equally peaceful and haunting ambiance. One important performative feature of the Nature theme is the sound of the expellation of breath. At the ends of phrases the pure flute timbre is distorted by downwards *glissandi* gestures, where the breath of the performer can be clearly heard. Mournful growls and wailing effects that mimic the sound of wild animal cries are heard. The character of the theme is defined as much by these guttural endings as its melodic structure. Coupled with the fact that the tuning of the instrument is not equally tempered, the sincere, imperfect character contributes to the perception of the theme as "naïve and beautiful."[36]

Not only is the material frequently heard unaccompanied, but the gestures are surrounded by space and "silence." Indeed, the space in between the phrases is a feature that is as important to the affect of the theme as the notes themselves. The space is more significant than a simple measured period of silence; it is a sensory and sensually perceived space. The solo instrument is heavily treated with digital reverberation, which is the remainder of sound that exists in a room after the source of the sound has stopped. Acoustic reflections provide a great deal of information about our everyday surroundings. For recordings of music to be aesthetically pleasing it is, consequently, necessary to use an appropriate type and amount of reverberation. Generally this imitates the live performance spaces in which music is normally heard. However, Danna's approach goes beyond the idea of faking natural room acoustics. Comparison of the original dry flute recordings—which were "close-miked" in Danna's studio—with the cues that are heard on the film illustrates the importance of the reverberation to the evocative character of the theme. Because reverberation primarily affects the perception of distance, the solo instrument sounds somewhat remote and reflective. The clearly perceptible long reverberation tail and the lack of any clear point of termination creates the effect of drawing the surrounding "silence" into the music as an active presence; the audience is encouraged to listen to the space. This technique is employed at the very outset of the film in the first part of cue 1M1 (see Figure 5.1).

The film opens in the darkness before dawn in the calm after the storm has passed. There are shots of a motionless train, covered in ice, which has stalled due to a downed power line. Paul Hood sits alone on the train reading a comic book. The opening sequence is a flash-forward, though this would not be apparent on an initial viewing, and it is the only chronological disjunction experienced in the whole film. The narrative starts in the future but then returns to the past in the first scene. The film then continues chronologically. Or the whole film can be read as memory. The use of reverberation is frequently used to articulate the idea of memories and the process of remembering, and combined with the flash-forward it helps to frame the film as Paul Hood's recollection. Certainly, the voice-over privileges Paul as a philosophical focal point. Aside from reflecting the natural environment, therefore, the flute melody and particularly the space surrounding it help focus, center, and objectify the opening voice-over.

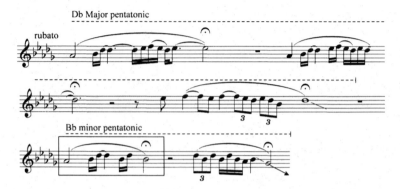

Figure 5.1: Nature Theme (transcribed): 1M1, 2M2A, and 3M4.
"Opening," "Bike Kiss," and "Roaming"
from *The Ice Storm*
By Mychael Danna.
Copyright © 1997 Fox Film Corp.
All Rights Reserved. Used by Permission.

In 1M1, the gaps between the musical gestures are not solely filled by reverberation tails, the sound design is also a vital part of the aural texture. Underneath the flute melody, gentle wind and rippling water— or melting ice—as well as "tinkling" bead noises can be heard. There is an interesting blurred boundary between score and sound design here that goes beyond the solo instrument's imitation of wildlife. On the first cut to a close-up of *The Fantastic Four* comic book repetitive scratching and a shimmering metallic sound are heard. It would be reasonable to assume that these sounds were created by the sound design team, but they were, in fact, generated by the composer using a shaker and Indian *nautch* bells. Danna also explains that some of the "tinkling" noises in the background were his creation (little stones hanging from string). As if to articulate this symbiosis further, when the final note of the solo Native American flute fades away, the sound of the train regaining power provides punctuation and completes the musical gesture. Like a relay race, the baton is passed from music to sound. The sequence then concentrates on the sound design of the train creaking and rumbling into life before the second half of cue 1M1 begins, some forty seconds later. Danna recognizes this space and unhurried approach as a particular quality of Ang Lee's films: "There is a sense of breath, the music has stopped and we are just listening to these sounds, it is very languid."[37]

With one exception, the Native American flute is only heard when the action is located outside. The instrument does not belong in the spaces in which the characters live. This reinforces the notion of the theme as the voice of nature. However, Schamus sees this representation as problematic.

> Certainly there is an easy but I think suspicious connection between "nature" and "Native American." I don't think it is that simple. I don't think there is an equation there, but I do think that there is a presence, that is to say, the natural environment, especially with these glass houses and the constant discourse reflected back from, through, and into those spaces in the suburbs, allows the presence of things like the Native American flute to take shape in interesting ways.[38]

That suspicious connection and discourse seems to be articulated in cue 3M4 "Roaming" where Ben is seen wandering around the Carver household in his boxer shorts. Although he is inside the house, the audience sees him from outside. The reflections of the woodland in the glass and images of the woodland itself surround him, merging into an indistinct visual landscape. Likewise, the perspective of the sound design is simultaneously external and internal. As Ben practices his golf swing in the Carvers' living room the "whoosh" is heard, but so are the sounds of the trees rustling in the wind outside. Nature is an all-pervading presence in Ben's life. The Native American flute, therefore, is not just a calling card, its function goes beyond a simple announcement of the presence of nature. It is unquestionably about man's relationship and reaction to nature. The film constantly contrasts the little problems that the characters have and the superficiality of their actions with the mysteriousness of the natural world in which they live.

It is striking that on the three occasions that the unaccompanied solo instrument is heard, the narrative is focused on individual characters. Cue 1M1 "Opening" is focused on Paul, 2M2A "Bike Kiss" focuses on Wendy, and 3M4 "Roaming" focuses on Ben. The material for each successive iteration of the cue is almost indistinguishable. Cue 2M2A "Bike Kiss" is the same as the initial opening statement of the theme in 1M1 except for the omission of the fourth phrase (i.e., boxed in Figure 5.1). In 3M4 "Roaming" the gestures are identical to 1M1, but the spaces in between the phrases are considerably longer.

Danna had, in fact, compiled different variations of the Nature theme for its successive entries, but Lee wanted the material to be the same on each occasion, a decision that according to Danna "made the music much more effective."[39] This effectiveness is, in part, due to the extra layers of meaning that the repetition of the thematic material generates in association with the individual characters. As well as references to the natural environment, the theme also highlights isolation and loneliness, and its simple restatement generates an effective metaphor for the relationship of characters to each other. As members of the same family they are inextricably connected, yet equally individualistic and dislocated.

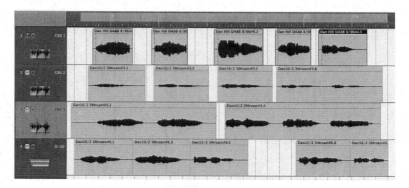

Figure 5.2: 3M4 "Roaming," Sequencer File, Audio Variations.
© 1996, reproduced by permission of Mychael Danna.

The audio waveforms for the four variations that Danna created for 3M4 "Roaming" are shown in Figure 5.2. Each horizontal track is a complete musical cue and each variation comprises five phrases based around improvised D♭/B♭ pentatonic recordings. However, they all use different elements and have slightly different structures. Principally, the composer experiments with the placement of space. The fourth track, for example, uses more space in the latter half of the cue than the other versions. The first track was eventually selected for use in the film.

There are three occasions when the Native American flute is not exclusively used as a solo instrument, but in conjunction with other instrumental resources. This happens extensively in the final cue, which will be examined later. On the other two occasions, 1M1 "Opening" and 2M2B "Bike Kiss," the solo flute is heard on its own before it subsequently joins the fuller ensemble, a further contrast between individuality and the group. In the second half of cue 1M1 "Opening" the Native American flute, gamelan, and orchestra are combined so that all the instrumental resources that Danna will use in the film are introduced. Two of the film's three themes are heard here, but attention is drawn to the texture rather than a focus on the statement of thematic material as a mnemonic. The cue functions like a postmodern overture. Although used sparingly, the Native American flute has the last word, growing out of the strings' final E♭ major chord. Its wailing gesture allows the music to glue over the spatiotemporal disjunction and dissolve into the next scene.

2M2B "Bike Kiss" provides a more extensive use of the Native American flute in combination with other instrumental forces. The cue begins as Wendy and Mikey kiss and a crane shot rises above them fully revealing the dried-out swimming pool, littered with fallen autumnal leaves, in which they are situated. It has become a cinematic cliché for crane shots to be used when characters embrace, resulting in dramatic, sweeping images, and a sense of soaring elation. Here, however, an altogether more objective and distant response is generated. The walls of the pool surround the characters, yet this "room" has no ceiling so they are simultaneously enclosed and exposed. The crane shot literally shatters their secluded space and provides the audience with a feeling of omniscience and distance. This is not a celebration of love or romance, but cool and detached sexual experimentation. A tracking shot traveling to the right with a view of the Carver house through the forest follows, and the action cuts to Ben and Janey in bed. Nature is framed by two emotionless sexual acts, performed first by the children and then by the adults, and the music is vital in generating an emotionally distant response to this sequence (Figure 5.3).

The strings play long held lines *senza vibrato* within a limited dynamic range, and a stifled harmonic structure centered on B♭ minor. There are occasional glimpses of G♭ Major but the bass remains on a B♭ pedal, creating a feeling of inertia. Removed from the rest of the gamelan ensemble, the solo *bonang* (a set of small, bulbous, gong-chimes) plays straight eighth notes and, in combination with the deer-skin drum and shaker, help provide regular pulsation that prevents the cue from grinding to a halt. There are no syncopations or rhythmic surprises. It is music that is rooted in stillness with the exception of the rhythmically free-flowing Native American flute.

The individuality of the Native American flute is further highlighted by the tuning, as the flute is slightly sharper than the rest of the ensemble, particularly on the held E♭ pitches.[40] This quirky characteristic generates an unsettled mood. A fundamental feature of the combination of instruments is that they remain somewhat separate,

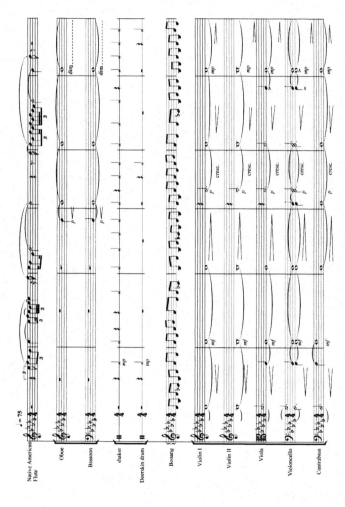

Figure 5.3: 2M2B "Bike Kiss," measures 5–10. From *The Ice Storm*.
By Mychael Danna. Copyright © 1997 Fox Film Corp.
All Rights Reserved. Used by Permission.

creating a skewed narrative atmosphere. The differing elements are layered on top of each other, but are never truly consolidated into a single statement. This interpretation is supported by the fact that, in contrast to the Nature theme, the solo *bonang* actually states the Negative Zone theme, which we shall examine presently. The score in Figure 5.3 approximates to the sounding pitches and it is clear that the *bonang* must have been recorded a whole tone higher before the audio materials were pitch shifted down to fit into the B♭ minor tonal center. There is consequently a juxtaposition of Nature with the Negative Zone, which adds further layers of signification to a scene already rich in contrasts between the natural world and doubtful moral actions.

Negative Zone

The Negative Zone theme is normally played by and associated with the gamelan ensemble. Gamelan is not a soloist's art; players are expected to be proficient in all of the instruments of the ensemble and the music is, above all else, about the special rapport between the musicians. The idea of a community in harmony with itself is in direct contrast to the characters in *The Ice Storm*.

This is the conceptual framework of the theme, but beyond this there are many other layers of meaning that the ensemble is potentially able to convey. On a purely sonic level gamelan has an icy quality that reflects both the eponymous natural event and the emotional coolness of the characters. Indeed, emotional detachment and restraint are central features of Javanese gamelan music. The order and structure of the music limits emotion to such an extent that musicians hope to realize a state of detachment.

> This state beyond emotion is what the Javanese call *iklas*. The refinements of all Javanese art and etiquette are designed to help one achieve this ideal state where one is at pure peace, untouched by emotion.[41]

In addition, the construction of gamelan music is often mechanical with numerous interlocking layers, creating repetitive music that is simultaneously rhythmic and inert, an appropriate characterization of the existential vacuum in which many of the characters find themselves. Another important aspect is that gamelan music can sound childlike and deceptively naïve, evoking music boxes or musical toys, which is particularly relevant in a film where the boundary between adult authority and juvenile irresponsibility is practically nonexistent. The decision to use gamelan therefore generates rich layers of meaning.

Before exploring the use of the theme, it is necessary briefly to outline some of the features of the Sundanese gamelan *degung* ensemble that Danna recorded. This will not be an exhaustive survey of gamelan music, for which there are many other excellent sources of information.[42] Sundanese gamelan *degung* normally have far fewer instruments than Central Javanese gamelan ensembles, which are arguably better known in the West. As with all gamelan music, the *degung* ensemble is organized into separate, yet interrelated, functional instrumental groups that express various aspects of time, melody, or structure. The music is cyclical and each piece derives from a primary structural pattern of tones, or *patokan*, that determines the duration of the cycle. A single *patokan* may serve as the outline for a large number of melodies and is played by the *jenglong*, six medium-sized hanging gongs suspended from the same frame. The end of each cycle is marked by the low pitched *gong ageng*. The *gong* and *jenglong*, therefore, define the phrase division or what is referred to as the colotomic structure. The barrel drum, named *kendang*, acts as a timekeeper, coordinator, and controller of dynamics. The so-called nuclear melody in classical gamelan *degung* is carried by the *bonang*. In modern gamelan *degung*, however, this is often performed by a female vocalist instead. The bamboo flute plays embellishments and two metallophones play abstractions of the nuclear melody, helping to create a rich polyphonic texture. Other instruments such as wooden xylophones or a bowed lute may be included according to the context. This type of music inevitably emphasizes polyphonic texture rather than harmony. Many layers of overlapping and interlocking melodic material are derived from the same basic thematic skeleton.

The instruments that Danna used for *The Ice Storm* are shown in Table 5.3, and a comparison with the full resources that were available (see chapter 4, Figure 4.8) reveals that he did not use the *kacapi* (stringed zither) or either of the bamboo flutes (*suling degung* or *suling tembang*). The *kacapi* would not normally play as part of the full ensemble, but would accompany the flute in interludes between pieces. Danna might have replaced the Native American flute with an Indonesian bamboo flute, but the Native American flute was more conceptually rich and more clearly separated and individualized from the rest of the ensemble. Danna explains that "without expecting people to have cultural anthropology degrees, the Native American flute still makes its point without words, without preaching, and in an emotionally stirring way. That would have been less direct with the gamelan flutes."[43]

Instrument	Range	Description
peking	Ab_4–C_6	high-pitched metallophone, with bars laid out in a single row
panerus	Ab_3–C_5	low-pitched metallophone, with bars laid out in a single row
bonang	C_4–G_6	two rows of seven small bulbous gongs lined up in an L shape
gambang	C_3–Db_5	wooden xylophone
jenglong	C_3–C_4	six medium, bulbous, hanging gongs suspended from the same frame
gongs: ageng and kempul	C_1 Ab_2	ageng: large hanging gong, 80–100 cm in diameter. kempul: smaller hanging gong 30–40 cm in diameter
kendang	N/A	set of drums, one double-sided (low and medium pitch), three single-side drums (three high pitches)

Table 5.3: Gamelan Ensemble Used by Danna in *The Ice Storm*.

While Danna's score pays homage to the formalized construction of gamelan *degung* music, it is not restricted by the weight of tradition. For example, even though the *bonang* is the main melody instrument, the idea of using it in isolation from the rest of the ensemble, as Danna does in cue 2M2B, would be alien to Javanese musical aesthetics and would sound "empty and unsatisfying."[44] Yet, to a Western cinema audience a rigid adherence to authentic features of formal construction would be of little significance, both musically and dramatically. Danna does not therefore pastiche gamelan music, but instead the available resources are used to create materials that serve the musical and dramatic purpose. According to some writers, this type of approach is more sincere than striving for authenticity.

> This brings about the interesting situation of the non-Western influence being there in the thinking, but not in the sound. This is a more genuine and interesting form of influence because while listening one is not necessarily aware of some non-Western music being imitated. Instead of imitation, the influence of non-Western musical structures on the thinking of a Western composer is likely to produce something genuinely new.[45]

It is fitting that Steve Reich's words about the influence of non-Western music on Western composers appear here, because it is crucial to acknowledge the importance of the post-sixties American minimalist school on the construction of the Negative Zone theme. Composers such as La Monte Young, Lou Harrison, Morton Feldman, Terry Riley, and Steve Reich were looking to Asian music for inspiration during the 1960s and 1970s, and ideas about the structure of musical materials derived from the aesthetics of gamelan were developed. Furthermore, university music departments subsequently began to teach world music, and the first sets of gamelan instruments began to appear in the West. Indeed, Danna became particularly fascinated by both world music and minimalism while a university student in Toronto.

Those influences are clearly evident in the first appearance of the Negative Zone theme, cue 1M8 "Train" (Figure 5.4). In its original form, the theme approximates to the key of C minor, in Western terms. It contains a flattened supertonic which adds an idiosyncratic color to what is essentially a driving rhythmic pattern, and the recurrent accents at the fifth help propel the movement forward. The initial material stated by the solo *bonang*, but later doubled on *pizzicato* violins and violas, is varied in the context of differing time signatures that help to create unpredictable phrase lengths.

Figure 5.4: 1M8 "Train," Negative Zone Theme. Measures 1–6.
From *The Ice Storm*.
By Mychael Danna.
Copyright © 1997 Fox Film Corp.
All Rights Reserved. Used by Permission.

One of the functions of the music in this cue is to generate momentum that characterizes the morning commute from the suburbs. At 122 BPM the music drives the action forward reflecting and supporting the hustle and bustle of the rush hour. Generally, the film is slow and contemplative, and moments such as this provide a valuable structural contrast. However, that rhythmic energy is a by-product of a deeper interpretative possibility that the cue provides. On the train platform, numerous anonymous commuters wear identical grey coats, and later an absent-minded Ben sits in a board meeting. The latter half of 1M8 "Train" shows Elena at a book fair, looking over a series of self-help texts. The clockwork construction of the cue highlights the idea of characters as cogs in an impersonal machine, emphasizing the regularity, tedium, and emptiness of their daily lives. The minimalist music is simultaneously rhythmically propulsive, harmonically static, and melodically constrained. There is movement but no direction. On the surface the combination of music and image reflects a nervous energy, but underneath it equally conveys the paralysis of life.[46]

The cue develops into an increasingly intricate series of syncopated and interlocking polyphonic lines (Figure 5.5), distributed between various instrumental sub groups. The *spiccato* violas and *bonang* play a recurrent eighth-note pattern, the *jenglong*, second violins, and *pizzicato* double bass interlock with a separate figure played by the flute, the *peking* and *panerus* (the two metallophones), and the first violins. The doublings contain occasional differences that exist mainly to exploit the particular ranges of the instruments. For example, in measure twenty-eight the viola pattern is altered from the *bonang* so that the *pizzicato* notes remain in the middle register. The fact that the music is organized into a stratified polyphonic structure, the strings are used percussively (*pizzicato* or *spiccato*), and the woodwinds are heavily articulated and play abstractions of the Negative Zone theme, suggests that the whole ensemble functions like a giant gamelan. The basic principle is that all material is directly related to and derived from the same thematic cell.

Even the *arco* cello phrase (measure 27) is derived from the basic Negative Zone material but moves at a slower rate and consequently provides a melodic counterbalance to the rhythmic movement. This melodic paraphrase appears frequently and prominently in combination with the theme itself and is characterized by an initial rising phrase followed by oscillation between the minor sixth, fifth, and perfect fourth. This oscillation is always resolved by a return to the perfect fifth, minor third, and then the tonic (Figure 5.6).

The melodic pattern reinforces the central minor tonality, but also emphasizes the importance of the perfect fifth. Indeed, the first appearance of the paraphrase melody in 1M8 "Train" is heard in consecutive fifths on the oboe and clarinet. It is varied rhythmically in every statement, but always functions melodically, moving more slowly than the accompanying rhythmic Negative Zone theme in the gamelan.

Cue 2M6 "Shoplift," which shows Elena riding a bicycle into town, entering a local pharmacy, and stealing some make-up, also incorporates the Western instruments into a gamelanesque structure. The material is closely related to 1M8 "Train," not least because both cues use the same tempo. However, the orchestration is somewhat lighter in 2M6 "Shoplift." As Elena is seen riding her bicycle, a syncopated *jenglong* ostinato supports the Negative Zone theme that is played solely by the *pizzicato* violins, and a solo concert flute plays a gentle variation of the paraphrase melody. The delicate texture of the first half of this cue provides an arguably more "feminine" representation that also highlights Elena's emotional fragility.

Figure 5.5: 1M8 "Train," Ending, Measures 25–30. From *The Ice Storm*. By Mychael Danna. Copyright © 1997 Fox Film Corp. All Rights Reserved. Used by Permission.

Figure 5.6: Negative Zone, Basic Paraphrase Melody.
From *The Ice Storm*.
By Mychael Danna.
Copyright © 1997 Fox Film Corp.
All Rights Reserved. Used by Permission.

Figure 5.7: 2M6 "Shoplift," Measures 28–32.
From *The Ice Storm*.
By Mychael Danna.
Copyright © 1997 Fox Film Corp.
All Rights Reserved. Used by Permission.

It is unsurprising, given the limited gamelan pitch ranges available, that the Negative Zone materials are frequently developed through coloristic difference and contrasting orchestration rather than extensive reinventions of the theme itself. The importance of the orchestration is highlighted in one of the few moments of direct correspondence between music and physical gesture in the film (Figure 5.7). Once inside the pharmacy Elena examines make-up products. As the camera tracks slowly towards her the musical texture is reduced from a mixed gamelan, wind, and string ensemble to solo *bonang* which plays a recurrent, alternating minor third. The gesture immediately creates suspense which is compounded by a single 6/4 measure that delays resolution for an extra two beats. When the camera has drawn close to Elena, the *bonang* pattern is dampened creating an even more intimate and expectant texture. At the moment that Elena decides to put the lipstick into her cardigan pocket, the *bonang* is suddenly unmuted and joined by the cello section playing the Negative Zone theme, and a syncopated pattern on the *jenglong* and the *gambang*. The *cor anglais* also emerges at this point and takes the melodic lead. It is the first time in the film that either the *gambang* or the *cor anglais* are used, and the latter is not heard again in the film. Consequently, this dramatic moment is marked by significant coloristic transformation where orchestration drives the narrative gesture. The next cut, a shot of Elena reflected in a security mirror stealing more products, is accented by the first entry in the film of the *gong ageng*. This is lowest of the gongs and in traditional gamelan is the most structurally important as it is used to mark the end of a cycle.

The Negative Zone theme is associated with events that form part of the characters' fruitless pursuit of meaning or satisfaction. Equally, the theme represents both physical journeys and metaphorical transitions, as has already been witnessed. In 2M3 "Walk," the Negative Zone theme accompanies Ben as he ambles home through the woods after his affair with Janey. The Nature theme might have been used here instead, but the use of the Negative Zone theme at a steady, cyclical 100 BPM suggests that the seemingly dangerous and exciting sexual encounter may be just as unsatisfying as the zombie-like journey to work. The use of this theme here also creates a musical bridge between the Carver and Hood households.

The use and meaning of the Negative Zone theme in cue 3M3 "Dinner" could also be questioned as it would seem to provide rather too bleak a commentary on the Hoods' Thanksgiving meal. Even though it is ritualized, this is one of the few moments of family unity that the film represents. However, the music is heard only at the very end of the scene and is the shortest cue in the whole film. This would suggest that the principal function of the music is to provide a smooth transition to the next sequence where Ben and Janey attempt another sexual encounter. The music does not encroach upon the action in either scene, rather it appears in between as a connecting structure. Ben and Janey's tryst is eventually aborted because he is anxious about his wife's suspicions and Janey resents being reminded of the emotional consequences of their actions. There is a conflict between the pursuit of pleasure and its potential emotional cost on the family. The proximity of the Thanksgiving dinner scene and the affair already suggest this reading, but the placement of the cue makes a more direct connection.

Cue 6M1 "Bathroom" is a delicate variation of the Negative Zone theme which shows Elena finding her husband, immediately after her brief sexual encounter with Jim. She lets Ben know that she is going home and asks him to sleep-off his intoxication on the Halfords' couch. One potential reading of this gentle cue is that it represents the affection that the married couple still hold for each other. The flute paraphrase melody is touching, but the use of the quiet, static, muted, and reduced strings—there is no double bass section—and the extremely slow tempo expresses a form of subdued, insular emotionality (Figure 5.8). Another potential reading, therefore, is that the score empathizes with Elena. The solo concert flute has already been specifically associated with her on its only other appearance in the film thus far. She attempted to take revenge on her husband by having sex with her neighbor, but the experience was demeaning and humiliating. The score helps to highlight the loneliness, emptiness, and despair that Elena feels, but which she is not able to express or discuss with her husband.

In its various forms the Negative Zone theme pervades the film as the most frequently used score material. Because it represents a concept rather than a place or a person, it is free to suffuse the narrative creating multiple layers of meaning. The theme can function as a precursor or postlude, it can generate rhythm or equally suggest inertia, it can suggest regularity and irregularity, it can suggest sophistication or naïvety, and it can generate transitions or equally suggest stasis. The fact that the meaning is often ambiguous and open to multiple interpretations is a direct consequence of placing the gamelan ensemble in a narrative context that forces the audience to question its significance.

Figure 5.8: 6M1 "Bathroom," Negative Zone, Measures 5–12.
From *The Ice Storm*.
By Mychael Danna.
Copyright © 1997 Fox Film Corp.
All Rights Reserved. Used by Permission.

Family

The most striking feature about the Family theme is its cyclical quality (Figure 5.9). The tonal center is established by the octave B♭ of the first two notes and is reinforced by a bass B♭ pedal note in the second measure. The melodic pattern in the first measure ends on an unresolved major ninth, falls to a minor seventh, but finally settles on the tonic B♭ in the final measure, before the whole phrase is repeated. This two-measure phrase is frequently looped. Like the concept of the family that is explored in *The Ice Storm*, the theme maintains its stability despite a number of destabilizing elements. It would seem to encapsulate Paul Hood's definition of the family as articulated in his first voice-over: "Your family is the void you emerge from and where you return to when you die."

Figure 5.9: Family.
From *The Ice Storm.*
By Mychael Danna.
Copyright © 1997 Fox Film Corp.
All Rights Reserved. Used by Permission.

The first statement of the theme in the film occurs in the second half of cue 1M1. A flash-forward shows Paul Hood returning home to New Canaan from his trip to New York; the train has stalled and the journey has taken all night. The score here provides an aural representation of thawing ice with subtle and carefully controlled orchestration. It symbolizes both the dissolution of the storm and the advent of a new emotional season. Entries for half-section string tremolos played *sul tasto*, flute and oboe trills, and unmeasured vibraphone tremolos run at different speeds generating a shimmering texture. Eventually all four vibraphone players contribute to the orchestration and the Family theme is heard on the gamelan in the home key of B♭ minor.

However, a comparison of the Family theme with the pitches available to Danna on the gamelan *degung* ensemble (C–D♭–E♭–G–A♭) raises a challenging question. Due to its intervallic structure the theme is simply not possible on any of the available instruments. Even pitch shifting the audio recordings would not resolve this. For example, the major ninth at the end of the first measure would not be obtainable in the *degung* mode and would have to be changed to a minor ninth. Danna explains that the "theme was originally for vibes, but we felt it lacked the gravitas needed."[47] This realization appears to have occurred late in the process as the orchestrator's score for 1M1 clearly shows the theme, originally intended for vibraphone four, crossed out and replaced with a doubling of vibraphone two (see Figure 5.10).

As the Family theme could not be performed by the real gamelan ensemble, its first statement in the film is, in fact, computer generated from a mixture of Roland *saron* and *kenong* samples. Without prior knowledge of this aspect of the scoring it would be difficult to identify

Figure 5.10: 1M1 "Opening" Part 2, Thawing Ice, Measures 14–17.
Section from Orchestrator's Handwritten Score.
From *The Ice Storm*.
By Mychael Danna.
Copyright © 1997 Fox Film Corp.
All Rights Reserved. Used by Permission.

Figure 5.11: 1M1 "Opening" Part 2, Family Theme Ending.
From *The Ice Storm*.
By Mychael Danna.
Copyright © 1997 Fox Film Corp.
All Rights Reserved. Used by Permission.

the theme as computer generated, it is a convincing and successful integration. The fact that the theme is quiet in the mix, low in register (starting on B♭₂), and shrouded in the shimmering texture of the real instruments deceives the ear into believing that the instrument is real. The two-measure theme is treated like an ostinato and is repeated eight times before the end of the cue. Above this, dovetailing neatly with the end of Paul Hood's voice-over and coinciding with a shot of his family, who are waiting for him at the train station, a more direct version of the theme using only four notes is heard. Its anacrusis A♭ leads onto the final three notes of the original theme: D♭, C, B♭. Since the cue has been so heavily rooted in a static B♭ minor the harmonization of this moment—B♭m, D♭ᵐᵃʲ⁷, E♭—is particularly striking and uplifting. The Dorian mode, whose significance was discussed in chapter 4, clearly drives the harmonization. The flattened seventh (A♭) and the sharpened sixth degree (G♮), essential features of the Dorian mode, also define the D♭ᵐᵃʲ⁷ and E♭ harmonies (Figure 5.11). The full significance of this harmonic color may not be apparent at this stage of the film, but it will eventually be understood as an affirmation of family unity.

The idea of family unity is supported by the next two incarnations of the Family theme. Both are associated with Ben and the relationship he has with his children. Cue 3M1 "Pick Up Paul" is heard when Ben collects his son from the train station. The *gambang*, *kendang*, hand drums, and hand percussion improvise around basic patterns, creating rhythmic movement that represents the car journey; the *kendang* is directed to play "sparse and groovy." Aside from the rhythmic movement central to the cue, the *peking* and *panerus* also create a naïve, music-box quality through alternating minor thirds. This is particularly relevant because Ben initiates an embarrassing discussion about the facts of life with his son. The issue of adult responsibility and rites of passage are explored in the scene and the music plays with the notion of who, in fact, is the more responsible and self-aware of the two family members. Interestingly, the cue starts in an unpredictable 7/4, but as soon as the theme enters the time signature reverts to a more stable 4/4, reinforcing the importance, strength, and incontrovertible permanence of the family. Later in the film, however, a revised version of the cue (3M6 "Drive") accompanies Ben and Elena on their way to the Carver household when it is clear that their marriage is at its most volatile. On this occasion, the Family theme is not stated and the music remains in an unstable 7/8 throughout.

Cue 3M6 "Toes Cold" represents a moment of honest affection between Ben and his daughter, as he carries Wendy home after he has caught her "fooling around" with Mikey. The irony of the fact that Ben was, only a few moments earlier, wandering around the Carver household semi-naked in anticipation of a sexual encounter with Janey is not lost on the audience. Yet, somehow the display of real love between a father and daughter transcends this. The scene is extremely moving precisely because it is one of the few genuine displays of emotion by characters in the film (Figure 5.12). Played initially by the strings, the Family theme enters when Ben holds his daughter, the spotting highlighting the important moment of physical contact. The theme is then played by the solo piano—the first time that this has occurred in the film—which is arguably a more domestic and intimate orchestration. Finally, a single statement of the four-note version of the theme appears on the clarinet. The cue is remarkably sparse, exemplifying restraint rather than suddenly overloading the moment with sentiment.

It could be argued that the influence of the Dorian mode is, once again, experienced in this cue. However, the G♮ that is heard in the fourth measure is only fleeting and is contrasted with G♭s from the fifth measure onwards. While the Dorian mode insinuates itself in the various cues that have been examined thus far, after the storm has passed it becomes more prominent. In 6M2 "Janey," rather than being used to characterize the harmony, the mode is used melodically.

The struggle to create this particular cue in relation to the temp track has already been explored in chapter 4, a journey that highlighted the contrapuntal and modal characteristics of the score. The narrative and structural significance of these features is all too apparent in the finished cue. The interweaving lines between oboe and clarinet suggest Janey's confused state of mind as she returns home. The use of the Dorian mode as melodic driver seems to break away from the harmonic framework that has encased the score up until this point. The shroud of restraint is gradually shed, and generates a sense of emotional unraveling at an important moment of realization and awakening. Equally though, the Family theme is stated on the piano underneath the interweaving contrapuntal lines. This might seem unusual for a scene that is focused on only one person, but the score hints at what is missing in Janey's life. As she lies in the fetal position, a symbolic return to the womb, the importance of emotional bonds to the family are strikingly apparent. Two important ideas are foregrounded by the music during this cue—the process of emotional unraveling and the importance of the family—and these thematic concepts are finally resolved in 6M4 "Bowl."

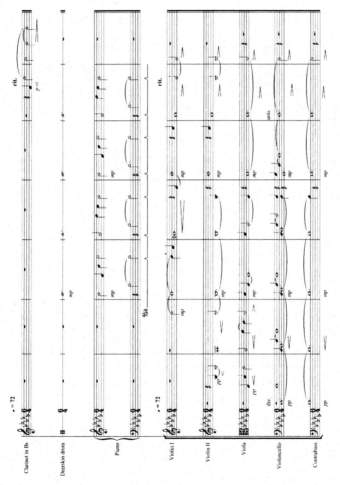

Figure 5.12: 3M5 "Toes Cold," Complete. From *The Ice Storm.*
By Mychael Danna. Copyright © 1997 Fox Film Corp.
All Rights Reserved. Used by Permission.

6M4 "Bowl"

Throughout *The Ice Storm* the filmmaking strategies employed help maintain an objective distance from the characters. Squyres describes this as an approach that asks the audience to step back "almost like an anthropologist would."[48] However, in the final cue of the film that objective distance is broken down, a transformation that is all the more powerful because of the emotional coldness that has been witnessed throughout. As the characters experience an emotional awakening in the aftermath of the storm so the audience is provided with reasons to empathize with them. There is a literal and metaphorical thawing. This is not to suggest that the score suddenly bursts into melodramatic musical gestures which would be out of context for the film and out character for the composer. The emotional release is as subtle and carefully controlled as the score elsewhere in the film.

Cue 6M4 "Bowl" is so named because it begins on a shot of the glass bowl that was used during the key party. There is very little dialogue during the sequence. In fact, there is no dialogue in the sense of conversational exchange between characters. Paul's voice-over is an internal monologue, the train guard's announcement is pure information, Ben's shocked explanation of what happened to Mikey is understandably brief and incomplete, and the last words in the film are simply Elena calling out Ben's name. Yet, a great deal of meaning and narrative resolution is expressed within the nine-and-a-half-minute sequence and the score is vital in its articulation. James Schamus explains that a transformation takes place from words to sounds and images, so that "music replaces dialogue as the center of consciousness of the movie."[49]

The sequence features a number of different locations and events including: Jim and Elena's return from the key party, Elena's discovery of Wendy and Sandy in bed together, Ben's discovery of Mikey's body, Paul returning home on the train from New York, the arrival of Mikey's body at the Carver household, Jim's reaction to the death of his son, Janey awakening, and the Hood family picking up Paul from the train station. Schamus explains that "there is a lot of cross-cutting, so the score really pulls everything together."[50] But the score does more than simply glue the events into a unified narrative experience. In fact, the way the score is structured defines the narrative trajectory of the sequence, allowing the audience to experience a powerful emotional journey. Danna's score is divided into five sections, which are labeled A to E in Table 5.4.

Table 5.4: 6M4 "Bowl," Structure.

Time (mins.)	0	0.5	1	1.5	2	2.5	3	3.5	4	4.5	5	5.5	6	6.5	7	7.5	8	8.5	9	9.5
Narrative Action	Bowl	Jim and Elena return to Carver household.	Wendy and Sandy in bed.		Ben discovers Mikey's body.		Train regains power.	Paul on the train. Train begins to move.		Shots of ice melting.	Ben brings Mikey's body to Carver household. Jim takes Mikey's body inside.			Wendy hugs Sandy.	Janey woken by crying. / Thawing landscape.	Paul returns to New Canaan station.	Paul sees his family waiting for him.	Hood family inside car.	Cut to black; credits.	Score Ends.
Section	A			B				C		D			E							
Thematic Material	Negative Zone			Transition (Nature)				Transition (Thawing)		Negative Zone (paraphrase)			Family							
Time Signature	6/4							5/4		3/4			6/4							
Tempo	♩=71									♩=48			♩=72							
Tonal Center	Cm			→			→	Cm		Cm			Bbm							
Ensemble	peking, panerus, bonang, jenglong, gongs, strings (no basses)			Native American flute, nautch bells, synth: log drums, jenglong, bonang, strings.				fl., 2 vibes (4 players), strings.		fl., cl., bsn., 2 vibes (4 players), synth gamelan, strings.			fl., ob., cl., bsn., synth gamelan, Native American flute, Indian deerskin drum, piano, solo violin, solo cello, strings.							

Two principal large-scale transitions occur through this sequence, a transformation from the dominance of the Negative Zone theme to the Family theme, and a concurrent shift from C minor to B♭ minor, the "home" key of the score. The sense of resolution provided by these transitions results in an important narrative foregrounding of family unity. The score, therefore, contributes to the presentation of the family as an archetype that resonates with the audience far beyond the localized events that the characters experience.

There is also a large-scale transition in terms of the instrumentation and orchestration of the music. The cue begins with unaccompanied gamelan ensemble but this instrumental texture is gradually reduced, eventually becoming a single line for synthesized gamelan before disappearing completely into the increasingly prominent strings. The icy quality of the gamelan sound gradually melts away as the cue progresses.

In the context of the whole film, the gamelan at the very opening of the cue is at its most "music box"-like. Contributing to this quality are the high *peking* and *panerus* which play a fragmented version of the Negative Zone theme in canon, first two beats then one beat apart. The innocent, mechanical character is enhanced by the lack of the pitch D♭, a defining feature of the original Negative Zone theme. Indeed, D♭ is consistently avoided. The repeated E♭ highlighted in Figure 5.13, for instance, should theoretically be a D♭. Yet in the eighteen measures that comprise Section A, the pitch D♭ is heard only once. The simplicity of the score at this point defines a starting point of naïvety for the emotional awakening that the characters are about to experience. The gamelan is at its most restricted.

Figure 5.13: 6M4 "Bowl," Section A, Measures 4–6.
From *The Ice Storm.*
By Mychael Danna.
Copyright © 1997 Fox Film Corp.
All Rights Reserved. Used by Permission.

Ben's discovery of Mikey's body (Section B) is one of the most striking moments within the sequence. The gamelan texture is reduced and the solo *jenglong* takes the lead, the *gong ageng* and *bonang* provide very occasional punctuation. Every downbeat is accented by a heavily reverberated synthesized log drum and *nautch* bells, adding dramatic weight to the realization that Mikey has died. However, it is not solely the change in instrumentation that is conspicuous, but also the harmonic structure. The *jenglong* plays an insistent octave pedal note C affirming the tonal center, but around this other elements constantly disrupt the supposed stability. The strings, for example, initially alternate between C minor and variations of E♭ minor harmonies, then after a sudden shift between F minor and E♭ minor, and finally resolve from B♭ minor to C minor. The parallel minor chord harmony constantly pulls away and then returns to the C pedal giving the impression of modulation though none has actually taken place. It is as if the music attempts to escape from the strict tonal boundaries that have encased it thus far but is unable to do so. Nonetheless, the process of emotional awakening has been set in motion by the discovery of the body.

Given Mikey's association with nature it is unsurprising that the Native American flute features prominently in this section of the score. Yet the flute does not play the Nature theme as it has been stated throughout the film. The melodic material still retains the free-spirited improvisatory character, but the pentatonic framework is now extended to B♭ natural minor. This expansion makes C♮s available to the flute, which in turn allows it to be situated within the general C minor tonal center. Although the difference is subtle, the Native American flute is less constrained than it has been in the past, and the melodic phrases employ greater intervallic extension and more *glissandi*. Furthermore, the Native American flute is especially sharp against the rest of the ensemble. Michel Chion argues that an out of tune instrument has a "materializing effect"[51] where the work of the emitter of the sound is accentuated "instead of allowing us to forget the emitter in favor of the sound itself."[52] The characteristically inconsistent intonation generates a wonderfully unsettling and unstable quality that reflects the vulnerable and volatile situation in which Ben now finds himself.

As Section B draws to a close, shots of the train regaining power are shown—its lights flicker back to life—and the visual gesture is cross-faded with a dying aural gesture. Danna employs a high-pitched elk antler—an instrument fashioned from the branched horns found in pairs on the head of elk that are shed annually—and the Native American flute in a joint downwards *glissando* that fades into silence.

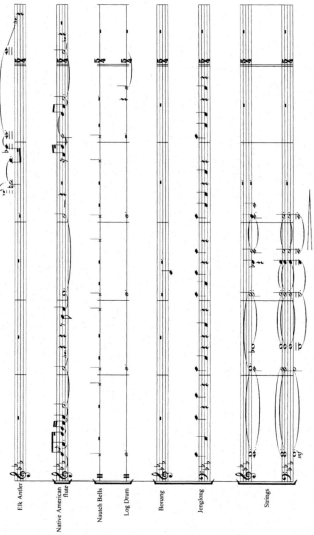

Figure 5.14: 6M4 "Bowl," Section B, Ending, Measures 33–38.
From *The Ice Storm*. By Mychael Danna.
Copyright © 1997 Fox Film Corp.
All Rights Reserved. Used by Permission.

Earlier in the film the sound design focused on Mikey's last breaths. Here the only entry of the elk antler in the entire score provides a symbolic mirror image to that realistic sound, a metaphorical final expellation of breath that emphasizes the irrevocability of the circumstance (Figure 5.14). The tuning, harmonic structure, gestural patterns, and instrumentation throughout the section have generated an atmosphere of transitional instability. The score has shifted from the naïve, harmonically static gamelan opening to a more volatile state. The emotional landscape has begun to change.

The transformation that has been hinted at in the score thus far is now pushed forward in Section C. It is a trajectory that can lead in only one narrative direction. In a shimmering depiction of melting ice, the score is literally defrosted. The material is similar to that which was heard in cue 1M1 "Opening" and is constructed from vibraphone, flute, and string *tremolandi* running at different speeds. Initially, the tonality is unclear but it eventually situates itself in C minor. As in the flash-forward, the focus is on Paul Hood and the return to service of the train that will take him back to New Canaan. Therefore, the physically and emotionally representative defrosting is allied with a return to the family. The score is in transition, the physical and metaphorical thawing provides a pivot point after which the thematic material is heard in a different way. Growing out of the shimmering textures, therefore, a modified statement of the Negative Zone theme is heard in Section D.

This penultimate section is concerned with the return of Mikey's body to the Carver household and the initial reactions to his death. Throughout the film, the Negative Zone theme has been played by the metallophone instruments from the gamelan ensemble, often the solo *bonang*. However, following the defrosting of the score in Section C, the theme is transferred to the first violins with the rest of the strings providing harmonic support. Above this a solo clarinet plays an extended version of the Negative Zone paraphrase melody. The music is arguably the "warmest" statement of the material that has been heard in the film. Certainly the change from brittle gamelan at the very opening of the sequence to the smoother string and clarinet sound, via this symbolic thawing, provides a vital narrative transition. The Negative Zone theme has been transformed, requiring reevaluation of the detachment that it has previously conveyed. This simultaneously suggests that the characters' isolationism has in some way contributed towards the tragic event, but also that a change in their actions may now occur. Gamelan textures are still present in Section D, but the musical material is synthesized (the real gamelan ceased playing at the end of Section B). Rather than stating the Negative Zone theme with its characteristic eighth-note movement, the synthesized gamelan now plays regular quarter-note harmonies based on either C minor or Ab^{maj7}. The softened orchestration challenges the selfish individualism of the existential nihilist agenda that the characters have pursued throughout the film.

Jim's reaction to the death of his son is an extraordinarily powerful and genuine outpouring of emotion. The score acknowledges and embraces this emotional awakening, an awakening that has been steadfastly avoided throughout the film. It is interesting to note that the precise moment that Jim cries over Mikey's body is where Section E, the final part of the score, begins (Figure 5.15). The entry of the Indian deerskin drum and *gong ageng* on each downbeat is gesturally similar to the material that accompanied Ben's discovery of Mikey's body in Section B, making a structural link between the two father figures. Indeed, I would argue that the final scenes of the film and the score support not only a reading of emotional thawing but particularly of masculine emotional thawing.

The concept of stifled male emotion and its representation has been widely discussed in film, cultural, and psychological studies.[53] For our purposes, it is interesting to note that this was a particular social preoccupation of the 1970s, when the patriarchal order appeared to be in crisis. Writing only one year after the film is set, for example, Warren Farrell argued that men are "emotionally constipated" with real emotion somehow stuck in their system.[54] This bodily metaphor served to emphasize willfully contained masculinity as a danger. If, as Stanley Aronowitz later wrote, men are the "victims of the emotional plague by the imperative of always having to be in control," then emotional release is both inevitable and cathartic.[55] The final sequences of *The Ice Storm* explore the nature of this emotional release as Jim, Sandy, and Ben, but not Elena or Janey, are witnessed crying.

Both the Family theme and a new tonal center are introduced in the final section. However, the transition to these new materials occurs gradually, almost hesitantly. As has already been seen, the Family theme contained pitches that were not possible on the real gamelan ensemble, so it is stated by the synthesized gamelan. It is initially fragmented, becoming more recognizable in measure 85, where the strings tentatively introduce the new tonal center of Bb minor, and a full statement of the theme doubled by the piano then appears in measure 90. The family has been disrupted but will be reformed. It is important to reflect on the spotting of this staggered appearance of the Family theme. The marker list—a means of identifying structural and narrative moments of significance—contained within the sequencer file for this cue reveals that Danna specifically pinpointed the moment where

Wendy hugs Sandy. Earlier in the film, as Wendy was carried home by her father, the moment of physical contact acted as a spur for the release of the Family theme. Here also a hug finally releases the Family theme. The camera circles round the two children eventually focusing on Sandy's tearful face, and in the background Jim's wailing becomes increasingly prominent. As the emotional outpouring intensifies, therefore, the theme becomes more recognizable (Figure 5.15).

One of the central characteristics of the Family theme, its cyclical quality, is fully exploited as the cue continues to build. There have been no solo string passages anywhere in the score thus far, but as the narrative increasingly focuses on the Hood family, both solo cello and solo violin respectively state the theme. Like a mantra, each repetition affirms and reinforces the emotional impact, building to a climax as Paul descends from the train. The simple act of a family waiting for one of their own provides a powerful narrative and emotional resolution, in part, because this scene has already been witnessed at the very opening of the film. The full significance of the imagery and musical materials at that stage would not have been entirely clear. However now, given everything the Hood family has experienced, the scene acquires a remarkable strength and poignancy. The individualism that the characters have exhibited disappears as they realize their vulnerability and how precious they are to each other. Through a carefully structured release the sequence, indeed the whole film, has been building to this moment. The Family theme proper is given an expansive statement by the piano, synthesized gamelan, solo violin, and solo cello, and simultaneously a paraphrase of the theme is stated by the woodwinds from measure 102 onwards (Figure 5.16). The Dorian mode that Danna has avoided using throughout the sequence drives the harmonization at this important moment of revelation. The block harmony—B♭m, D♭^{maj7}, E♭—provides a powerful, uplifting statement in support of the permanence and unity of the family.

As the film draws to a close, the texture of the score is reduced to delicate strings and piano. The final moments show Ben breaking down and weeping in the car surrounded by his family. He looks at his son as if to say something, but does not or can not, and then bursts into tears. Earlier, Jim and Sandy's tears arguably fell into stereotyped, socially acceptable masculine displays of emotion (moments of family grief, the horrors of war, when a favorite sports team loses, and so on). But Ben's sudden outpouring at the end of the film has no such justification. Tom Lutz argues that the flashpoint for tears is often "the character's recovery of his or her proper social role, after an exciting foray into social disruption, but that return is always a notably compromised or transformed version of the role."[56] There is some relevance here to Ben who may be regaining his social role as a responsible father, but the scene also provides a richer representation of emotion that goes beyond this melodramatic model. His expression of emotion is simultaneously genuine and intimate. It acknowledges the wrong that Ben has done and the guilt that he feels. It reflects the emotional stress that he has experienced, the relief that his own son is safe and well, and the joy that the family is unified despite all that has occurred. It is a complex of emotions that Ben can no longer contain, a catharsis that must be shared with his family.

Matching his emotional expression the score begins to swell as Ben cries, continuing past the cut to black and into the final credits. This type of approach is relatively uncommon. Typically the score would fade out towards the end credits, and different music— sometimes a pop song—would act as a structural marker to signify the end of the film. However, at the end of *The Ice Storm* the cue continues for a further thirty seconds into the credits sequence. This approach keeps the audience in a state of suspended emotional tension and also invites them to contemplate further what has just been experienced. Rather than bringing the narrative events to an absolute conclusion the scoring approach opens up further interpretative possibilities. The images have finished but the narrative continues.

Cue 6M4 "Bowl" is a relatively rare example of a continuous, extended score sequence. The sheer length of the cue allows Danna to create a series of goal-oriented musical structures within a large-scale transition that builds beyond the narrative images into the credits. Through careful configuration of its internal thematic, harmonic, instrumental, and orchestrational resources, the cue guides the audience through a narrative journey from cold to warm and from restraint to release. But the cue is also part of a larger scoring concept and structure that employs only three themes, restricted tonal range, subdued orchestration, and sparse spotting as its principal tools. The restraint employed in the score throughout the film and its deliberate weighting towards the end defines the powerful emotional journey that the audience takes with the characters.

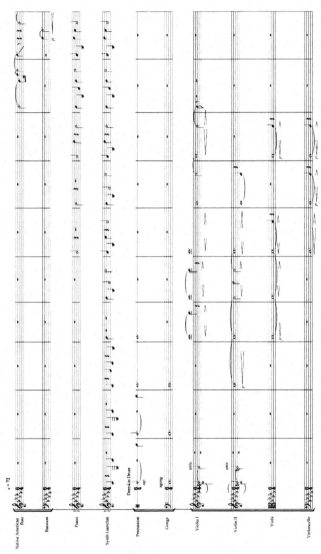

Figure 5.15: 6M4 "Bowl," Section E, Family Theme Entry, Measures 81–90.
From *The Ice Storm*. By Mychael Danna.
Copyright © 1997 Fox Film Corp.
All Rights Reserved. Used by Permission.

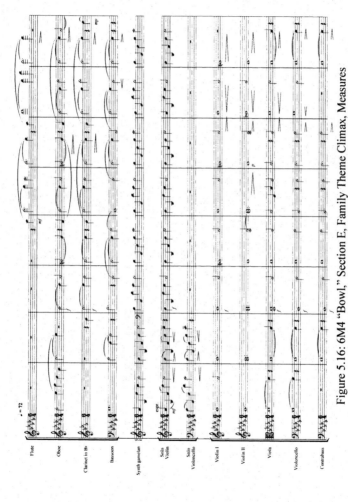

Figure 5.16: 6M4 "Bowl," Section E, Family Theme Climax, Measures 99–106. From *The Ice Storm*. By Mychael Danna. Copyright © 1997 Fox Film Corp. All Rights Reserved. Used by Permission.

Fade to Black: "I Can't Read"

The very final music in the film is the reworking of the song "I Can't Read," originally written by David Bowie and Reeves Gabrels in 1989. Tin Machine, the name of both the band and the album, marked an important shift in Bowie's musical development. It allowed him to jettison the expectations of the mainstream audience he had attracted as a solo artist during the 1980s, moving on to the critically respected albums of the 1990s. Tin Machine had a back-to-basics, hard rock sound with simple production, as opposed to Bowie's previous two extravagantly produced solo albums. Given Bowie's vast influence, perennial popularity, and iconic status from the 1970s onwards the decision to employ him in any capacity in the film is fascinating. Steyermark explains that the production team had

> explored with Bowie whether he wanted to be involved with either writing a score or contributing to it. I mean just to feel him out, we never expected that he would want to do the score, and we were not sure that it was necessarily the best idea, but we thought that somehow he might be involved.[57]

The proposal that Bowie would write an end credit song emerged from these discussions. It is not clear whether the initial intention was for an original composition or a revised version of an existing song. However, Steyermark was adamant that the song should not simply be "slapped on" the credits with only a passing relevance to the film.[58] This may explain why a song from *The Rise and Fall of Ziggy Stardust and the Spiders from Mars* was not chosen as raw material for development. Such a choice could have generated exciting modernization of a historical "document" mirroring the themes of transformation that are central to the narrative. However tracks from the 1972 concept album would have been too well known and heavily loaded with their own narrative and cultural associations: glam rock, androgyny, and science fiction. The general strategy for the source music was to favor less identifiable songs in order to inspire vague memories and an uneasy feeling. The lyrics of "I Can't Read" could also be adapted more easily to the film and seemed to provide a more useful blank canvass on which to develop materials.

A screening was arranged for Bowie on September 27th 1996 in New York so that he could tailor the song specifically to the narrative mood and emotional content of the film.[59] This screening was almost certainly of VERSION 8 of the edit and included Danna's most recent score demos. Steyermark explains that the production team wanted the song to grow organically out of the score so that when "Bowie's voice came in it would be a cathartic moment, it would be like the final release."[60] Typically, the music that is heard on credits sequences would have a different mood and quality from the music that has been heard at the end of the film. However, here the song forms an important completion of the musical trajectory defined by the score and provides further confirmation of a general narrative strategy of restraint and release. Equally, it is clear that the soundworld of Danna's score was influential in Bowie's revision of the song.

There are some interesting transformations made to the original song in terms of structure, lyrics, harmony, tempo, and instrumentation. The alterations employed generate a more contemplative, less extroverted track. Both versions are in the same key, but the revision avoids upbeat major tonality in the chorus, creating a uniformly dark mood. The revised version is much slower than the original punchy rock song; acoustic guitars, including a nylon strung guitar, replace the heavily distorted guitars, there is no drum kit or any percussion in the updated version, and a synthesizer string pad is added and generates a washy harmonic texture. In essence the original pacey, hard rock sound is transformed into an intimate soundworld that sits more comfortably with the score.

These revisions also serve to focus attention on the lead vocal. The fact that Steyermark highlights the entry of the voice—not the entry of the song—as a cathartic moment suggests that the choice of track was of secondary importance to the choice of singer. Bowie's distinctive vocal quality was intended to resonate with the audience, but in an unfamiliar context. In the original song, Bowie's voice has an upfront, brash, nasal quality located in the mask of the face, whereas in the revised version the throat is more relaxed resulting in a mellow and rounded quality. This change in vocal quality may be partially caused by the natural physiological changes of an artist respectively in his early thirties and early forties at the time of recording, but the difference is also deliberately performative. It is a more sensitive and gentle rendition of the song.

The song used in the film consists of two verses, an instrumental break, and finally the chorus. The structural difference from the original is largely defined by the slower tempo and the timing limitations of the credit sequence.[61] The lyrics of the first verse and chorus are only slightly altered, while those of the second verse are entirely rewritten (Figure 5.17). Schamus explains that Bowie had initially prepared a "version of the song with lyrics that referenced the film explicitly, but I remember Ang asking him to remove the overt references."[62] Consequently, the extant film version is profitably ambiguous and suggests greater vulnerability than the original lyric.

For example, a comparatively minor change in the third line of the first verse: "I don't *know*" rather than "I don't *care*" accentuates uncertainty rather than a brash lack of concern. The new second verse is entirely comprised of questions that refer back to the film. It is much less confident and secure, and creates a deliberate open-ended narrative. The last line of this verse: "Can I Feel? Can I please?" also has a number of meanings. As a verb "please" could refer to giving enjoyment or pleasure. However, as an adverb the meaning is altered, especially given the question that immediately precedes it. The phrase could be read as a request, an almost imploring statement: please allow me to feel.

I Can't Read (original)	I Can't Read (film version)
I can't read and I can't write down,	I can't read and I can't write down,
I don't know a book from countdown,	I don't know a book from countdown,
I don't care which shadow gets me,	I don't know which shadow gets me,
All I've got is someone's face.	All I've got is someone's face.
Money goes to money heaven,	Can I see a family smile?
Bodies go to body hell,	Can I reach tomorrow?
I just cough and catch the chase,	Can I walk a missing mile?
Switch the channel watch the police car.	Can I feel? Can I please?
	Instrumental
CHORUS	**CHORUS**
I can't read shit anymore.	I can't read shit anymore,
I just sit back and ignore.	I just sit back and ignore.
'Cause I just can't get it right, can't get it right,	I just can't seem to get it right, get it right.
I can't read shit, I can't read shit.	I can't read shit, I can't read shit.

Instrumental

When you see a famous smile,
No matter where you run your mile,
To be right in that photograph,
Andy where's my fifteen minutes?

CHORUS

Figure 5.17: "I Can't Read" © 1989 David Bowie and Reeves Gabrels.
Reproduced by permission of Jones Music America/RZO Music.

An interesting feature of both the original song and the film version is the final phrase of the chorus: "I can't read shit." Without specific knowledge of the written lyrics, one might hear the phrase as: "I can't reach it." This suggests helplessness and fate playing against the individual. Bowie's performance enjoys this ambiguity as he does not clearly articulate the consonants. Both phrases express powerlessness, but ambiguity surrounds the song's parting shot that could represent an inability to fulfill desires or literal excreta.

Conclusions

The soundtrack for *The Ice Storm* is one of the most conceptually rich, subtle, and effective of the 1990s. Each element contributes towards a multilayered and yet integrated soundworld that lingers in the memory, not only because of the scope of the tragedy at the conclusion of the film, but because of the controlled journey towards it that the soundtrack helps create. Restraint is the principal device employed and through the precise combination of sound design, source music, song, and score, emotion is skillfully withheld and released.

The sound design rarely contains more than the most delicate traces of wind, water, or ice. Deliberately reduced textures—the presence of absence—generate subtle precursors or meaningful "silences," across a spectrum of embodied and encoded sounds. The use of the varied source music materials generates historical, cultural, and social locators, which for some audience members will trigger memories of the early 1970s. But this is not pure anthropology, other audience members find themselves immersed in an honest 1970s atmosphere that avoids kitsch representation of the period. The sparse score employs a fascinating mixture of classical Western instruments, gamelan and Native American flute. Using only limited thematic material it succeeds in activating the imagination of the audience. Indeed, the soundtrack as a whole creates layers of signification that provide the audience with an opportunity to engage personally with the text. All too often contemporary films and film soundtracks suffocate themselves in their own completeness; there is not enough space for contemplation. The accomplishment of *The Ice Storm* is its concentration on ambiguity as a central articulating device rather than succumbing to the causal aesthetics of mainstream storytelling. It is undoubtedly true that the collaborative processes employed by the creative team were fundamental in shaping this understated yet multifaceted work. However, there is one further collaborative process that is central to *The Ice Storm*, the collaboration of the audience with the film. It is clear that this collaborative aspect was a principle motivating factor in the decisions made by the production team. It is fitting, then, that the final words belong to the composer himself, because as Danna explains, film is

> a collaboration between the film and the person who is watching the film. You need their processing. It is not a film until it is being processed in somebody's brain. Part of the art is to leave something up to the person. Those discoveries are what give you a thrill.[63]

Notes

Chapter 1

1. Mychael Danna in Doug Adams, "Man of a Thousand Phrases," *Film Score Monthly*, Vol. 3, No. 1 (January 1998), 35.
2. Mychael Danna, e-mail to author, January 6th 2003.
3. Mychael Danna, interviewed by author, July 27th 2002.
4. Danna, interviewed by author, July 27th 2002.
5. Danna, e-mail to author, January 6th 2003.
6. Handel: *Water Music/Music for the Royal Fireworks*, RCA Victor Symphony Orchestra, 9026 61207 (1959); *9 Symphonien*, Berlin Philharmonic Orchestra, Gundula Janowitz soprano, Hilde Rössel-Majdan mezzo-soprano, Waldemar Kmentt tenor, Walter Berry bass, Deutsche Grammophon Five Disc set, 429 036–2 (1961–62).
7. Danna, interviewed by author, July 27th 2002.
8. Danna, interviewed by author, July 27th 2002.
9. Danna, interviewed by author, July 27th 2002.
10. All pieces are published by Frederick Harris Music Co. Ltd., Oakville, Ontario, Canada.
11. Danna, e-mail to author, January 6th 2003.
12. Danna, interviewed by author, July 27th 2002.
13. The Mellotron was an electronic organ built by Harry Chamberlain that allowed multitrack recording and limited "sampling." It became popularized by The Kinks, The Rolling Stones, and The Beatles' song "Strawberry Fields Forever" (1967).
14. Danna, interviewed by author, July 27th 2002. Progressive rock is music that follows traditional rock music instrumentation for the most part, yet also stretches the confines of the traditional pop or rock song. It is frequently influenced by a variety of non-rock musical styles and is usually complex, dynamic, and multi-dimensional, as exemplified by bands such as Pink Floyd or Emerson, Lake and Palmer.
15. Mychael Danna, interviewed by author, April 25th 2003.
16. Danna, interviewed by author, April 25th 2003.
17. Danna, interviewed by author, April 25th 2003.
18. CD liner notes, Danna and Clément, *A Gradual Awakening*, SL0010 (1984). Danna and Clément, *Summerland*, CHACD030 (1985).
19. Liner notes from the initial American release of Brian Eno's *Ambient 1/Music for Airports*, PVC 7908–AMB 001 (1978).

20. Tim Clément, interviewed by Linda Kohanov, CD liner notes. Danna and Clément, *North of Niagara*, HS11049–2 (1995).

21. Danna, interviewed by author, July 27th 2002.

22. Danna, interviewed by author, July 27th 2002. A *bîn* is a double clarinet of India and Pakistan consisting of two single-reed parallel pipes inserted into a gourd; one pipe serves as a drone, the other as a chanter. It is played by snake-charmers throughout Pakistan and India.

23. Elliot L. Tepper, "Immigration Policy and Multiculturalism," in *Ethnicity and Culture in Canada: The Research Landscape*, ed. J. W. Berry and J. A. Laponce (Toronto: University of Toronto Press, 1994), 102.

24. Danna, interviewed by author, July 27th 2002.

25. For a detailed survey of minimalism and its cultural context see Keith Potter, *Four Musical Minimalists* (Cambridge: Cambridge University Press, 2000).

26. Danna, interviewed by author, July 27th 2002.

27. Danna, interviewed by author, July 27th 2002.

28. Danna, interviewed by author, July 27th 2002.

29. Walter Buczynski, e-mail to author, March 31st 2003.

30. Buczynski, e-mail to author, March 31st 2003.

31. Danna, interviewed by author, July 27th 2002.

32. Mychael Danna, "An Interview with Mychael Danna," September 14th 2004. http://www.soniccontrol.com/university/article.php?category=filmtv&ID=35 (accessed June 6th 2006).

33. Buczynski, e-mail to author, March 31st 2003.

34. Danna, interviewed by author, July 27th 2002.

35. Danna, interviewed by author, July 27th 2002.

36. Danna, interviewed by author, July 27th 2002.

37. Atom Egoyan, interviewed by author, March 5th 2003.

38. Egoyan, interviewed by author, March 5th 2003.

39. Egoyan, interviewed by author, March 5th 2003.

40. Egoyan, interviewed by author, March 5th 2003.

41. Danna, "An Interview with Mychael Danna," www.soniccontrol.com

42. Danna, "An Interview with Mychael Danna," www.soniccontrol.com

43. Danna, interviewed by author, July 27th 2002.

44. Chacra Alternative Music, NM010 (1987) and NM011 (1988).

45. Mira Nair, interviewed by author, April 29th 2003.

46. Nair, interviewed by author, April 29th 2003. *Umrao Jaan*, directed by Muzaffar Ali (1981).

47. Danna, interviewed by author, April 25th 2003.

48. A *rag* or *raga* is a fundamental scalic building block of all Indian music.

49. For more information about Danna's working relationship with Mira Nair see John Kenneth Muir, *Mercy in Her Eyes: The Films of Mira Nair* (New York: Applause Theatre and Cinema Books, 2006).

50. Bruno Nettl, *The Study of Ethnomusicology: Thirty-one Issues and Concepts* (Urbana and Chicago: University of Illinois Press, 1983/2005), 30.

51. During the 1960s the Brill Building exemplified the concept of vertical integration. A songwriter could make the publishers' rounds until someone had bought their music. On another floor an arrangement or a lead sheet could be created, copies could be made in the duplication office, or musicians who were frequently "hanging

around" could be hired to record a demo in one of the many studios. Then the song could be presented to recording companies, artists' managers or radio promoters, as all were located within one edifice. For more information see Ken Emerson, *Always Magic in the Air: The Bomp and Brilliance of the Brill Building Era* (London: Viking, 2005).

52. Danna, interviewed by author, July 27th 2002.
53. Alex Steyermark, interviewed by author, April 10th 2003.
54. Danna in Adams, "Man of a Thousand Phrases," 37.
55. Danna, interviewed by author, July 27th 2002.
56. Danna in Adams, "Man of a Thousand Phrases," 37.
57. Vera John-Steiner, *Creative Collaboration* (Oxford: Oxford University Press, 2000), 5.
58. The *ney* (pronounced as in *Neigh*bor) is an ancient Middle Eastern end-blown flute played in slightly varying forms from Morocco to Pakistan.
59. Danna, interviewed by author, April 25th 2003.
60. Mychael Danna in Randall D. Larson, "The Film Music of Mychael Danna," *Soundtrack*, Vol. 21, No. 83 (Fall 2002), 32.
61. Danna, interviewed by the author, April 25th 2003.
62. Danna in Larson, "The Film Music of Mychael Danna," 33.
63. Mychael Danna, interviewed by Paul Tonks, Toronto International Film Festival, September 10th 2002.
64. Justin Wyatt, *High Concept, Movies and Marketing in Hollywood* (Austin: University of Texas Press, 1994).
65. Tino Balio, "A Major Presence in All of the World's Important Markets: The Globalization of Hollywood in the 1990s," in *Contemporary Hollywood Cinema*, ed. Steve Neale and Murray Smith (London: Routledge, 1998), 59.
66. Richard Maltby, "'Nobody knows everything': Post-classical Historiographies and Consolidated Entertainment," in *Contemporary Hollywood Cinema*, ed. Steve Neale and Murray Smith, (London: Routledge, 1998), 37.
67. Wyatt, *High Concept*, 60.
68. Mychael Danna, e-mail to author, April 5th 2003.
69. Maltby, "Nobody knows everything," 36.
70. Mychael and Jeff Danna have co-composed music for a number of projects from the late 1980s onwards. These include Victor Sarin's disturbing psychological thriller *Cold Comfort* (1989) and Timothy Linh Bui's *Green Dragon* (2002). CD projects include *A Celtic Tale: The Legend of Deirdre*, Hearts O'Space 1106–2 (1996), and *A Celtic Romance: The Legend of Liadain and Curithir*, Hearts O'Space 11084–2 (1997). Space does not permit a detailed study of this work.
71. Danna in Larson, "The Film Music of Mychael Danna," 35.

Chapter 2

1. Mychael Danna in Doug Adams, "Man of a Thousand Phrases," *Film Score Monthly*, Vol. 3, No. 1 (January 1998), 40.
2. Jonathan Kramer, "The Nature and Origins of Musical Postmodernism," in *Postmodern Music/Postmodern Thought*, ed. Judy Lochhead and Joseph Auner (New York and London: Routledge, 2002), 14; Jean-François Lyotard, *The Postmodern*

Condition: A Report on Knowledge, trans. Geoff Bennington and Brian Massumi (Minneapolis: University of Minnesota Press, 1984); Umberto Eco, *Postcript to the Name of the Rose*, trans. William Weaver (San Diego: Harcourt Brace Jovanovich, 1984).

3. Mychael Danna in Randall D. Larson, "The Film Music of Mychael Danna," *Soundtrack*, Vol. 21, No. 83 (Fall 2002), 33.

4. Danna in Adams, "Man of a Thousand Phrases," 35.

5. Walter Murch, "Sound-Design: The Dancing Shadow," in *Projections 4: Film-makers on Film-making* (London: Faber and Faber, 1995), 247.

6. Mychael Danna, e-mail to author, 16th June 2006.

7. The library music in the film was provided by Chris Stone Audio, a Toronto based library music production company and consultancy. Of Italian descent, Annunzio Paolo Mantovani (1905–1980) moved to England with his family in 1912. His orchestra was a cornerstone of easy listening music for over thirty years. After the Second World War, he abandoned live performance and focused on recording. Spending hours in the studio developing microphone placement and other recording techniques he formulated a distinctive, lush, cascading string sound.

8. A study of the use of reverberation and other audio processing techniques in film music has yet to emerge, but its importance in the articulation of narrative in *Felicia's Journey* suggests that an appropriate methodology is sorely needed in the development of film music studies. Danna's sequencer files, for example, show how he uses a Lexicon LXP-5 audio effects processor controlled from within his sequencer environment to generate reverberation, pitch shift, and delay effects.

9. Atom Egoyan, interviewed by author, March 5th 2003.

10. In Gaelic the last two lines of text are: *Monaur gan sinn 'ár bpósadh/ Nó'r bórd luinge 'triall 'un siubhail.*

11. See Michel Chion, *The Voice in Cinema* (New York: Columbia University Press, 1999), 23–37; and *Audio-Vision: Sound on Screen* (New York: Columbia University Press, 1994), 129–131.

12. Chion, *The Voice in Cinema*, 21.

13. In *Sunset Boulevard* (Wilder, 1950) the acousmatic voice, in this case the central narrator, also speaks from beyond the grave.

14. Egoyan, interviewed by author, March 5th 2003.

15. Chion, *The Voice in Cinema*, 23–37.

16. Egoyan, interviewed by author, March 5th 2003.

17. In response to the demise of the tonal system of composition, musicians in the early twentieth century looked for new approaches to composing that would restore a sense of coherence to music. One such approach was devised by Arnold Schoenberg, who formulated what is now known as serial composition or the "twelve-tone" system. It is a system where complete equality of all twelve chromatic pitches is achieved.

18. Jonathan Romney points out that this shot is modeled on Hitchcock's *Suspicion* (1941). Jonathan Romney, *Atom Egoyan* (London: British Film Institute, 2003), 151.

19. Andrew Lockington, interviewed by author, May 21st 2003. Lockington was Danna's assistant between 1997–2002.

20. Egoyan, interviewed by author, March 5th 2003.

21. See Gwendolyn Audrey Foster, *Women Filmmakers of the African and Asian Disapora: Decolonizing the Gaze, Locating Subjectivity* (Carbondale and Edwardsville: Southern Illinois University Press, 1997), 111–127.

22. Mira Nair, interviewed by author, April 29th 2003.

23. Ellen Cheshire, *Ang Lee* (Harpenden: Pocket Essentials, 2001), 16.

24. Ang Lee in Chris Berry, "Taiwanese Melodrama Returns with a Twist in *The Wedding Banquet*," *Cinemaya*, Issue 21 (Fall 1993), 54; see also Wei Ming Dariotis and Eileen Fung, "Breaking the Soy Sauce Jar: Diaspora and Displacement in the Films of Ang Lee," in *Transnational Chinese Cinemas: Identity, Nationhood, Gender*, ed. Sheldon Hsia-Peng Lu (Honolulu: University of Hawaii Press, 1997): 187–220.

25. Georgina Born and David Hesmondhalgh, eds., *Western Music and Its Others: Difference, Representation and Appropriation in Music* (Berkeley: University of California Press, 2000), 41.

26. Geoff Pevere, "No Place Like Home: The Films of Atom Egoyan," in *Exotica* (Toronto: Coach House Press, 1995), 26.

27. Egoyan, interviewed by author, March 5th 2003.

28. Mychael Danna, interviewed by author, April 25th 2003.

29. Danna, interviewed by author, April 25th 2003.

30. Danna in Adams, "Man of a Thousand Phrases," 35.

31. Edward Said, *Orientalism* (London and Henley: Routledge and Kegan Paul, 1978); see also, Bill Ashcroft, Gareth Griffiths, and Helen Tiffin, eds., *The Empire Writes Back: Theory and Practice in Postcolonial Literatures* (London and New York: Routledge, 1989); Bryan S. Turner, *Orientalism, Postmodernism and Globalism* (London and New York: Routledge, 1994).

32. Steven Feld, "The Poetics and Politics of Pygmy Pop," in Georgina Born and David Hesmondhalgh, eds., *Western Music and Its Others: Difference, Representation and Appropriation in Music* (Berkeley: University of California Press, 2000), 274.

33. John Hutnyk, *Critique of Exotica: Music, Politics and the Culture Industry* (London and Sterling Virginia: Pluto Press, 2000), 6.

34. Hutnyk, *Critique of Exotica*, 6.

35. Simon Frith, "The Discourse of World Music," in Georgina Born and David Hesmondhalgh, eds., *Western Music and Its Others: Difference, Representation and Appropriation in Music* (Berkeley: University of California Press, 2000), 311; see also Eric Hobsbawm and Terence Ranger, eds., *The Invention of Tradition* (Cambridge: Cambridge University Press, 1983).

36. British rule in India was from 1776–1947.

37. The song was written by Ravi Sharma. *Aadmi Sadak Ka* was the last film that the director Devendra Goel made before he died in 1978.

38. For more information see Gregory D. Booth, "Traditional Practice and Mass Mediated Music in India," *International Review of the Aesthetics and Sociology of Music*, Vol. 24, No. 2 (December 1993): 159–174.

39. Nair, interviewed by author, April 29th 2003. Nino Rota is an Italian composer, most famous for his scores for Fellini films.

40. Nair, interviewed by author, April 29th 2003.

41. When Danna was asked to score *Monsoon Wedding* he was in the process of organizing his own Hindu marriage ceremony. In a curious case of life imitating art, he married Aparna Bhargava in the summer of 2001. Danna explains that it was "with a strange sense of familiarity that I beheld my own wedding that summer, though there wasn't a cloud in the sky." Liner notes, *Monsoon Wedding*, CD 74321 89824–2 (2001).

42. Danna, interviewed by author, April 25th 2003.

43. The Church of Saint Gayane, Etchmiadzin, is located near Armenia's capital city, Yerevan.

44. Mychael Danna, "Atom Egoyan and Mychael Danna Lecture/Presentation," January 13th 2003. NUMUS Inc. and Wilfrid Laurier University, Waterloo, Ontario, Canada.

45. Danna, "Lecture/Presentation," January 13th 2003.

46. Mychael Danna, interviewed by Paul Tonks, Toronto International Film Festival, September 10th 2002.

47. Danna, "Lecture/Presentation," January 13th 2003.

48. Claudia Gorbman, "Scoring the Indian: Music in the Liberal Western," in Georgina Born and David Hesmondhalgh, eds., *Western Music and Its Others: Difference, Representation and Appropriation in Music* (Berkeley: University of California Press, 2000), 250.

49. Jonathan Bellman, ed., *The Exotic in Western Music* (Boston: Northeastern University Press, 1998), xii.

50. Nair, interviewed by author, April 29th 2003.

51. Egoyan, interviewed by author, March 5th 2003.

52. Russell Lack, *Twenty-four Frames Under: A Buried History of Film Music* (London: Quartet Books, 1997), 169.

53. Miguel Mera, "Representing the Baroque: The Portrayal of Historical Period in Film Music," *The Consort: Journal of the Dolmetsch Foundation*, Vol. 57 (2001): 3–21.

54. Coined by film critic B. Ruby Rich writing in the *Village Voice*, New Queer Cinema refers to the appearance of films dealing openly and sometimes aggressively with queer culture, politics, and identity on the independent film circuit in the early nineties. For more information see Michele Aaron, ed., *New Queer Cinema: A Critical Reader* (Edinburgh: Edinburgh University Press, 2004).

55. The choir used was The Hilliard Ensemble.

56. In Renaissance music the *cantus firmus* was any type of antecedent melody used as a basis for a later polyphonic composition.

57. Royal S. Brown, *Overtones and Undertones: Reading Film Music* (Berkeley: University of California Press, 1994), 43.

58. Danna, interviewed by author, April 25th 2003.

59. *Musica ficta* is the term used to describe notes that lie outside the diatonic framework of medieval plainchant. There are many theoretical treatises defining which accidentals are acceptable and under which circumstances.

60. Danna, interviewed by author, April 25th 2003.

61. Danna in Adams, "Man of a Thousand Phrases," 35.

62. Atom Egoyan, in *Formulas for Seduction: The Cinema of Atom Egoyan*, directed by Eileen Anipare and Jason Wood, Black and White Productions, 1999. The stories collected by Jacob and Wilhelm Grimm in the early 1800s were attempts to preserve Germanic folktales. The frequently dark, cruel, and moralistic stories have remained consistently popular with children and adults alike.

63. Robert Browning, *The Pied Piper of Hamelin*, illustrations by Kate Greenaway (London and New York: Frederick Warne, 1888).

64. Danna in Adams, "Man of a Thousand Phrases," 37.

65. *Organum* is a type of Medieval polyphony that consisted of parallel movement of instrumental voices over a drone.

66. For more information about branding see: David A. Aaker and Erich Joachimsthaler, *Brand Leadership* (New York: Free Press, 2000); Bernd H. Schmitt and

Alex Simonson, *Marketing Aesthetics. The Strategic Mmanagement of Brands, Identity, and Image* (New York: Free Press, 1997).

67. The Dalai Lama is effectively Tibet's Head of State in exile, but he is also a spiritual leader. When the Dalai Lama dies, Buddhists believe that he will be reborn within another mortal body. In 1937, after a vigorous search a two-year-old boy, Tenzin Gyatso, was named as the fourteenth Dalai Lama. In 1950 Communist China attacked Tibet and the Dalai Lama fled to India in 1959. China replaced the Tibetan government with an autonomous region of the Chinese Democratic Republic. In 1967 the Red Guards destroyed thousands of holy sites, thus weakening the backbone of Tibetan civilization. Over the decades the Dalai Lama has been a firm advocate of nonviolence and has continued to seek genuine autonomy for his homeland, a land that China considers to be an integral part of its territory. In 1989 he received the Nobel Prize for peace. The Chinese believe Communism liberated the Tibetans from a feudal theocracy and that Tibet has developed considerably under their rule. Others have claimed human rights abuses, as well as cultural and ecological destruction.

68. Ang Lee, director's commentary, *The Hire*, BMW Films, 2001.

69. Temp tracks are preexistent recordings used during postproduction in order to help focus the ideas of the production team and the composer.

70. James M. Welsh, "Action Films: The Serious, the Ironic, the Postmodern," in *Film Genre 2000: New Critical Essays*, Wheeler Winston Dixon, ed. (Albany: State University of New York Press, 2000), 169.

71. The term "dick flick," increasingly used by film scholars, was coined in response to and as the antithesis of the term "chick flick," which characterized certain types of movies that appealed particularly to women.

72. Lee, *The Hire*.

73. Mychael Danna in Doug Adams, "Danna in Demand," *Film Score Monthly*, Vol. 6, No. 9 (October/November, 2001), 16.

74. Danna in Adams, "Danna in Demand," 16.

75. As revealed by the score in Danna's sequencer file.

76. Jeanne Lamon, e-mail to author, May 24th 2003.

77. The song "One More Color" is taken from Jane Siberry's album *The Speckless Sky*, Duke Street Records, DSMD 31019 (1985); "Courage" is taken from The Tragically Hip album *Fully Completely*, MCA, MCLD19314 (1992).

78. Danna plays the harmonium in the Sam Dent Band.

79. Allan F. Moore, *Rock: The Primary Text* (Aldershot: Ashgate, 2001), 52.

80. Moore, *Rock: The Primary Text*, 53.

81. It is also clearly evident in the music of Thomas Newman and James Newton Howard for example.

82. Standard contemporary concert tuning for the A above middle C is A = 440hz. However, the historically informed performance movement has settled into a situation where three pitch levels are generally used: A = 392hz for French Baroque, A = 415hz for German Baroque, and A= 430hz for Classical works.

Chapter 3

1. Ang Lee in Oren Moverman, "The Angle on Ang Lee," *Inter/view* (September 1997), 68.
2. Peter Matthews, "The Big Freeze," *Sight and Sound* (February 1998), 12.
3. Robert Sklar, "The Ice Storm," *Cineaste*, Vol. XXIII, No. 2 (1997), 42.
4. Lizzie Francke, "The Ice Storm," *Sight and Sound* (February 1998), 42.
5. http://www.genesiskel.com/screening_room/thumbs_up2.htm (6th June 2006).
6. Ellen Cheshire, *Ang Lee* (Harpenden: Pocket Essentials, 2001), 63. It is interesting to note that there are many similarities between the scores for *The Ice Storm* and *American Beauty* (1999). Thomas Newman's score for *American Beauty* won him worldwide recognition and critical acclaim, yet in terms of style and function its precedent is *The Ice Storm*.
7. David Thomson, "Riding with Ang Lee," *Film Comment*, Vol. 35, No. 6 (November/December, 1999), 9.
8. Ang Lee, in *The South Bank Show*, directed by Daniel Wilde, first broadcast, ITV 1, UK, July 13th (2003).
9. WASP = White Anglo-Saxon Protestant.
10. Matthews, "The Big Freeze," 12.
11. James Schamus, *The Ice Storm: The Shooting Script* (London: Nick Hern, 1997), xiii.
12. Janet Wasko, *Hollywood in the Information Age: Beyond the Silver Screen* (Cambridge: Polity Press, 1994), 41.
13. Good Machine was a staunch supporter of independent filmmaking and filmmakers, and had a particularly important role in nurturing young talent. For example, from the early to mid nineties, Good Machine worked with Tod Haynes on *Poison* (1991), Edward Burns on *The Brothers McMullen* (1995), Nicole Holofcener on *Walking and Talking* (1996), and Tod Solondz on *Happiness* (1998), among many other projects. Focus Features was formed from the 2002 divisional merger of USA Films and Good Machine.
14. Emanuel Levy, *Cinema of Outsiders: The Rise of American Independent Film* (New York: New York University Press, 1999), 1–9.
15. Levy, *Cinema of Outsiders*, 501.
16. James Schamus in Todd Lippy, "James Schamus and Ted Hope," in *Projections 11: New York Film-makers on Film-making*, ed. Todd Lippy (London: Faber and Faber, 2000), 8.
17. Ang Lee in Mary Hardesty, "Ang Lee on Directing in an Ice Storm," *Directors Guild of America Magazine*, Vol. 22, No. 4 (1997), 51.
18. Matthews, "The Big Freeze," 12.
19. Matthews, "The Big Freeze," 12.
20. Ang Lee in I. Blair, "The Ice Storm," in *Film and Video* (October 1997), 48.
21. James Schamus, interviewed by author, January 5th 2006.
22. Schamus, *The Ice Storm: The Shooting Script*, ix–xiii, 145–149.
23. Schamus, *The Ice Storm: The Shooting Script*, ix.
24. Schamus, *The Ice Storm: The Shooting Script*, x.
25. Schamus, *The Ice Storm: The Shooting Script*, 148.
26. Matthews, "The Big Freeze," 12.

27. Ang Lee in James Schamus, *The Ice Storm: The Shooting Script*, viii.
28. Rick Moody, *The Ice Storm* (London: Abacus, 1994), 132.
29. Schamus, *The Ice Storm: The Shooting Script*, x.
30. Janet Maslin, "Suburbanites Pure as Driven Slush," *New York Times*, September 26th (1997), 14.
31. Matthews, "The Big Freeze," 13.
32. Thomas S. Hibbs, *Shows About Nothing: Nihilism in Popular Culture from the Exorcist to Seinfeld* (Dallas: Space Publishing, 1999), 126.
33. Friedrich Nietzsche, *The Gay Science*, trans W. Kaufmann (New York: Vintage Books, 1882/1974), section 134: 108.
34. For example, Helmut Thielicke, *Nihilism: Its Origin and Nature, with a Christian Answer*, trans. J. W. Doberstein (New York: Schocken, 1970).
35. For example, Jean-Paul Sartre, *Being and Nothingness: An Essay on Phenomenological Ontology* (London: Routledge, 1957/2003).
36. Karen L. Carr, *The Banalization of Nihilism* (Albany: State University of New York Press, 1992), 18.
37. Hibbs, *Shows About Nothing*, 126.
38. Hibbs, *Shows About Nothing*, 125.
39. Ian H. Smith, "Ang Lee," in *Fifty Contemporary Filmmakers*, ed. Yvonne Tasker (London and New York: Routledge, 2002), 230–231.
40. Hibbs, *Shows About Nothing*, 128.
41. The filmmakers clearly provide the audience with clues about the film's existential nihilist themes, as Dostoevsky is consistently acknowledged by scholars as one of the foremost writers in the existential nihilist school. See for example: Constantin V. Ponomareff, *On the Dark Side of Russian Literature 1709–1910* (New York: Peter Lang, 1987).
42. Hibbs, *Shows About Nothing*, 128.
43. James Schamus in *The South Bank Show*, directed by Daniel Wilde, first broadcast, ITV 1, UK, July 13th (2003).
44. Hibbs, *Shows About Nothing*, 126.
45. Lee in Moverman, "The Angle on Ang Lee," 65.
46. James Christopher, "Forbidden Love, Hidden Romance," *The Times*, The Knowledge supplement, December 17th (2005), 10.
47. Sheng-Mei Ma, "Ang Lee's Domestic Tragicomedy: Immigrant Nostalgia, Exotic/Ethnic Tour, Global Market," in *Journal of Popular Culture*, Vol. 30, No.1 (1996), 193.
48. Lee in Moverman, "The Angle on Ang Lee," 65, 68.
49. Ang Lee was a student at a high school in which his father was headmaster. The expectations of the young Lee were, consequently, augmented. He was also a very quiet, dreamy child and it was only when he discovered acting that he grew in confidence. Lee's father finally accepted his son's chosen profession after *Eat Drink Man Woman* (1994) received international praise.
50. Lee, *South Bank Show*.
51. Lee, *South Bank Show*.
52. See Francis Jennings, *The Invasion of America: Indians, Colonialism, and the Cant of Conquest* (Chapel Hill: University of North Carolina Press for the Institute of Early American Thought, 1976); Robert F. Berkhofer Jr., *The White Man's Indian: Images of the American Indian from Columbus to the Present* (New York: Vintage

Books, 1978); James W. Loewen, *Lies My Teacher Told Me: Everything Your American History Textbook Got Wrong* (New York: New Press, 1995).

53. Margaret Mead, *Coming of Age in Samoa: A Psychological Study of Primitive Youth for Western Civilisation* (New York: Harper Perennial, 1928/2001).

54. James Schamus in *The South Bank Show*, directed by Daniel Wilde, first broadcast, ITV 1, UK, July 13th (2003).

55. Cheshire, *Ang Lee*, 57–58.

56. Schamus, *South Bank Show*.

57. Ang Lee in Brooke Comer, "Eat Drink Man Woman: A Feast for the Eyes," *American Cinematographer*, Vol. 76, No. 1 (1995), 62.

58. Cheshire, *Ang Lee*, 58. For more information about the Watergate scandal, see Stanley I. Kuter, *Wars of Watergate: The Last Crisis of Richard Nixon* (New York: W. W. Norton, 1992).

59. Cheshire, *Ang Lee*, 58.

60. Matthews, "The Big Freeze," 14.

61. Hibbs, *Shows About Nothing*, 128.

62. Hibbs, *Shows About Nothing*, 128.

63. Lee in Moverman, "The Angle on Ang Lee," 65.

64. Lee in Moverman, "The Angle on Ang Lee," 65.

65. Wei-Ming Tu, *Confucian Thought: Selfhood as Creative Transformation* (Albany: State University of New York Press, 1985), 35–50.

66. Frederick W. Mote, *Intellectual Foundations of China* (New York: Alfred A. Knopf, 1971), 19.

67. During shooting of *The Hulk*, Ang Lee would retreat to a miniature rock garden, of his own construction, as a means of calming and focusing his mind on the challenges that remained ahead. The importance of the physical, material sensation of the rocks and their organic connection to man is tied into a fundamental Confucian understanding of the world.

68. Lee in Moverman, "The Angle on Ang Lee," 65.

69. Smith, "Ang Lee," *Fifty Contemporary Filmmakers*, 231.

70. Noël Carroll, *Beyond Aesthetics: Philosophical Essays* (Cambridge: Cambridge University Press, 2001), 128.

71. Tu, *Confucian Thought*, 40.

72. Lee in Schamus, *The Ice Storm*, vii.

73. Sklar, "The Ice Storm," 41.

74. Matthews, "The Big Freeze," 14.

75. Ang Lee in David E. Williams, "Reflections on an Era," *American Cinematographer*, Vol. 78, No. 10 (1997), 57.

76. James Schamus in David E. Williams, "Reflections on an Era," *American Cinematographer*, Vol. 78, No. 10 (1997), 64.

77. Frederick Elmes in David E. Williams, "Reflections on an Era," *American Cinematographer*, Vol. 78, No. 10 (1997), 64.

78. Elmes in Williams, "Reflections on an Era," 57.

79. Cheshire, *Ang Lee*, 61.

80. Lee in Williams, "Reflections on an Era," 57.

81. Elmes in Williams, "Reflections on an Era," 62.

82. Ang Lee in Mary Hardesty, "Ang Lee on Directing in an Ice Storm," *Directors Guild of America Magazine*, Vol. 22, No. 4 (1997), 51.

83. Francke, "The Ice Storm," 14.
84. Matthews, "The Big Freeze," 14.
85. Matthews, "The Big Freeze," 14.
86. Matthews, "The Big Freeze," 14.
87. Sklar, "The Ice Storm," 42.
88. Lee in Williams, "Reflections on an Era," 57.

Chapter 4

1. Noël Carroll, *Beyond Aesthetics: Philosophical Essays* (Cambridge: Cambridge University Press, 2001), 180.
2. William K. Wimsatt and Monroe C. Beardsley, "The Intentional Fallacy," in *The Verbal Icon: Studies in the Meaning of Poetry* (Lexington: University of Kentucky Press, 1954), 3–18. For more information on the intention versus interpretation debate see Monroe C. Beardsley, *Aesthetics* (New York: Harcourt, Brace and World, 1958); Roland Barthes, "The Death of the Author," in *Image-Music-Text* (London: Fontana Press, 1977), 142–148; Gary Iseminger, ed. *Intention and Interpretation* (Philadelphia: Temple University Press, 1992); Michel Foucault, "What Is an Author?" in Paul Rabinow, ed., *The Foucault Reader* (New York: Pantheon, 1984), 101–120.
3. David Hesmondhalgh, "International Times: Fusions, Exoticism, and Antiracism in Electronic Dance Music," in *Western Music and Its Others: Difference, Representation and Appropriation in Music*, Georgina Born and David Hesmondhalgh, eds. (Berkeley: University of California Press, 2000), 281.
4. Carroll, *Beyond Aesthetics*, 159.
5. In the field of electronic music a sequencer was originally any device that recorded and played back a sequence of control information for an electronic musical instrument. In the 1980s and 1990s the term referred almost exclusively to computer software for recording, playing back, and editing MIDI and audio. Since the late nineties and early noughties the term Digital Audio Workstation (DAW) has been preferred. Popular examples include Logic, Cubase, Performer, and Reason.
6. For an excellent case study discussion of the strengths and weaknesses in examining composer's sketches see Barry Cooper, *Beethoven and the Creative Process* (Oxford: Clarendon Press, 1990).
7. *Auteur* theory is a way of reading and appraising films which was originally advocated by François Truffaut in 1954, and is frequently associated with the *nouvelle vague* and critics who wrote for *Cahiers du cinéma*. It is perhaps less a theory than a critical method. In essence, it champions the idea that a film, or a body of work, by a director reflects their personal artistic vision and preoccupations, as if they were the work's "author." See John Caughie, *Theories of Authorship: A Reader* (London: Routledge, 1981).
8. A click-track is a type of metronome beat that allows musicians to synchronize accurately to the film. In an orchestral recording session it is common for all of the players and the conductor to receive the click-track through headphones while recording.
9. Mychael Danna, interviewed by author, July 27th 2002.
10. Faxes from Ross Katz and Anthony Bregman at Good Machine to Mychael Danna, September 24th 1996.

11. Ang Lee in Mary Hardesty, "Ang Lee on Directing in an Ice Storm," *Directors Guild of America Magazine*, Vol. 22, No. 4 (1997), 49.

12. Tim Squyres, interviewed by author, February 17th 2006.

13. Danna, interviewed by author, July 27th 2002.

14. Danna, interviewed by author, July 27th 2002.

15. Danna, interviewed by author, July 27th 2002.

16. One sequencer file has been excluded from this analysis, as it is not directly relevant to the development of the score. This is labeled Fox OscarContender CD and was created on December 4th 1996 at 15:12 and modified on the same day at 19:55. It is a medley of audio tracks for submission and consideration for the 1997 Academy Awards.

17. Within Danna's *Ice Storm* materials (e.g., notes, memos, etc.) there are numerous printed versions of the shooting script, including some with his own annotations.

18. Films tend to be constructed in 15–20 minute segments, called reels.

19. For the purposes of royalty collection all music used within a film is registered with a royalty collection agency such as ASCAP (in the USA) or the PRS/MCPS (in the UK). The cue sheet submitted to these collection agencies provides the most accurate account of all the music that is used within a particular film.

20. Danna also composes some cues which appear to be completely isolated; despite the fact that they were written for specific sequences they did not lead to a causal development of material. This is particularly evident in three cues which only appear in VERSION 6 and VERSION 8. By the tenth version of the edit, these pieces were replaced by preexistent tracks.

21. Alex Steyermark, interviewed by author, April 10th 2003; James Schamus, interviewed by author, January 5th 2006.

22. The Yamaha TX-7 was the rack-mounted version of the DX-7 that was first released in 1983. It remains one of the most influential digital synthesizers in the history of music technology. It used a revolutionary system of FM synthesis which gives it its distinctive sound quality. Briefly, FM (Frequency Modulation) synthesis is where the output of one oscillator (modulator) is used to modulate the frequency of another oscillator (carrier). These oscillators are called operators. For more information see Martin Russ, *Sound Synthesis and Sampling* (Oxford: Focal Press, 2004).

23. Flanging is created by mixing a signal with a slightly delayed copy of itself, where the length of the delay is constantly changing.

24. Danna, interviewed by author, July 27th 2002. Wendy Carlos, *Switched-on Bach*, CBS Masterworks, MK7194 (1968).

25. For more information on the Moog see Trevor J. Pinch and Frank Trocco, *Analog Days: The Invention and Impact of the Moog Synthesizer* (Cambridge: Harvard University Press, 2002).

26. Chick Corea's album *Light as a Feather*, Verve, CD 73145571152 (1973) and Miles Davis's *In a Silent Way*, Legacy, CD 69699865562 (1969) featured the Rhodes.

27. Steyermark, interviewed by author, April 10th 2003.

28. Lee in Steyermark, interviewed by author, April 10th 2003. It appears that discussions about possible approaches to the score took place between four main production personnel: Ang Lee (director), Tim Squyres (editor), Alex Steyermark (music supervisor), and Mychael Danna (composer).

29. Danna, interviewed by author, July 27th 2002.

30. Gamelan is a form of music originating in the islands of Indonesia in South East Asia. Gamelan music is played by an orchestra consisting primarily of metal-keyed percussion instruments (metallophones) and gongs, but also including hand or stick drums, flutes, and occasionally also bowed instruments and bamboo rattles. No two gamelan sets are the same. Most of the gamelan music heard in the West is either from Java or Sunda (West Java), or Bali. The styles of gamelan from Java and Bali are strikingly different. Javanese and Sundanese gamelan tends to be softer and quite hypnotic in nature. Balinese gamelan is often much louder, more flamboyant, and dramatic, but can also include quieter, contemplative pieces.

31. Ang Lee in David Handelman, "Cheat Drink Man Woman," *Premiere (USA)*, Vol. 2, No. 3 (November, 1997), 113.

32. Danna, interviewed by author, July 27th 2002.

33. Danna's recorded audio files reveal that a number of different instruments were played by Dan Cecil Hill, including elk antlers. The elk antlers can be heard briefly in the final cue 6M4 "Bowl."

34. Danna, interviewed by author, July 27th 2002.

35. In North Indian *Kathak* dance, the performers are often referred to as *nautch* girls. As part of their costume the performers commonly wear ankle bells and it seems that these are what Danna refers to as *nautch* bells. He will have learned about *Kathak* dance during the making of the film *Kama Sutra*.

36. Danna, interviewed by author, July 27th 2002.

37. Danna, interviewed by author, July 27th 2002.

38. Danna, interviewed by author, July 27th 2002. Mark Duggan from the Evergreen Club gamelan ensemble also recalls that Lee was "enchanted by the sound of the gamelan . . . and he even played some of the gamelan instruments with us." E-mail to author, September 13th 2005.

39. The Evergreen Club was Canada's first professional gamelan ensemble, formed in 1983 by composer Jon Siddall. It continues to commission and perform contemporary repertoire: http://www.evergreenclubgamelan.ca/ (August 20th 2005).

40. Mark Duggan, e-mail to author, September 13th 2005.

41. Traditionally the gamelan is learned aurally. A variety of musical notations have been introduced and experimented with since the end of the nineteenth century. In present-day Java, cipher notation is frequently used as a teaching and analytical device. The system includes information about pitch, rhythm, and the colotomic structure of the piece. The colotomic instruments, i.e., the gongs, *kempul, kenong, kethuk*, and *kempyang*, use a special notation from which one is expected to infer the actual part.

42. Duggan, e-mail to author, September 13th 2005.

43. One cent is one-hundreth of an equally tempered semitone.

44. Danna, interviewed by author, July 27th 2002. It is interesting to note that in subsequent projects, Danna has sampled the actual instruments of the Evergreen Club gamelan ensemble so that in terms of pitch he can accurately demonstrate how the music will actually sound before it is recorded live.

45. Kathryn Kalinak, *Settling the Score: Music and the Classical Hollywood Film* (Madison: University of Wisconsin Press, 1992), 192.

46. Kalinak, *Settling the Score*, 192.

47. Although we cannot be sure of the date, one of Danna's handwritten notes, hastily sketched during a screening, contains comments about the first few cues of the film, a melodic pattern in 5/4 time and the question "Temp too heavy?" One wonders if

this comment relates to the "Before Night Falls" cue and its use in the sequence when Ben walks home. Importantly, Danna's comment suggests an active engagement with the temp score rather than a rejection of it.

48. Steyermark, interviewed by author, April 10th 2003.

49. Steyermark, interviewed by author, April 10th 2003. I would argue that the existence of the temp track is symptomatic of working methods where the composer is employed in the final stages of postproduction. Some of the problems highlighted by composers in relation to the temp track could be eliminated if they were simply engaged at an earlier stage in the filmmaking process.

50. George Burt, *The Art of Film Music* (Boston: Northeastern University Press, 1994), 221.

51. Danna, interviewed by author, July 27th 2002.

52. One of the first modifications was the sharing of the solo clarinet melody (NYC ICE STORM MIDI FILES: From Ice Janey) between both oboe and clarinet (EARLY VERSIONS: From Janey NYC8/30). In terms of chronology, it is important to note that the cues that appear in the folder NYC ICE STORM MIDI FILES were actually composed before the equivalent cue in the EARLY VERSIONS folder, as is revealed by the metadata.

53. Steyermark, interviewed by author, April 10th 2003.

54. I do not wish to suggest that directors should employ musical terminology when speaking to composers. My own experience is that this can in fact be more detrimental and constraining than helpful. Nonetheless, the training of composers and directors needs to address more adequately the issue of communication so that appropriate language and collaborative methodologies can be developed.

55. A number of film composers are reputedly known as "hummers," a derogatory term for people who lack the skills and knowledge to create a score and require the help of many other assistants, composers, arrangers, and orchestrators to complete this aspect of their work.

56. Mychael Danna, interviewed by author, April 25th 2003.

57. Danna, interviewed by author, April 25th 2003.

58. Nicholas Dodd, e-mail to author, May 28th 2003.

59. Jamie Hopkings, e-mail to author, February 17th 2006.

60. Hopkings, e-mail to author, February 17th 2006.

61. Hopkings, e-mail to author, February 17th 2006.

62. Hopkings, e-mail to author, February 17th 2006.

63. Hopkings, e-mail to author, February 17th 2006.

64. Ang Lee in James Schamus, *The Ice Storm: The Shooting Script* (London: Nick Hern, 1997), vii.

65. It is worth noting, for example, that the character of the Hulk in *The Hulk* (2003) is performed by Lee himself using motion capture technology. The CGI monster takes on the director's physical movements.

66. Danna bought an instrument which had "little stones hanging from strings" and was in essence similar to a set of wind chimes. This was used as part of the texture in 1M1 "Opening." Mychael Danna, presentation at Royal College of Music, September 30th 2003.

67. Philip Stockton, interviewed by author, April 15th 2003.

68. Danna explains that his score for the film *Shattered Glass* (Ray, 2003) underwent drastic structural reorganization at the final mix, with many of his cues being

re-edited and moved to different locations. The finished result, from Danna's point of view, weakened the effectiveness of the score.

69. Stockton, interviewed by author, April 15th 2003.

70. Squyres, interviewed by author, February 17th 2006.

71. Mychael Danna, e-mail to author, January 10th 2006.

72. Danna, presentation at Royal College of Music, September 30th 2003.

Chapter 5

1. Mychael Danna, interviewed by author, July 27th 2002.

2. Danna, interviewed by author, July 27th 2002.

3. Philip Stockton, interviewed by author, April 15th 2003.

4. Rick Altman with McGraw Jones and Sonia Tatroe, "Inventing the Cinema Soundtrack: Hollywood's Multiplane Sound System," in *Music and Cinema*, James Buhler, Caryl Flinn, and David Neumeyer, eds. (Hanover and London: Wesleyan University Press, 2000), 339–359.

5. Timings and all analytical materials discussed in this chapter refer to NTSC/Region 1 DVD version of the film (Cat. 2001224). The mass-distribution of DVDs allows scholars to examine primary texts in detail; however, timings are not consistent across different regions and this can have an impact on analysis. For example, *The Ice Storm* lasts 113 minutes on a region 1 DVD, but is only 108 minutes long on a region 2/PAL DVD. There is a corresponding alteration of pitch which can be misleading in pitch/harmonic analyses.

6. Alex Steyermark, interviewed by author, April 10th 2003. David Bowie, "I Can't Read," *Tin Machine*, EMI: 5219100 (1989). One of the most important and influential concept albums of the 1970s was Bowie's *The Rise and Fall of Ziggy Stardust and the Spiders from Mars*, EMI: 5219000 (1972).

7. Pierre Bourdieu, *Distinction: A Social Critique of the Judgment of Taste* (London: Routledge and Kegan Paul, 1984), 18.

8. Anahid Kassabian, *Hearing Film; Tracking Identifications in Contemporary Hollywood Film Music* (London and New York: Routledge, 2001), 141–144.

9. Kassabian, *Hearing Film*, 79.

10. Tim Squyres, interviewed by author, January 17th 2006.

11. Stockton, interviewed by author, April 15th 2003.

12. For a discussion of the conflict between art and craft in sound design studies see Gianluca Sergi, "In Defence of Vulgarity: The Place of Sound Effects in the Cinema," in *Scope: An Online Journal of Film Studies*, Issue 5 (June 2006). http://www.scope.nottingham.ac.uk/article.php?issue=5&id=129 (June 6th 2006).

13. Walter Murch, "Dense Clarity—Clear Density," http://www.ps1.org/cut/volume/murch.html (January 9th 2006).

14. Murch, "Dense Clarity—Clear Density."

15. Murch, "Dense Clarity—Clear Density."

16. James Schamus, *The Ice Storm: The Shooting Script* (London: Nick Hern, 1997), 146.

17. Stockton, interviewed by author, April 15th 2003.

18. James Schamus, interviewed by author, January 5th 2006.

188 Notes

19. Squyres, interviewed by author, January 17th 2006.
20. Squyres, interviewed by author, January 17th 2006.
21. Steyermark, interviewed by author, April 10th 2003.
22. Frank Zappa, *Overnight Sensation*, Rykodisc, RCD 10518 (1973).
23. Frank Zappa, "On Junk Food for the Soul," *New Perspectives Quarterly*, Vol. 4, No. 4 (Winter 1998), 26.
24. Eric D. Nuzum, *Parental Advisory: Music Censorship in America* (London: HarperCollins, 2001), 145–147.
25. For more on Zappa see Ben Watson, *Frank Zappa: The Negative Dialectics of Poodle Play* (London: Quartet, 1994). It is an overblown work of obsession and idolization, but with a great deal of intelligence and critical insight. Alternatively, read Zappa's own words: Frank Zappa, *The Real Frank Zappa Book* (New York: Simon and Schuster, 1989). Among other things, Zappa devotes two chapters in this autobiography to the censorship debate.
26. Jim Croce, *I Got A Name*, ABC Records, ABCX/D–797 (1973). Croce died in a plane crash on September 20th 1973, and the album was released posthumously adding to its popularity.
27. Elton John, *Madman Across the Water*, Universal, 9824029 (1971).
28. Squyres, interviewed by author, January 17th 2006.
29. Traffic, *The Low Spark of the High Heeled Boys*, Island Records, 842779 (1971); Free, *Free Live!* Universal, 586228 (1971).
30. Squyres, interviewed by author, January 17th 2006.
31. Harry Nilsson, *Nilsson Schmilsson*, RCA, 57265 (1971).
32. Peter Matthews, "The Big Freeze," *Sight and Sound* (February 1998), 12.
33. Royal S. Brown, *Overtones and Undertones: Reading Film Music* (Berkeley: University of California Press, 1994), 239.
34. Mychael Danna, e-mail to author, March 22nd 2006.
35. Mychael Danna, presentation at Royal College of Music, September 30th 2003.
36. Danna, presentation, September 30th 2003.
37. Danna, presentation, September 30th 2003.
38. Schamus, interviewed by author, January 5th 2006.
39. Danna, presentation, September 30th 2003.
40. I have chosen not to use microtonal notation for musical examples featuring the Native American flute as in many cases it would be unnecessarily complicated.
41. Jennifer Lindsay, *Javanese Gamelan* (Kuala Lumpur: Oxford University Press, 1979), 39.
42. Neil Sorrell, *A Guide to the Gamelan* (London: Faber, 1990); Lindsay, *Javanese Gamelan* (1979); Max L. Harell, *The Music of the Gamelan Degung of West Java*, Ph.D. dissertation (Los Angeles: University of California, 1974); R. Anderson Sutton, *Traditions of Gamelan Music in Java: Musical Pluralism and Regional Identity* (Cambridge: Cambridge University Press, 1991); also see entries on "Sunda" and "An Introduction to Java" in *The Garland Encyclopedia of World Music*, Terry E. Miller and Sean Williams, eds., Vol. IV: Southeast Asia (New York and London: Routledge, 1998–2002).
43. Mychael Danna, e-mail to author, February 15th 2006.
44. Lindsay, *Javanese Gamelan*, 38.
45. Steve Reich, *Writings About Music* (London: Universal Edition, 1974), 40.

46. This combination of music and image employs the same kind of conceptual strategy as Godfrey Reggio's *Koyaanisqatsi* (1983), which uses a minimalist score by Philip Glass to support the notion of life out of balance.

47. Mychael Danna, e-mail to author, November 1st 2005.

48. Squyres, interviewed by author, January 17th 2006.

49. Schamus, interviewed by author, January 5th 2006.

50. Schamus, interviewed by author, January 5th 2006.

51. Michel Chion, *Audio-Vision: Sound on Screen* (New York: Columbia University Press, 1994), 115.

52. Chion, *Audio-Vision*, 116.

53. For a fascinating exploration of the subject see Milette Shamir and Jennifer Travis, eds., *Boys Don't Cry? Rethinking Narratives of Masculinity and Emotion in the U.S.* (New York: Columbia University Press, 2002).

54. Warren Farrell, *The Liberated Man Beyond Masculinity: Freeing Men and Their Relationships with Women* (New York: Random House, 1974), 71.

55. Stanley Aronowitz, "My Masculinty," in *Constructing Masculinity*, Maurice Berger, Brian Wallis, and Simon Watson, eds. (New York: Routledge, 1995), 320.

56. Tom Lutz, "Men's Tears and the Roles of Melodrama," in *Boys Don't Cry? Rethinking Narratives of Masculinity and Emotion in the U.S.*, Milette Shamir and Jennifer Travis, eds. (New York: Columbia University Press, 2002), 189.

57. Steyermark, interviewed by author, April 10th 2003.

58. Steyermark, interviewed by author, April 10th 2003.

59. This took place on Friday September 27th 1996 at the Broadway Screening Room in New York. Fax from Anthony Bregman, September 24th 1996.

60. Steyermark, interviewed by author, April 10th 2003.

61. It is worth noting that Steyermark truncated the song to fit the end credits. The version of the song that is heard on the soundtrack CD is longer and contains an extra verse and chorus.

62. James Schamus, e-mail to author, January 17th 2006.

63. Mychael Danna, interviewed by author, July 27th 2002.

Bibliography

Aaker, David A. and Erich Joachimsthaler. *Brand Leadership*. New York: Free Press, 2000.

Aaron, Michele, ed. *New Queer Cinema: A Critical Reader*. Edinburgh: Edinburgh University Press, 2004.

Adams, Doug. "Danna in Demand." *Film Score Monthly*, Vol. 6, No. 9 (October/November 2001): 14–17.

———. "Man of a Thousand Phrases." *Film Score Monthly*, Vol. 3, No. 1 (January 1998): 34–40.

Alemany-Galway, Mary. *A Postmodern Cinema: The Voice of the Other in Canadian Film*. Lanham, Md, and London: Scarecrow Press, 2002.

Altman, Rick with McGraw Jones and Sonia Tatroe. "Inventing the Cinema Soundtrack: Hollywood's Multiplane Sound System." In *Music and Cinema*, edited by James Buhler, Caryl Flinn, and David Neumeyer. Hanover and London: Wesleyan University Press, 2000: 339–359.

Aronowitz, Stanley. "My Masculinity." In *Constructing Masculinity*, edited by Maurice Berger, Brian Wallis, and Simon Watson. New York: Routledge, 1995: 307–320.

Ashcroft, Bill, Gareth Griffiths and Helen Tiffin, eds. *The Empire Writes Back: Theory and Practice in Postcolonial Literatures*. London and New York: Routledge, 1989.

Balio, Tino. "A Major Presence in All of the World's Important Markets: The Globalization of Hollywood in the 1990s." In *Contemporary Hollywood Cinema*, edited by Steve Neale and Murray Smith. London: Routledge, 1998: 58–73.

Barthes, Roland. *Image-Music-Text*. London: Fontana Press, 1977.

———. *S/Z*. trans. Richard Miller. New York: Hill and Wang, 1974.

Beardsley, Monroe C. *Aesthetics*. New York: Harcourt, Brace and World, 1958.

Bellman, Jonathan, ed. *The Exotic in Western Music*. Boston: Northeastern University Press, 1998.

Berkhofer, Robert F. Jr. *The White Man's Indian: Images of the American Indian from Columbus to the Present*. New York: Vintage Books, 1978.

Berry, Chris. "Taiwanese Melodrama Returns with a Twist in *The Wedding Banquet*." *Cinemaya*, Issue 21 (Fall 1993): 52–54.

Blair, I. "The Ice Storm." *Film and Video* (October 1997): 48–50, 59.

Booth, Gregory D. "Traditional Practice and Mass Mediated Music in India." *International Review of the Aesthetics and Sociology of Music*, Vol. 24, No. 2 (December 1993): 159–174.

Born, Georgina and David Hesmondhalgh, eds. *Western Music and Its Others: Difference, Representation and Appropriation in Music*. Berkeley: University of California Press, 2000.

Bourdieu, Pierre. *Distinction: A Social Critique of the Judgment of Taste*. London: Routledge and Kegan Paul, 1984.

Brown, Royal S. *Overtones and Undertones: Reading Film Music*. Berkeley: University of California Press, 1994.

Browning, Robert. *The Pied Piper of Hamelin*. Illustrations by Kate Greenaway. London and New York: Frederick Warne, 1888.

Buhler, James. "Analytical and Interpretive Approaches to Film Music (2): Analysing Interactions of Music and Film." In *Film Music Critical Approaches*, edited by Kevin J. Donnelly. Edinburgh: Edinburgh University Press, 2001: 39–61.

Burt, George. *The Art of Film Music*. Boston: Northeastern University Press, 1994.

Carroll, Noël. *Beyond Aesthetics: Philosophical Essays*. Cambridge: Cambridge University Press, 2001.

Carr, Karen L. *The Banalization of Nihilism*. Albany: State University of New York Press, 1992.

Caughie, John. *Theories of Authorship: A Reader*. London: Routledge, 1981.

Cheshire, Ellen. *Ang Lee*. Harpenden: Pocket Essentials, 2001.

Chion, Michel. *Audio-Vision: Sound on Screen*. New York: Columbia University Press, 1994.

———. *The Voice in Cinema*. New York: Columbia University Press, 1999.

Christopher, James. "Forbidden Love, Hidden Romance," *The Times*, The Knowledge supplement, December 17th (2005): 9–10.

Comer, Brooke. "Eat Drink Man Woman: A Feast for the Eyes." *American Cinematographer*, Vol. 76, No. 1 (1995): 62–67.

Cooper, Barry. *Beethoven and the Creative Process*. Oxford: Clarendon Press, 1990.

Dariotis, Wei Ming and Eileen Fung. "Breaking the Soy Sauce Jar: Diaspora and Displacement in the Films of Ang Lee." In *Transnational Chinese Cinemas: Identity, Nationhood, Gender*, edited by Sheldon Hsia-Peng Lu. Honolulu: University of Hawaii Press, 1997: 187–220.

Eco, Umberto. *Postcript to the Name of the Rose*. Trans. William Weaver. San Diego: Harcourt Brace Jovanovich, 1984.

Emerson, Ken. *Always Magic in the Air: The Bomp and Brilliance of the Brill Building Era*. London: Viking, 2005.

Farrell, Warren. *The Liberated Man Beyond Masculinity: Freeing Men and Their Relationships with Women*. New York: Random House, 1974.

Feld, Steven. "The Poetics and Politics of Pygmy Pop." In *Western Music and Its Others: Difference, Representation and Appropriation in Music*, edited by Georgina Born and David Hesmondhalgh. Berkeley: University of California Press, 2000: 254–279.

Foster, Gwendolyn Audrey. *Women Filmmakers of the African and Asian Disapora: Decolonizing the Gaze, Locating Subjectivity.* Carbondale and Edwardsville: Southern Illinois University Press, 1997.

Foucault, Michel. "What Is an Author?" In *The Foucault Reader,* edited by Paul Rabinow. New York: Pantheon, 1984: 101–120.

Francke, Lizzie. "The Ice Storm." *Sight and Sound* (February 1998): 42.

Frith, Simon. "The Discourse of World Music." In *Western Music and Its Others: Difference, Representation and Appropriation in Music,* edited by Georgina Born and David Hesmondhalgh. Berkeley: University of California Press, 2000: 305–322.

Gorbman, Claudia. "Scoring the Indian: Music in the Liberal Western." In *Western Music and Its Others: Difference, Representation and Appropriation in Music,* edited by Georgina Born and David Hesmondhalgh. Berkeley: University of California Press, 2000: 234–253.

———. *Unheard Melodies: Narrative Film Music.* Bloomington: Indiana University Press, 1987.

Handelman, David. "Cheat Drink Man Woman." *Premiere (USA),* Vol. 2, No. 3 (November 1997): 98–115.

Hardesty, Mary. "Ang Lee on Directing in an Ice Storm." *Directors Guild of America Magazine,* Vol. 22, No. 4 (1997): 48–51.

Harell, Max L. *The Music of the Gamelan Degung of West Java,* Ph.D. dissertation. Los Angeles: University of California, 1974.

Hesmondhalgh, David. "International Times: Fusions, Exoticism, and Antiracism in Electronic Dance Music." In *Western Music and Its Others: Difference, Representation and Appropriation in Music,* edited by Georgina Born and David Hesmondhalgh. Berkeley: University of California Press, 2000: 280–304.

Hibbs, Thomas S. *Shows About Nothing: Nihilism in Popular Culture from the Exorcist to Seinfeld.* Dallas: Space Publishing, 1999.

Hobsbawm, Eric and Terence Ranger, eds. *The Invention of Tradition.* Cambridge: Cambridge University Press, 1983.

Hutnyk, John. *Critique of Exotica: Music, Politics and the Culture Industry.* London and Sterling, Va.: Pluto Press, 2000.

Iseminger, Gary, ed. *Intention and Interpretation.* Philadelphia: Temple University Press, 1992.

Jennings, Francis. *The Invasion of America: Indians, Colonialism, and the Cant of Conquest.* Chapel Hill: University of North Carolina Press for the Institute of Early American Thought, 1976.

John-Steiner, Vera. *Creative Collaboration.* Oxford: Oxford University Press, 2000.

Kalinak, Kathryn. *Settling the Score: Music and the Classical Hollywood Film.* Madison: University of Wisconsin Press, 1992.

Kassabian, Anahid. *Hearing Film: Tracking Identifications in Hollywood Film Music.* New York and London: Routledge, 2001.

Kramer, Jonathan. "The Nature and Origins of Musical Postmodernism." In *Postmodern Music/Postmodern Thought,* edited by Judy Lochhead and Joseph Auner. New York and London: Routledge, 2002: 13–26.

Kuter, Stanley I. *Wars of Watergate: The Last Crisis of Richard Nixon*. New York: W. W. Norton, 1992.

Lack, Russell. *Twenty-four Frames Under: A Buried History of Film Music*. London: Quartet Books, 1997.

Larson, Randall D. "The Film Music of Mychael Danna." *Soundtrack*, Vol. 21, No. 83 (Fall 2002): 32–35.

Levy, Emanuel. *Cinema of Outsiders: The Rise of American Independent Film*. New York: New York University Press, 1999.

Lindsay, Jennifer. *Javanese Gamelan*. Kuala Lumpur: Oxford University Press, 1979.

Lippy, Todd. "James Schamus and Ted Hope." In *Projections 11: New York Film-makers on Film-making*, edited by Todd Lippy. London: Faber and Faber, 2000: 2–18.

Loewen, James W. *Lies My Teacher Told Me: Everything Your American History Textbook Got Wrong*. New York: New Press, 1995.

Lutz, Tom. "Men's Tears and the Roles of Melodrama." In *Boys Don't Cry? Rethinking Narratives of Masculinity and Emotion in the U.S.*, edited by Milette Shamir and Jennifer Travis. New York: Columbia University Press, 2002: 185–204.

Lyotard, Jean-François. *The Postmodern Condition: A Report on Knowledge*. Trans. Geoff Bennington and Brian Massumi. Minneapolis: University of Minnesota Press, 1984.

Ma, Sheng-Mei. "Ang Lee's Domestic Tragicomedy: Immigrant Nostalgia, Exotic/Ethnic Tour, Global Market." *Journal of Popular Culture*, Vol. 30, No.1 (1996): 191–202.

Maltby, Richard. "'Nobody knows everything': Post-classical Historiographies and Consolidated Entertainment." In *Contemporary Hollywood Cinema*, edited by Steve Neale and Murray Smith. London: Routledge, 1998: 21–44.

Maslin, Janet. "Suburbanites Pure as Driven Slush." *New York Times*, September 26th (1997): 1, 14.

Matthews, Peter. "The Big Freeze." *Sight and Sound* (February 1998): 12–14.

Mead, Margaret. *Coming of Age in Samoa: A Psychological Study of Primitive Youth for Western Civilisation*. New York: Harper Perennial, 1928/2001.

Mera, Miguel. "Representing the Baroque: The Portrayal of Historical Period in Film Music." *The Consort: Journal of the Dolmetsch Foundation*, Vol. 57, (2001): 3–21.

Miller, Terry E. and Sean Williams, eds. *The Garland Encyclopedia of World Music*, Vol. IV: Southeast Asia. New York, London: Routledge, 1998–2002.

Moody, Rick. *The Ice Storm*. London: Abacus, 1994.

Moore, Allan F. *Rock: The Primary Text*. Aldershot: Ashgate, 1993/2001.

Mote, Frederick W. *Intellectual Foundations of China*. New York: Alfred A. Knopf, 1971.

Moverman, Oren. "The Angle on Ang Lee." *Inter/view* (September 1997): 64–68.

Muir, John Kenneth. *Mercy in Her Eyes: The Films of Mira Nair*. New York: Applause Theatre and Cinema Books, 2006.

Murch, Walter. "Sound-Design: The Dancing Shadow." In *Projections 4: Film-makers on Film-making*, edited by Todd Lippy. London: Faber and Faber, 1995: 237–251.

Nettl, Bruno. *The Study of Ethnomusicology: Thirty-one Issues and Concepts.* Urbana and Chicago: University of Illinois Press, 1983/2005.

Neumeyer, David and James Buhler. "Analytical and Interpretive Approaches to Film Music (1): Analysing the Music." In *Film Music Critical Approaches*, edited by K. J. Donnelly. Edinburgh: Edinburgh University Press, 2001: 16–38.

Nietzsche, Friedrich. *The Gay Science.* Trans W. Kaufmann. New York: Vintage Books, 1882/1974.

Nuzum, Eric D. *Parental Advisory: Music Censorship in America.* London: HarperCollins, 2001.

Pevere, Geoff. "No Place Like Home: The Films of Atom Egoyan." In *Exotica.* Toronto: Coach House Press, 1995: 9–41.

Pinch, Trevor J. and Frank Trocco. *Analog Days: The Invention and Impact of the Moog Synthesizer.* Cambridge: Harvard University Press, 2002.

Ponomareff, Constantin V. *On the Dark Side of Russian Literature 1709-1910.* New York: Peter Lang, 1987.

Potter, Keith. *Four Musical Minimalists.* Cambridge: Cambridge University Press, 2000.

Reesman, Bryan. "Mychael Danna, Globe-trotting Visionary." *Mix: Professional Audio and Music Production*, Vol. 26, No. 6 (May 2002): 125–126, 138–142.

Reich, Steve. *Writings About Music.* London: Universal Edition, 1974.

Romney, Jonathan. *Atom Egoyan.* London: British Film Institute, 2003.

Russ, Martin. *Sound Synthesis and Sampling.* Oxford: Focal Press, 2004.

Said, Edward. *Orientalism.* London and Henley: Routledge and Kegan Paul, 1978.

Sartre, Jean-Paul. *Being and Nothingness: An Essay on Phenomenological Ontology.* London: Routledge, 1957/2003.

Schamus, James. *The Ice Storm: The Shooting Script.* NHB Shooting Scripts. London: Nick Hern, 1997.

Schmitt, Bernd H. and Alex Simonson. *Marketing Aesthetics: The Strategic Management of Brands, Identity, and Image.* New York: Free Press, 1997.

Sergi, Gianluca. "The Sonic Playground: Hollywood Cinema and its Listeners." In *Hollywood Spectatorship: Changing Perceptions of Cinema Audiences*, edited by Melvyn Stokes and Richard Maltby. London: BFI Publishing, 2001: 121–131.

———. "In Defence of Vulgarity: The Place of Sound Effects in the Cinema." *Scope: an online journal of film studies*, Issue 5 (June 2006). http://www.scope.nottingham.ac.uk/article.php?issue=5&id=129

Shamir, Milette and Jennifer Travis, eds. *Boys Don't Cry? Rethinking Narratives of Masculinity and Emotion in the U.S.* New York: Columbia University Press, 2002.

Sklar, Robert. "The Ice Storm." *Cineaste*, Vol. XXIII, No. 2 (1997): 41–42.

Smith, Ian H. "Ang Lee." In *Fifty Contemporary Filmmakers*, edited by Yvonne Tasker. London and New York: Routledge, 2002: 227–235.

Sorrell, Neil. *A Guide to the Gamelan*. London: Faber, 1990.
Sutton, R. Anderson. *Traditions of Gamelan Music in Java: Musical Pluralism and Regional Identity*. Cambridge; Cambridge University Press, 1991.
Tepper, Elliot L. "Immigration Policy and Multiculturalism." In *Ethnicity and Culture in Canada: The Research Landscape*, edited by J. W. Berry and J. A. Laponce. Toronto: University of Toronto Press, 1994: 95–123.
Thielicke, Helmut. *Nihilism: Its Origin and Nature, with a Christian Answer*. Trans. J. W. Doberstein. New York: Schocken, 1970.
Thomson, David. "Riding with Ang Lee." *Film Comment*, Vol. 35, No. 6 (November/December 1999): 4–9.
Turner, Bryan S. *Orientalism, Postmodernism and Globalism*. London and New York: Routledge, 1994.
Tu, Wei-Ming. *Confucian Thought: Selfhood as Creative Transformation*. Albany: State University of New York Press, 1985.
Wasko, Janet. *Hollywood in the Information Age: Beyond the Silver Screen*. Cambridge: Polity Press, 1994.
Watson, Ben. *Frank Zappa: The Negative Dialectics of Poodle Play*. London: Quartet, 1994.
Weis, Elizabeth. "Eavesdropping: An Aural Analogue of Voyeurism." In *Cinesonic: The World of Sound in Film*, edited by Phil Brophy. Sydney: AFTRS, 1998: 79–108.
Welsh, James M. "Action Films: The Serious, the Ironic, the Postmodern." In *Film Genre 2000: New Critical Essays*, edited by Wheeler Winston Dixon. Albany: State University of New York Press, 2000: 161–176.
Williams, David E. "Reflections on an Era." *American Cinematographer*, Vol. 78, No. 10 (October 1997): 56–65.
Wimsatt, William K. and Monroe C. Beardsley. "The Intentional Fallacy." In *The Verbal Icon: Studies in the Meaning of Poetry*. Lexington: University of Kentucky Press, 1954: 3–18.
Wyatt, Justin. *High Concept, Movies and Marketing in Hollywood*. Austin: University of Texas Press, 1994.
Zappa, Frank. "On Junk Food for the Soul." *New Perspectives Quarterly*, Vol. 4, No. 4 (Winter 1998): 26–29.
———. *The Real Frank Zappa Book*. New York: Simon and Schuster, 1989.

Index

temp track, 23, 39, 40, 92, 103–9,
116, 154
Tennyson, Alfred Lord, 43
thanksgiving, 49, 50, 62, 98, 122,
148
Tibet, 38
Tideland, 15
Tin Machine, 119, 167
tone row. see serialism
Toronto, 2, 5, 7, 9, 10, 13, 28, 39,
41, 43, 100, 144
The Tragically Hip, 41, 42
Trevor, William, 19
tuning, 43, 102–3, 118, 135, 139,
161, 179n82

Umrao Jaan, 10
University of Toronto, 5

Vanity Fair, 15, 27, 43
Vaughan, Malcolm, 20

Vietnam, 46
voice-over, 37, 52, 53, 58, 59, 66,
136, 151, 153, 156

Water, 15
Watergate, 46, 49, 65, 120
Weaver, Sigourney, xvii
The Wedding Banquet, 60
Where the Truth Lies, 15
Wimsatt, William, 77
Wings of Desire, 10
Witherspoon, Reese, 43
workstation set-up, 79-80
world music, 5–6, 12, 17, 27, 29,
32–33, 38, 104, 144; see ethnic
music

Zappa, Frank, 123, 128–29,
188n25
Ziggy Stardust, 119, 167

About the Author

MIGUEL MERA is widely published in music and moving image studies from music in historical drama to the use of popular songs in contemporary cinema. He is coeditor of *European Film Music* (Ashgate, 2006) and is a senior lecturer at the Royal College of Music. Miguel also composes music for film and television; his work has been screened at the Venice and London film festivals, among others, and broadcast on television throughout the world.